SPORT PSYCHOLOGY

This book offers a student-friendly introduction to the discipline of sport psychology. All the key psychological issues in sport are explored and illustrated with sporting examples. Throughout, difficult questions are raised: are athletes born or made? Does participating in sport affect personality? What impact do cultural beliefs have on personal sporting development? These complex issues are weighed up to provide a detailed overview of the topic. Matt Jarvis has substantially revised and expanded his original coverage of the subject from his highly successful book *Sport Psychology* (published by Routledge in 1999). Here he provides a succinct but comprehensive account of major theory and research in sport psychology, whilst maintaining the readable style and student-centred approach which made the previous book so successful.

Key issues covered include:

- personality and sport
- attitudes to sport
- aggression in sport
- the social factors affecting performance
- arousal and anxiety
- motivation and skill acquisition.

There is an emphasis not merely on learning about sport psychology, but also on developing critical and creative thinking. In addition, the book includes chapters on conducting research and writing essays in sport psychology, as well as reflective exercises throughout the text.

Written by a successful author who has experience of teaching at sixth form and undergraduate level, this book will be useful to undergraduates in sport science and leisure management, those studying for the BAQTS and PGCE in physical education, and those studying A-level psychology or sports studies.

Matt Jarvis teaches psychology at Totton College and is Visiting Lecturer at Southampton University.

Sport Psychology

A Student's Handbook

Matt Jarvis

Routledge
Taylor & Francis Group

LONDON AND NEW YORK

First published by Routledge
27 Church Road, Hove, East Sussex, BN3 2FA

Simultaneously published in the USA and Canada
by Routledge
270 Madison Avenue, New York, NY 10016

Routledge is a part of the Taylor & Francis Group

Copyright © 2006 Routledge

Typeset in Palatino by RefineCatch Ltd., Bungay, Suffolk
Printed and bound in Great Britain by TJ International Ltd., Padstow, Cornwall
Cover design by Hybert Design

British Library Cataloguing in Publication Data
A catalogue record for this book is available from the British Library

Library of Congress Cataloging in Publication Data
Jarvis, Matt, 1966–
   Sport psychology : a student's handbook / Matt Jarvis.
     p. cm.
   Includes bibliographical references and index.
   ISBN 1 -84169-581-5 (hardcover) – ISBN 1-84169-582-3 (softcover)
    1. Sports – Psychological aspects – Handbooks, manuals, etc.   I. Title.
GV706.4.J37 2005
796.01—dc22
ISBN10: 1-84169-581-5 (hbk)   ISBN13: 978-1-84169-581-5 (hbk)
ISBN10: 1-84169-582-3 (pbk)   ISBN13: 978-1-84169-582-2 (pbk)

Contents

List of figures and tables

Figures

Tables

Preface to the second edition

Following the success of the first edition of *Sport Psychology*, which was written primarily for A-level students, the aim of this second edition is to make the book of more use to students at undergraduate level. To achieve this, I have tried to maintain the informal, user-friendly style of the first edition, but I have also added substantially to the content. Thus, the text is much more detailed and up-to-date, featuring a more comprehensive range of theories and numerous studies from the last 5 years. Chapters 2–9 cover the essential topics in sport psychology; personality and sport, attitudes to sport, aggression and sport, social factors affecting performance, arousal and anxiety, motivation, and the acquisition of skill and expertise. Throughout the book, I have rejected utterly the 'just do it' attitude that characterises some sport science literature. Instead there is an emphasis on thrashing out difficult issues, including the questions of whether athletes are born or made, and whether sport is really character building.

For real understanding of sport psychology, it is necessary to have a reasonable understanding of the nature of psychology itself. One of the things I have tried to do in this second edition is to put across to those new to studying psychology at this level the nature of the discipline. In Chapter 1, the reader is introduced to the distinction between theory and research and the range of theoretical approaches that make up psychology. However, psychology is as much a way of thinking as a set of theories and studies. I have tried to introduce the reader to the skills of critical and creative thinking prized by psychologists, and to encourage the use of these higher thinking skills throughout the book with a series of reflective exercises.

Also of use to those new to psychology should be the final two chapters. In Chapter 10, I review the major research methods used in sport psychology. This should help students both to understand more deeply the research they have studied already and to plan their own research. Chapter 11 aims to teach students what is expected in a psychology essay, and to guide them through the process of planning and constructing an essay. Again there is an emphasis on applying higher-level thinking skills to psychological theory and research, and this chapter should crystallise the understanding of creative and critical thinking encouraged throughout the text.

Introduction 1

Learning objectives

By the end of this chapter you should be able to:

- define sport psychology
- give a brief history of the discipline
- understand what sport psychologists do and who is entitled to use the designation
- explain the purpose of theory and research in psychology, and describe some major research methods used in sport psychology
- recognise the major approaches to psychology
- begin to think critically about psychological theory and research.

What is sport psychology?

Because there are many ways in which we can apply psychology to sport and, given the wide range of activities that different cultures regard as sport, it is helpful to adopt quite a broad definition of sport psychology. In 1996, the European Federation of Sport Psychology (FEPSAC) produced such a broad definition, which, slightly simplified, reads, '*Sport psychology is the study of the psychological basis, processes and effects of sport.*' This of course begs the questions, what is sport and what is psychology? Although many athletes would insist that sport necessarily includes an element of competition, the term 'sport' is used, both in the FEPSAC definition of sport psychology, and throughout this book, in the broadest sense, including any physical activity for the purposes of competition, recreation, education or health. Psychology is often defined as 'the science of mind and behaviour' (Gross, 2005). Later in this chapter, we can take a brief overview of psychology and begin to learn how to think critically and creatively about psychological theory and research.

Sport psychology (or sports psychology, as some prefer) is thus a broad church. Many American sport psychologists draw a sharp distinction between academic sport psychology, which focuses on all the factors affecting participation and performance in sport, and applied sport psychology, which focuses purely on applying psychology to enhance athletic performance (e.g. Cox, 2001). At the time of writing, European writers generally do not subscribe to this rather rigid distinction (Kremer & Scully, 1994), and this book crosses freely between academic and applied sport psychology. The topics covered here, personality, attitudes, aggression, stress and anxiety, group dynamics, motivation and skill acquisition, should be both of academic interest and applicable to working with athletes and, in some cases, spectators.

A brief history of sport psychology

Sport psychology has existed in some form for almost as long as psychology itself. The first recorded study in sport psychology took place at the close of the nineteenth century. Norman Triplett (1898) performed what is often cited as the first experiment in social psychology as well as the first in sport psychology. Triplett investigated the phenomenon of *social facilitation*, in which performance is affected by the presence of others (this is discussed in detail in Chapter 6). He demonstrated that cyclists tended to cycle faster when racing against other cyclists than they did alone. Triplett did not pursue further sport-related research, however, and it was not until the 1920s that the discipline of sport psychology was formally established.

In 1925, Coleman Griffith set up the Athletic Research Laboratory at the University of Illinois. Griffith, who also put sport psychology on the map by establishing a university course, publishing two major textbooks and acting as a consultant to professional sports teams, is often called the 'father of sport psychology'. The early path of sport psychology did not run smoothly, however, and the Athletic Research Laboratory closed in 1932 due to lack of funds.

Between the 1930s and the 1960s (at least in the Western world), there was little activity in the field of sport psychology. In the Soviet Union, sport psychology emerged as a discipline shortly after the Second World War. It is of course difficult to obtain accurate information about the practice of Soviet psychology during the Cold War, but it is commonly believed that, during the 1960 Melbourne Olympics, Eastern European teams employed sport psychologists (Kremer & Scully, 1994). Certainly, we know that, by the early 1970s, East German and

Soviet teams were routinely employing sport psychologists to enhance athletic performance in international events.

Sport psychology reappeared in the USA in the 1960s, and was taken up in Britain and the rest of Europe a few years later. The area has since expanded worldwide to become one of the fastest growing new academic disciplines. Interestingly, until very recently, the study of sport psychology was firmly located in the domain of sport sciences as opposed to within psychology. This may be changing, however. In 1986, the American Psychological Association officially recognised sport psychology as a branch of psychology, and in 1993 the British Psychological Society formed a Sport and Exercise Psychology Section, which has now become a full division of the society.

What is a sport psychologist?

We can think of this question in two ways; first, who can call himself or herself a sport psychologist, and second, what do sport psychologists do? To address the first question, currently, in Britain, there is no compulsory registration of sport psychologists; therefore, in theory, anyone can call himself a sport psychologist. In reality, of course, it would be highly unethical for anyone not properly trained to use the title 'psychologist' in any context. At the time of writing, legislation is being brought in which will place legal limits on the use of the term. The British Association of Sport and Exercise Sciences (BASES) keeps a register of approved sport psychologists. At the 1998 annual conference, the British Psychological Society (BPS)'s Sport and Exercise Psychology Section (now 'Division') approved the principle of granting the title *Chartered Sport Psychologist* to appropriately qualified people. At the time of writing, legislation is at the consultation stage to restrict certain titles, including *Chartered Sport* and *Exercise Psychologist*, to those on a register, to be maintained by the Health Professions Council. To register with BASES as a sport psychologist, one needs either a first degree in psychology and a higher degree in sport science *or* a first degree in sport science and a higher degree in sport psychology. To achieve chartered status from the BPS, it is necessary to have a BPS-approved first degree in psychology and BPS-approved postgraduate training, including supervised practice. There is currently no such approved postgraduate training. A similar situation exists in the USA, where, although the American Psychological Association (APA) has a Division of Sport Psychology (Division 47), it does not accredit courses.

There is some controversy surrounding the accreditation of sport psychologists. The BASES scheme for registration of sport psychologists has existed only since 1992, and many people who were already working as sport psychologists chose not to join the register or were unqualified to do so. Anshel (1992) has pointed out that many of those working full-time with athletes do not have the time, resources or inclination to pursue the lengthy procedures necessary to become registered, and that registration thus excludes some of the Britain's most experienced practitioners. On the other hand, compulsory registration would provide a measure of protection for the public from dubious or underqualified practitioners.

With regard to the second question, the work carried out by sport psychologists is quite varied. The European Federation of Sport Psychology (1996) recognises three interrelated tasks for sport psychologists:

- *research*; investigation into all aspects of the psychology of sport, both theoretical and applied
- *education*; teaching students, officials and athletes about sport psychology
- *application*; assessment of and intervention in psychological problems connected to sport. This can involve consulting to whole teams or counselling of individuals.

The BPS Division of Sport and Exercise Psychology is particularly committed to research, education and application in particular areas, as shown in Box 1.1:

Box 1.1 Areas of focus for the BPS Division of Sport and Exercise Psychology

- psychology of elite performance
- individual and group processes in sport
- motor skill acquisition and performance
- motivational issues in sport and exercise
- psychological factors in adoption and maintenance of exercise behaviour
- sport, exercise and mental health
- professional practice in sport and exercise psychology.

Because sport psychology is now such a broad field, it is becoming impossible for sport psychologists to keep up with all aspects of their discipline. Nowadays, you will find that many sport psychologists have become highly specialised. For example, psychologists may specialise in the study of motivation (see Chapter 8). They may carry out research into motivation, teach coaches about motivation and perhaps work with individual athletes to improve their motivation.

For those new to psychology

For readers new to psychology, before ploughing into the specifics of sport psychology, it is perhaps worth taking some time to overview the nature of psychology in general, and to begin to learn to think like a psychologist. To understand psychology, it is necessary to understand what we mean by the terms 'theory' and 'research', and to be familiar with the different theoretical approaches psychologists can draw upon to understand a phenomenon.

Theory and research

The writings of psychologists largely consist of two very important elements: theory and research. A psychological *theory* is intended to explain why something takes place. For example, in Chapter 7, we can look at a range of theories that aim to explain the relationship between arousal, anxiety and sporting performance. It is tempting to ask, 'which is right?' when confronted by a range of alternative theories; however, it is rare in psychology for a single theory to hold all the answers. Usually, each theory is helpful in its own way because it helps us understand and think about a different aspect of the situation.

The term 'research' is a very broad one, and is used by psychologists in different fields to mean rather different things. However, a simple definition appropriate to sport psychology is the gathering and analysing of data (information).[1] Often, though not necessarily, this is done in order to test an idea or *hypothesis*. For example, we might hypothesise that team players are more sociable than athletes in individual sports. There are many procedures by which data can be gathered. Some of the more important research methods used in sport psychology are outlined in Box 1.2.

---

[1] This definition would not be universally acceptable in psychology. In social psychology, for example, it would not be adequate, as there is a field of 'theoretical research' that overlaps between the generating of theory and data gathering.

> **Box 1.2** Some of the research methods used in sport psychology
>
> - **Experiment**: involves comparing people's responses or performance under two or more artificially created conditions. For example, we might set up two conditions in which basketball players are either punished or rewarded as they train, and thus measure the effect punishment and reward has upon their motivation and performance.
> - **Quasi-experiment**: involves comparing two or more naturally occurring groups. For example, we might be interested in comparing the personality characteristics of athletes in individual and team sports, or comparing men's and women's attitudes to boxing.
> - **Survey**: involves asking questions or asking for responses to suggestions. This can be done verbally (interview) or on paper (questionnaire). Surveys are useful in investigating attitudes and motives.
> - **Observation**: involves systematically watching people's behaviour in particular circumstances. We might use observation, for example, to see how frequency of aggression changes in response to losing in a contact sport.
> - **Correlation**: involves measuring two or more variables and seeing how they are related. In a positive correlation, as one variable increases, so does the other. An example of such a correlation is that between physical size and hostility. In a negative correlation, as one variable increases, the other decreases. An example of this is the relationship between experience as a martial artist and hostility – as experience increases, hostility declines.

Approaches to psychology

The BPS recognises five aspects of or approaches to the study of psychology. These are individual differences, social psychology, cognitive psychology, physiological psychology and developmental psychology. Examples of how each of these approaches can be applied to sport psychology are shown in Table 1.1.

From Table 1.1 it is quickly apparent that there is considerable overlap between the five approaches and that in practice they are not distinct from one another. For example, attitudes are an aspect of social psychology because they affect our interpersonal behaviour, but they also vary from one person to another; thus, they are also studied as an aspect of individual differences. Similarly, personality is most obviously an aspect of individual differences; however, we can understand the reasons why we differ in our personality with reference to physiological processes and developmental processes.

Approach	Main focus of approach	Examples in sport psychology
Individual differences	Variation in the characteristics of individuals	Personality, attitudes to sport, motivation, anxiety
Social psychology	Ways in which people interact with one another	Attitudes to sport, aggression, team cohesion, team leadership
Cognitive psychology	Ways in which the mind processes information	Skill acquisition, motivation, imagery
Physiological psychology	The relationship between biological and psychological functioning	Arousal and performance, biological basis of personality traits
Developmental psychology	The processes of development of psychological functions and characteristics across the lifespan	Social learning, gender development, personality development

Table 1.1 Applying psychological approaches to understanding sport

Theoretical orientations in psychology

An alternative way to classify approaches to psychology is in terms of its theoretical orientations. Unlike other sciences, which tend to have broad agreement about the fundamentals of what they study, how and to what end, psychology is made up of different theoretical schools, each of which takes a different view of the subject. Table 1.2 shows some of the major theoretical orientations in psychology and examples of their contributions to sport psychology.

Some psychologists operate very much within a single theoretical framework and can be said to have a distinct orientation, whilst others dip into different orientations and approaches as required. This latter is called an eclectic approach.

Theoretical orientation	Underlying assumptions	Examples of applications in sport psychology
Behavioural (learning)	• Focus is on observable behaviour • Behaviour is acquired by learning	Social learning of attitudes, personality, aggression

Table 1.2 Major theoretical orientations in psychology

Table 1.2 continued

Theoretical orientation	Underlying assumptions	Examples of applications in sport psychology
Cognitive	• Focus is on mental processes • Mental processes underlie behaviour and emotion	Cognitive anxiety Cognitive aspects of motivation
Psychodynamic	• Focus is on the unconscious mind • There are unconscious influences on us, including instinct and early experience	Personality development Unconscious factors in attitudes Instinct and aggression
Humanistic	• Focus is on human potential and growth	Achievement motivation
Physiological	• Focus is on physiological processes • Physiology underlies psychological processes	Trait theories of personality Arousal and somatic anxiety
Social	• Focus is on interpersonal and group processes • Social situation affects psychological processes	Social facilitation Team membership

Reflective exercise

Consider the following scenario. John, a middle-aged man who has not taken part in sport since school (when he was a talented athlete), decides to start regular exercise. He gets into the habit of running, in which he takes considerable pleasure and which helps him lose weight and feel more energetic. After several months, John achieves a standard high enough to enter in a local race, where he records a creditable time.

- From a behavioural perspective, John is receiving reinforcement in the form of weight loss, increased energy and improved times. He is thus learning that running is a good thing so he continues.
- From a cognitive perspective, John is processing information about running. He believes his running makes him healthier and more attractive, and will help him live longer.
- From a psychodynamic perspective, there are likely to be unconscious influences on John's behaviour, perhaps related to his age. He might be unconsciously trying to recapture his youth or responding to a fear of ageing and death.

- From a humanistic perspective, John never fulfilled his early potential as an athlete and is seeking to achieve as much as he can in this area.
- From a physiological perspective, John is producing large quantities of endorphins, natural opiates, which induce 'runner's high'. Running and other vigorous exercise enhance mood because of the chemical changes they bring about.
- From a social perspective, we need to take a step back and consider the social situation in which John's behaviour takes place. For example, in the light of social norms of body type, we might see his behaviour as a response to social pressure to lose weight.

1. Which of these perspectives portrays John's behaviour in a positive light?
2. Which appeal to you as likely explanations of John's behaviour?

Learning to think like a psychologist: critical and creative thinking

Psychology is not just a collection of theory and research. To study psychology effectively, we also need to learn to think like a psychologist. Perhaps the most important aspect of thinking psychologically is *critical thinking*. This means that, although we try to rely on evidence rather than common sense, we are also careful not to take theory or research findings at face value. Whenever we encounter a psychological theory or study, we should ask ourselves certain questions. Box 1.3 indicates some key questions to ask when faced by a new theory, and Box 1.4 some questions to ask regarding a new piece of research.

Box 1.3 Critical thinking about theories

When you meet a new theory, try asking yourself the following questions. Not all questions will be equally useful for evaluating every theory, but between them they should give you some idea of its strengths and limitations.

1. *What evidence is the theory based on?* Is it, for example, based on only a single study? It is a strength if a theory is based on more than one source of information.
2. *Is there convincing evidence to support the theory?* Have there been many studies aiming to test the study? If so, how many provide firm support?
3. *Is there some evidence that clearly fails to support the theory?* Are there studies that suggest that in fact the theory may not be correct?

4. *Does the theory provide a complete explanation for a psychological phenomenon?* In other words, is there some important observation that the theory cannot easily explain. Is there another theory that explains that observation better?

Box 1.4 Critical thinking about studies

When you come across a new study, ask yourself the following questions. Like those for evaluating a theory, they should give you some idea about the strengths and limitations of the study.

1. *How large and representative is the sample size?* A common limitation of studies is that they involve a small group of participants, often undergraduate students. Are these results applicable to athletes at large?
2. *Will results generalise from one sport to another?* For example, will a 'fact' discovered about team players generalise to those pursuing individual sports or from contact to non-contact athletes?
3. *Was the study carried out in a controlled or natural setting?* If it was set up in an artificial setting, it is possible that participants did not behave naturally.
4. *How good are the measures used to record results?* For example, if a study involves measuring personality or attitudes, how good is the scale used to measure these? Generally, published tests are better than those put together for a single study.
5. *Is there another study that shows the opposite?* If so, think about what might differ between the studies. They might, for example, look at different sports or athletes playing at different levels.

Recently, psychologists have begun to recognise that creative thinking as well as critical thinking is an important aspect of being a good psychologist or psychology student (Sternberg, 1999; McGhee, 2001). We think creatively when we develop new ideas or think about a problem from a different angle. Box 1.5 suggests some examples of the type of questions you can ask yourself in order to think creatively about sport psychology.

Box 1.5 Questions and tasks to stimulate creative thinking

1. What things does this theory predict might happen in a sporting situation?
2. How could you test that idea? Design a study.
3. Could you design a programme to tackle a problem based on that theory?

---

4. What alternative explanations can you think of for the results of that study other than the one the authors have suggested?
5. Putting together the findings of these studies, can you suggest your own explanation for this phenomenon?

Summary and conclusions

Sport psychology has existed for around a hundred years, becoming widely accepted in the 1960s, and growing rapidly in influence at the time of writing. Sport psychologists conduct research, educate interested parties, such as coaches, and work directly with athletes to improve their performance. Some psychologists draw a distinction between academic and applied sport psychology, but this is controversial. Also controversial is the issue of accreditation of sport psychologists. Currently, there is a move toward accreditation in all the professions; however, there is some resistance in sport psychology, meaning that some of the most experienced practitioners have not sought accreditation.

For those new to studying psychology, it is important to understand some basics about the way the subject works. In particular, be clear about the distinction between theory and research, and be familiar with the five approaches to studying psychology and the theoretical orientations psychologists might adopt. You should also be aware that psychology involves critical and creative thinking about theory and research. Practise using the key questions in Boxes 1.3, 1.4 and 1.5 to develop your critical and creative thinking as you read this book.

Further reading

- FEPSAC (1996) Position statement of the FEPSAC: 1. Definition of sport psychology. *The Sport Psychologist* 10, 221–223.
- Kremer J & Scully D (1994) *Psychology in sport*. London, Taylor & Francis.
- LeUnes A & Nation JR (2002) *Sport psychology*. Pacific Grove, CA, Wadsworth.
- www.bases.org.uk/newsite/aboutbases.asp
- www.bps.org.uk/sub-syst/SPEX/index.cfm
- www.psyc.unt.edu/apadiv47/
- http://itp.lu.se/fepsac/

Personality characteristics and sporting behaviour 2

Learning objectives

By the end of this chapter you should be able to:

- define personality
- describe the trait approach to personality, with particular reference to the theories of Eysenck, Cattell, and Costa and McCrae
- discuss research into the relationship between personality traits and sporting participation, performance and choice of sport
- outline narrow-band theories of personality, with particular regard to sensation seeking, telic dominance, mental toughness and attentional style, and evaluate their relationship to sporting behaviour
- understand the relationship between situation and behaviour, and explain the interactional approach with particular reference to the profile of mood states.

One of the most basic questions faced by psychology is, 'Why are we all different?' Of course, in some ways, we are all much the same, as in the structure of our brains and the mechanisms of perception and memory. However, there are huge differences among us in the ways we think, feel and behave in response to particular situations. The psychology of personality is concerned with these individual differences. Pervin (1993) has offered a simple working definition of personality: 'Personality represents those characteristics of the person that account for consistent patterns of behaviour'. Broadly, four factors influence how we respond in any given situation: our genetic make-up, our past experience, the nature of the situation in which we find ourselves and our free will. Each of these factors is emphasised by one or more theories of personality.

Trait theories of personality emphasise the role of genetics in determining our individuality. Situational and interactional views place more emphasis on the particular situation and less emphasis on the nature of the individual in determining how we act. Trait, situational and interactional theories are all ambitious approaches to personality that aim to describe the entire nature of the person. Narrow-band theories are less ambitious, focusing on a single aspect of personality. None of the main theoretical approaches to personality place much emphasis on free will; that is, how we choose to think, feel and behave. Free will is a controversial idea in psychology. Although we may believe that we choose how to behave, it is always likely that we are influenced to some degree by our genetic make-up and our past experiences. The role of experience in personality development is dealt with in Chapter 3.

In some ways, the study of personality underlies all sport psychology. When we look in later chapters at such topics as attitudes, aggression, motivation and anxiety, what we are really interested in is how and why people differ in these aspects, and how we can modify these to improve athletic performance. The answers to many of these questions can be found in personality theory.

Trait theories

There are two main assumptions underlying the trait approach to personality. Firstly, an individual's personality is made up of certain key characteristics or traits. Traits are the stable, enduring characteristics of a person. Secondly, individuals differ in each trait, at least partly due to their genetic differences. Traits can be measured according to three factors: their frequency, their intensity and the range of situations to which they can be applied. For example, a trait that appears in most of the major theories is extroversion – how lively, sociable and impulsive an individual is. We are safe in saying that someone is highly extrovert if they display lively, sociable and impulsive behaviour, often to an extreme and in a variety of quite different situations.

Eysenck's theory

Eysenck (1952) initially proposed that personality could be completely described by just two traits, extroversion and neuroticism. *Extroversion* describes how lively, sociable and impulsive a person is, whilst *neuroticism* describes how emotionally stable they are. One question you might ask is why three different characteristics like liveliness, sociability and impulsivity are grouped together as one trait. The answer is that, through a mathematical process called *factor analysis*, Eysenck discovered that in most cases, it is the same people who tend to be lively, impulsive and sociable. When characteristic behaviours tend to cluster together in this way, we can say that they make up one trait. Extraversion and neuroticism can be measured by a personality test called the Eysenck Personality Inventory (EPI).

Some items from the EPI are shown in Box 2.1.

Box 2.1 Items from the Eysenck Personality Inventory (EPI)

	YES	NO
1. Do you often long for excitement?	[ ]	[ ]
2. Do you often need understanding friends to cheer you up?	[ ]	[ ]
3. Are you usually carefree?	[ ]	[ ]
4. Do you find it very hard to take no for an answer?	[ ]	[ ]
5. Do you stop and think things over before doing anything?	[ ]	[ ]

Questions 1, 3 and 5 are part of the extroversion (E) scale, whilst questions 2 and 4 are part of the neuroticism (N) scale. The E and N scales are each marked out of 24. A high score on the E scale would indicate that you are very extrovert whilst a low score would indicate that you are very introvert, that is, quiet, solitary, and not at all impulsive. A high score on the N scale would indicate that you are very neurotic, that is, emotionally unstable, whereas a very low score would indicate that you are a very stable, unflappable person. This is shown in Box 2.2.

Box 2.2 What EPI scores show

EPI score

introvert	1 2 3 4 5 6 7 8 9 10 11 12	E scale	13 14 15 16 17 18 19 20 21 22 23 24	extrovert
stable	1 2 3 4 5 6 7 8 9 10 11 12	N scale	13 14 15 16 17 18 19 20 21 22 23 24	neurotic

---

Most people score between 5 and 20 on each scale. In a later version of his theory, Eysenck (1975) added a third personality trait, psychoticism, a measure of how tender or tough-minded an individual is. This factor is incorporated into a third scale in Eysenck's later personality test, the Eysenck Personality Questionnaire (EPQ). By looking at

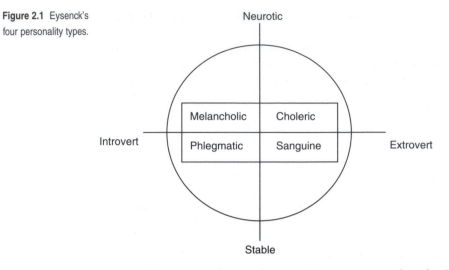

Figure 2.1 Eysenck's four personality types.

someone's extroversion and neuroticism, we can classify them as one of four personality types, or *temperaments*. These are shown in Figure 2.1.

Reflective exercise

Some of snooker's best-loved figures from the past two decades have included Jimmy White and Alex Higgins. They were known for both their outgoing personalities and their inspirational but inconsistent play. By contrast, Steve Davis and Stephen Hendry were more reserved players, who achieved more consistent results.

1. Suggest where each of these players might fall in Eysenck's personality types.
2. How might their personality traits have contributed to their success?

Eysenck (1966) explained extroversion and neuroticism as being primarily determined by the nature of the individual's nervous system. Introverts are more easily aroused by events than extroverts because of the sensitivity of an area of the brain called the *reticular activating system*; therefore, they require less stimulation to be comfortable. Introverts tend to seek out situations where there is relatively little stimulation, appearing quiet and solitary. Extroverts, who require more stimulation to achieve a comfortable level of arousal, respond by seeking out situations where there is more stimulation to be had. Their behaviour therefore tends to be more lively and sociable.

Eysenck saw neuroticism as being a result of the response of the individual's nervous system to stress. Those who score highly in neuroticism are thus those whose nervous system, in particular the *limbic system*, is highly responsive to stress and is slow to recover. Stable individuals are those whose nervous system responds less strongly to stress and then recovers more quickly.

Cattell's theory

Cattell disagreed with Eysenck's view that personality could be understood by looking at only three dimensions of personality. Instead he argued that it was necessary to look at a much larger number of traits in order to get a complete picture of someone's personality. Like Eysenck, Cattell used the mathematical technique of factor analysis to look at what types of behaviour tended to be grouped together in the same people. He identified 16 personality factors. Cattell's 16 personality traits are shown in Box 2.3.

Box 2.3 Cattell's 16 personality factors

reserved ↔ outgoing	unintelligent ↔ intelligent
stable ↔ unstable	humble ↔ assertive
sober ↔ happy-go-lucky	expedient ↔ conscientious
shy ↔ adventurous	tough-minded ↔ tender-minded
trusting ↔ suspicious	practical ↔ imaginative
forthright ↔ shrewd	placid ↔ apprehensive
conservative ↔ experimenting	group-dependent ↔ self-sufficient
undisciplined ↔ controlled	relaxed ↔ tense

Cattell produced a personality test similar to the EPI that measured each of the 16 traits. The 16PF, as it is called, has 160 questions in total, 10 questions relating to each personality factor. Examples of four items from the ego-strength (expedient-conscientious) scale are shown in Box 2.4.

Eysenck maintained that Cattell's 16 factors would fit neatly within his three. For example, the relaxed–tense factor, the placid–apprehensive factor, the relaxed–tense factor and the stable–unstable factor are all subsumed by Eysenck's trait of neuroticism. The argument between Eysenck and Cattell is really a mathematical one. To sport psychologists, what matters primarily is not who got his sums right, but which test is more useful in understanding sporting

> **Box 2.4** Items from the ego strength scale of the 16PF
>
> **1.** If you had your life to live over again, would you
> (a) want it to be essentially the same. OR   (b) plan it very differently?
>
> **2.** Do you ever have disturbing dreams?
>   (a) Yes   OR   (b) No
>
> **3.** Do your moods sometimes seem unreasonable to you?
>   (a) Yes   OR   (b) No
>
> **4.** Do you feel tired when you've done nothing to justify it?
>   (a) Rarely   OR   (b) Often

performance. Studies using Eysenck's and Cattell's theories and personality tests in relation to sport will be reviewed later in this chapter.

The five-factor model of personality

Arguably, the most popular trait theory in contemporary personality psychology is the five-factor model, developed by Costa & McCrae (1985); however, sport psychologists have been fairly slow to recognise its importance, and there are few published studies making use of it. The five factors in this model include extroversion and neuroticism (similar to Eysenck's traits). In addition, the trait of openness describes the individual's ability to appreciate new experiences and tolerate the unfamiliar. Open people are curious and imaginative. Individuals low in openness are conventional and narrow in their interests. Agreeableness (what we would call niceness in everyday speech) describes the extent to which one is compassionate and trusting, or hostile and ruthless. The final trait is conscientiousness, closely related to Cattell's trait of ego strength. Conscientiousness describes the extent of our organisation and persistence. Highly conscientious individuals are disciplined, punctual and ambitious.

Costa & McCrae (1985) developed a personality test known as the NEO-PI, an acronym which stands for the Neuroticism, Extroversion and Openness Personality Inventory. The first version just measured these three traits, and the name stuck when agreeableness and conscientiousness were added. The NEO-PI includes 181 statements to which respondents indicate their agreement on a 5-point scale ranging from 'strongly agree' to 'strongly disagree'. Box 2.5 shows four of the 40 items of the E-scale of the NEO-PI.

For these four statements, a high E-score is indicated by agreement with the statement. Some items, however, are reversed. Thus, agreement with the statement, 'You never smile when you talk to friends', would be scored negatively and reduce your E-score.

Research into traits and sporting behaviour

There has been a large volume of research into the relationship between personality traits, as measured by the EPI/EPQ, the 16PF and the NEO-PI, and sporting behaviour. Attempts have been made to distinguish athletes from non-athletes and successful performers from less successful performers. Sport psychologists have also looked at whether personality factors are associated with choice of sport.

Distinguishing athletes from non-athletes

Numerous attempts have been made to find out whether there is a fundamental difference between the personalities of athletes and non-athletes. Eysenck (1982) proposed that people scoring high on the extroversion and psychoticism scales of the EPQ are more likely to take up sport. Some though by no means all research has supported this hypothesis. Schurr et al (1977) tested 1500 American students with the 16PF, relating this to participation in sport, choice of sport and level of success. They found that athletes (defined as those in university teams) differed from non-athletes on three scales of the 16PF, being more independent and objective, and less anxious than the non-athletes.

Reflective exercise

Practise your critical thinking on the Schurr et al study.

1. Is the sample large enough and is it representative?
2. Was a good range of sports covered?
3. Was it conducted in a natural or artificial setting?

More recently, Francis et al (1998), using the EPQ, compared the personality of 133 Irish female students who participated in university hockey clubs with a control group of female students with no formal involvement in sport. The hockey players emerged as significantly higher in extroversion and psychoticism. Of course, university hockey players cannot necessarily be taken as representative of athletes as a whole. Clearly, students differ from other groups, and hockey is a team sport characterised by particularly high levels of group cohesion. In another study of 86 undergraduate athletes and a matched group of 86 non-athletes, McKelvie et al (2003) found no differences in extraversion between athletes and non-athletes, although athletes scored significantly lower in neuroticism; that is, they were more emotionally stable. Other studies have confirmed this relationship between neuroticism and sporting participation (e.g. Sevcikova et al (2000)). An interesting question is raised by research into the relationship between sporting participation and personality traits. Do people of a particular type seek out sport (this is known as the *gravitation* hypothesis), or does taking part in sport affect personality? Some early experiments (e.g. Ledwidge, 1980) suggested that neuroticism can be reduced by taking part in sport. However, studies also show that extraversion and neuroticism tend to be highly stable over time (e.g. McKelvie et al, 2003). This supports the gravitation hypothesis.

Distinguishing successful from unsuccessful athletes

An early attempt to use the idea of personality traits to identify successful athletes was that by Tutko and Ogilvie (1966). They proposed that successful people score highly on 11 personality traits: aggression, coachability, conscientiousness, determination, drive, emotional control, guilt proneness, leadership, mental toughness, self-confidence and trust. Tutko & Ogilvie produced a personality test called the Athletic Motivation Inventory (AMI) to measure these traits. Most sport psychologists agree that the AMI was seriously flawed, and contemporary research does not support the idea that the AMI can distinguish between successful and unsuccessful athletes.

Studies using superior personality tests have found some evidence that aspects of personality are associated with athletic success. Garland & Barry (1990) placed American college athletes in categories representing their level of skill. They were then tested with the 16PF. The statistical relationship between their athletic success and the personality factors measured by the 16PF was calculated. It emerged that tough-mindedness, extroversion, group dependence and emotional stability accounted for 29% of the variance in skill. This shows that although personality may have been one important factor in success, there were other, probably more important factors.

Although the five-factor model of personality has been under-utilised in sport psychology, one influential study using the NEO-PI has helped illuminate the relationship between success and personality. Piedmont et al (1999) administered the NEO-PI to 79 female footballers. The skill of the players was assessed by coaches and by game statistics (goals scored, possession, tackles won, etc.). Interestingly, extraversion and neuroticism were strongly correlated with coaches' ratings, but *not* with performance as judged objectively by game statistics. This suggests that either coaches' ratings *or* game statistics were invalid measures of performance. The only trait associated with objective performance was conscientiousness, high levels being associated with good performance.

Reflective exercise

Practise your critical and creative thinking on the Piedmont study.

1. Critically evaluate both the measures of performance used, coaches' ratings and game statistics.
2. Suggest ways in which you could investigate the validity of both these measures.

Although these results show that we have had moderate success in relating personality characteristics to success in sport, there are some important provisos to bear in mind. Firstly, not all studies have confirmed this type of relationship. For example, Davis (1991) attempted to predict success in the selection of professional ice hockey players in trials by measuring personality traits, and he found no relationship between selection and personality. Secondly, there are serious limits to the usefulness of knowing that there is a modest relationship between personality and success. Although we can help improve an individual's motivation and focus, and we can help athletes manage their anxiety, we cannot fundamentally change someone's personality. Neither, as Davis demonstrated, can we select people purely on the basis of their personality when there are more important factors, both psychological and physical, affecting performance.

Personality and choice of sport

Personality and sport has proved a rather more fruitful area of study, and some important differences between the personalities of success-ful athletes in different sports have emerged. This is perhaps unsurprising when we consider the varying demands of different sports. In the Schurr et al (1977) study, although relatively few differ-ences emerged between athletes and non-athletes, considerable dif-ferences were found between team and individual players. Team players emerged as more anxious and extrovert than individual competitors.

Another important distinction has emerged between the person-alities of those taking part in high- and low-risk sports. Breivik (1996) administered the 16PF to 38 elite Norwegian climbers and found a distinctive profile characterised by very high levels of stability, extra-version and adventure seeking. In another study, Freixanet (1999) administrated the EPQ to a range of high-risk sports participants, including 72 mountaineers, and a control group of low-risk athletes. The mountaineers and other high-risk athletes were characterised by significantly higher levels of extraversion and low levels of neuroti-cism. Other high-risk sports have also attracted attention. Using the NEO-PI, Diehm & Armatas (2004) compared the personality of 44 golfers (low-risk) and 41 surfers (high-risk). Surfers emerged as sig-nificantly higher on the openness scale, meaning that they were more open to new experiences (Figure 2.2).

Narrow-band theories of personality

Trait theories proper aim to be comprehensive accounts of personality, seeking to explain all variations in individual behaviour. However, in addition to these rather grand theories, there are a number of more modest theories that focus on specific aspects of personality. We call these narrow-band theories. Three narrow-band approaches to personality are worth a particularly close look: sensation-seeking, telic dominance and mental toughness.

Sensation seeking

Zuckerman (1978) identified sensation seeking as an aspect of person-ality. Sensation seeking reflects the amount of stimulation a person will seek. Zuckerman (1978) identified four separate factors that make

Figure 2.2 What personality differences can you see between golfers and surfers?

Copyright © Will & Deni McIntyre/Corbis

Copyright © Don Mason/Corbis

up sensation seeking, namely seeking of thrills and adventure, tendency to act on impulse, seeking of new experiences and vulnerability to boredom. Zuckerman has produced a personality test measuring sensation seeking. Some items from Zuckerman's scale are shown in Box 2.6.

Studies have found that sensation seeking, as measured by Zuckerman's scale, is positively related to drug-taking, sexual experimentation, public drunkenness and volunteering for high-risk activities. Clearly, the last is of interest to sport psychologists, who are interested in who chooses to participate in risky sports. In one study, Jack & Ronan (1998) assessed 166 athletes from both high-risk sports, such as hang-gliding, mountaineering and motor racing, and low-risk activities such as aerobics and golf, using Zuckerman's sensation-seeking scale. High scores on the Zuckerman scale were associated with participation in high-risk sports.

Telic dominance

The idea of telic dominance comes from the wider field of reversal theory (Apter, 1993), an approach to analysing human motivation that explains personality in terms of individual differences in motivational style. According to reversal theory, we all alternate between *telic* states, in which we avoid arousal, and *paratelic* states, in which we seek arousal. Some of us can be said to be dominated by telic states and others by paratelic states; that is, we spend most of our time in that state. We are thus said to be telic dominant or paratelic dominant. Murgatroyd et al (1978) have produced a 42-item personality test designed to measure telic dominance. Some items from Murgatroyd's Telic Dominance Scale (TDS) are shown in Box 2.7.

Kerr (1997) has suggested that telic dominance affects choice of sport, sporting achievement and the response of the individual to the pressure of competition. Because arousal is associated with high risk, we would expect highly paratelic-dominant people to prefer high-risk sports, whereas telic-dominant individuals might prefer more low-risk activities. This hypothesis was tested in a study by Chirivella & Martinez (1994), in which participants in a high-risk sport (parasailing) were compared for telic dominance with those opting for a medium-risk sport (karate) and a low-risk sport (tennis). As expected, there were significant differences between the three groups, para-sailors being the most paratelic dominant and tennis players the most telic dominant.

A number of studies have investigated the relationship between telic dominance and sporting achievement. Snell (1991), using the TDS, compared professional and amateur triathletes. No differences were found in serious-mindedness or planning orientation, but professionals scored significantly lower on arousal avoidance, suggesting that an important factor in success is being able to cope with the additional pressure (hence arousal) of professional-level sport.

Mental toughness

The term 'mental toughness' has been used for some time by athletes and commentators, but has only very recently become a focus of attention for sport psychologists. It has been defined in a range of ways, but a common thread in all these definitions seems to be the ability to cope with difficult circumstances. This manifests in a range of qualities, including coping with pressure of competition, coming back after failure, determination and resilience (Middleton et al, 2004). Jones et al (2002) carried out individual interviews and focus groups with international-level athletes in an attempt to clarify what the athletes saw as mental toughness. Interestingly, athletes framed mental toughness in *relativistic* terms, that is, in terms relative to other competitors: 'Mental toughness is having the natural or developed psychological edge that enables you to: 1. Generally cope better than your opponents with the many demands ... that sport places on a performer; and 2) Specifically, be more consistent and better than your opponents in remaining determined, focused, confident, and in control under pressure' (p 209).

There have been a number of attempts to measure mental toughness by self-rating inventories. Establishing a valid measure has not been made easier by difficulties in arriving at a precise definition. However, a number of such measures exist. Items from one such measure are shown in Box 2.8.

Box 2.8 Items from Goldberg's (1998) mental toughness questionnaire

(Answer T for True and F for False for each statement)

1) I frequently worry about mistakes.   T   F
2) I get really down on myself during performance when I mess up.   T   F
3) It's easy for me to let go of my mistakes.   T   F
4) If I start out badly, it's hard for me to turn my performance around.   T   F
5) I get distracted by what the coach thinks whenever I screw up.   T   F
6) I bounce back quickly from setbacks, bad breaks and mistakes.   T   F

Clough et al (2002) have attempted to explain mental toughness as a set of coping skills that combine to make the individual *hardy*, that is, able to thrive under pressure. The concept of hardiness was developed in the field of health psychology by Kobasa (1979), whose aim was to explain why a minority of people do not appear to experience stress in circumstances that would be unhealthy for most of us. Clough and colleagues identified four characteristics underlying hardiness.

- control; being able to keep emotions in check
- commitment; taking an active role in events
- challenge; a positive attitude to change
- confidence; self-belief.

Support for the importance of hardiness comes from a study by Golby et al (2003), in which 70 international rugby league players were assessed for mental toughness and hardiness by standard measures (the Psychological Performance Inventory and the Personal Views Survey, respectively). Hardiness emerged as a significant factor affecting performance. At the time of writing, however, there is little consensus about how mental toughness should be defined and explained. Given the importance accorded to it by athletes, this is a source of frustration and represents a failure by the discipline of sport psychology.

Attentional style

Nideffer (1976) proposed that athletes' personality can be classified according to their individual information-processing characteristics. More specifically, he believed that our attention (the cognitive processes by which we focus and maintain focus on particular sources of information) can be measured in terms of two dimensions, width and direction.

- *Width* refers to our tendency to take in a broad range of information as opposed to focusing very narrowly on one source of information whilst tuning out other sources.
- *Direction* refers to *where* we tend to focus our attention, and varies from internal (our own mental and physical state) to external (what is happening around us).

Clearly, there are times when it is beneficial to focus narrowly and others when a wider focus is preferable. For example, tennis players must be able to focus narrowly on the ball but also use a broad focus to establish which way the opponent is moving – and hence to plan their next stroke. Similarly, it is sometimes important to focus on ourselves and other times more important to be able to focus on external events. For example, a rugby forward might maintain an internal focus in a scrum to be sure he was pushing effectively but an external focus to follow the direction of the ball. Effective attenders are those who can rapidly switch the direction and width of their attention and who do not easily become overloaded by information. Effective attention is beneficial in all sports. However, success in some sports is particularly associated with a particular attentional skill. For example, karateka particularly value a broad external focus (called *zanshin*), which allows the fighter to detect an attack from any direction.

Attentional style is measured by means of a 144-item questionnaire, the Test of Attentional and Interpersonal Style (TAIS). This measures 17 dimensions of personality, of which six are concerned with attention. The following three scales measure positive aspects of attentional style:

- The broad external scale (BET) assesses the athlete's ability to focus on several external stimuli.
- The broad internal scale (BIT) assesses the ability to analyse information from several sources.
- The narrow focus (NAR) scale assesses the ability to focus narrowly on one stimulus.

We would expect high scores on these scales to be associated with good performance. The other three scales measure negative aspects of attentional style, and we would expect high scores to be associated with poor performance.

- The overload external (OET) scale assesses the athlete's tendency to become overloaded with external stimuli and make errors as a result.
- The overload internal (OIT) scale assesses the tendency to become confused when analysing too many sources of data simultaneously.
- The reduced focus (RED) scale assesses the tendency to maintain too narrow a focus.

Box 2.9 shows some items from the TAIS.

Box 2.9 Items from the TAIS

1. When people talk to me, I find myself distracted by the sights and sounds around me.
2. When people talk to me, I find myself distracted by my own thoughts and ideas.
3. All I need is a little information, and I can come up with a large number of ideas.
4. My thoughts are limited to the objects and people in my immediate surroundings.
5. I need to have all the information before I say or do anything.
6. The work I do is focused narrowly, proceeding in a logical fashion.

There is some evidence to support the usefulness of Nideffer's approach. In one study, Nideffer (1976) administered the TAIS to a range of world and Olympic champions and found that one particular subscale, measuring effective narrowing of attention, predicted the number of gold medals won. A more recent study by Baghurst et al (2004) supports the distinction between internal and external directions. Using the TAIS, the researchers identified seven novice rowers with a strongly internal attentional style and seven with a strongly external style. Each group completed two 15-minute rowing trials. In one condition, they were asked to focus on their digital display to maintain constant attention on their performance. In the other, they were required to dissociate from the task by doing sums. Interestingly, the individuals identified as internal by means of the TAIS rowed further in 15 minutes when focusing on their performance, whereas those identified as external by the TAIS rowed further when focusing on sums (an external focus). However, not all studies have found such supportive results, and several commentators have questioned the validity of the TAIS. One particular problem concerns the ability of athletes to reflect accurately on their own attentional processes. Of course, the TAIS relies on this, as it measures athletes' perceptions of their attentional abilities rather than the abilities themselves.

Discussion of the trait and narrow-band approaches

The usefulness of the trait approach largely depends on its success in measuring personality. Personality tests derived from trait theories, such as the EPI and the 16PF, are called self-rating inventories. There are numerous problems with this type of test, and, if you have ever filled in an EPI or EPQ and received a score, you would be well advised not to take the results too seriously. Tests like this have limited test–retest reliability; that is, if you test someone and then test them again a few days or weeks later, they will tend to give the same responses to only about 80% of the questions. Answers to this type of test are influenced by mood and the social desirability of the answers – most people would rather be seen as extrovert than introvert and as stable rather than neurotic. Who administers the test and how they do so (e.g. alone or in a group) can also affect people's responses.

Ultimately, the trait approach to personality has yielded some fascinating results, but has limited application in sport psychology. As already discussed, we cannot radically change someone's personality traits in order to make them a better athlete. Nor would it be wise to use personality traits as a way of selecting athletes – seeing people perform will always be a better test of their potential. One way in which the trait approach can be useful, however, is in profiling individual athletes so that the sport psychologist can identify the type of difficulties that they are likely to encounter. Personality profiling involves measuring an athlete on a number of personality scales and building up a picture of their strengths and weaknesses. We might, for example, find that when a promising athlete is profiled, their only weakness is in achievement motivation or competitive anxiety. A coach can benefit from knowing this and may choose to manage that athlete accordingly. However, the best profiles of this type do not just measure personality traits but other psychological factors as well. We can return to the issue of profiling when discussing the interactional approach.

Situational and interactional approaches

One of the problems with trait theories, and to some extent with narrow-band theories as well, is that they assume that the individual's behaviour is consistent across a variety of situations. This largely ignores the impact that the situation itself has on the person's response. Mischel (1968) put forward the situationalist approach. This was a radical theory that rejected entirely the idea of stable personality traits. Instead, Mischel proposed that people's responses to situations could be explained entirely by the specifics of the situation. Effectively, this is a rejection of the whole concept of personality.

Reflective exercise

Imagine you are about to compete in a practice sprint at your local college or club. There are a few friends around, but nobody is paying you too much attention. No other serious runners are taking part. Now imagine instead that you are lining up for the final of the Olympic 100 metres.

1. List all the aspects of these two situations you can think of that differ.
2. How might your response to these two situations differ?

Nowadays, virtually no psychologists would accept situationalism as a complete explanation of behaviour. Mischel (1990) has himself backtracked somewhat, whilst still maintaining the important point that the way individuals think, feel and act in different situations varies considerably more than we would expect if trait theory were entirely correct. The idea that our behaviour at any time is the product of an interaction between the situation and our personality is called the interactional view, first proposed by Bowers (1973).

Applying the interactional model to sport

The vignette in the reflective exercise above should illustrate the importance of situations. However, we can understand people's behaviour better if we look at how the situation interacts with their personality. You probably all know someone who is a friendly, jolly character who, in their social life, would not hurt a fly, yet, on the sports field seems almost uncontrollably aggressive. We cannot explain this person's actions by situation or personality alone. We know that they are not simply aggressive because their behaviour is not aggressive in other situations. We also know that competing on the sports field does not make the rest of us uncontrollably aggressive. Therefore, this individual's aggression when taking part in sport must result from some complex interaction between their personality and the sporting situation.

Cox (2001) has estimated the importance of various factors in sporting performance. Personality, situation and the interaction between personality and situation together account for less than half the variance in athletic performance, as shown in Figure 2.3.

Profiling moods

We know that, although we can produce profiles of athletes' personalities, this is not necessarily useful in predicting how well they will perform. However, the interactional model gives us another angle on profiling. Instead of trying to measure people's underlying personality traits, we can instead measure their mood at the time of performance. An athlete's mood at any one time is a product of both personality and situation; therefore, it is a much more valid measure of their psychological state during performance. McNair et al (1972) developed the Profile of Mood States (POMS), a 65-item questionnaire that assesses individuals on six scales: tension, depression, anger, vigour, fatigue and confusion. The POMS was originally developed for assessing the state of psychiatric patients, but it quickly caught on in the field of sport psychology.

Morgan (1979) have produced the mood profile for elite athletes, by measuring them on each of the POMS scales. Figure 2.4 shows the classic iceberg profile of an elite athlete. The flatter profile of the less successful athlete is also shown. Elite athletes score lower on most mood measures, notably on tension and depression, but higher on

Figure 2.3 The relative importance of personality, situation and other factors in athletic performance (from Cox, 2001).

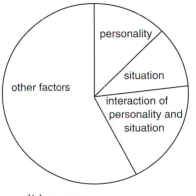

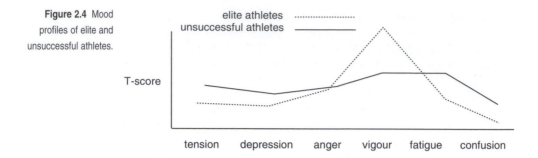

Figure 2.4 Mood profiles of elite and unsuccessful athletes.

vigour. Numerous studies have shown that elite athletes from a variety of sports do tend to exhibit the iceberg profile. Thus, Bell & Howe (1988) found iceberg profiles in triathletes, and Gat & McWhirter (1998) found the same pattern in cyclists. Beedie et al (2000) carried out a meta-analysis of previous studies relating POMS to performance. Meta-analysis is a statistical technique in which the results of previous studies are combined, weighting each study for sample size. In this case meta-analysis revealed that, taken across a range of sports, POMS profiles were fairly predictive of performance. Vigour, depression and confusion were particularly strongly associated with performance.

Discussion of the interactional approach

As the interactional approach looks at how individuals respond to specific sport-related situations, it is more useful than the trait approach for predicting athletic performance. Of course, in practice, the two approaches can be used together. When profiles of individual athletes are drawn up for training purposes, the best profiles include information about both personality and mood states.

In her review of personality research in sport, Vealey (1989) identified a shift away from trait measurement since the 1970s in favour of the interactional approach. However, this approach is not without its critics. Some sport psychologists reject the idea of testing athletes for mood or traits. Prapavessis (2000) points out that where studies compare average POMS scores of elite and unsuccessful athletes, these averages obscure wide individual differences. This was confirmed by a study of golfers (Hassmen et al, 1998), in which pre-performance moods were associated with performance in some players but not in others. Thus, there are highly successful performers who do not exhibit an iceberg profile. In general, POMS scores are only moderately predictive of performance.

Summary and conclusions

Considerable energy has been spent in the attempt to understand the relationship between sporting participation and achievement and personality. One approach involves looking at personality traits, stable aspects of personality with a partial genetic basis. The most influential trait theories are those of Eysenck, Cattell, and Costa and McCrae. They differ primarily in their view of the number of traits that make up personality. There is some evidence to suggest that some traits are associated with participation and success in sport; for example, sporting participants tend to be more extravert and stable than non-participants. However, results are mixed, and we should be wary about drawing too many hard and fast conclusions.

There are alternatives to the trait approach and these have been gaining ground in recent years. One alternative is the narrow-band approach, which, rather than breaking down all aspects of personality to traits, focuses on specific aspects of personality. Sensation seeking has received particular attention and is reliably associated with participation in high-risk sports. The quality of mental toughness is considered important by athletes but thus far has defied precise definition and explanation by sport psychologists. Attentional style appears to be a promising line of research, but there are questions over the validity of current measures. Another alternative to looking at traits is the interactional approach, which looks at the interaction between individuals and their situation; this may result, for example, in a profile of mood states. A substantial body of research has shown that, at least for many athletes, individual performance is associated with a distinctive 'iceberg' profile of mood states.

Self-assessment questions

1. Define personality. Your definition should take account of the trait, narrow-band and interactional perspectives.
2. Compare and contrast the trait theories of Eysenck and Cattell.
3. Critically discuss research into the relationship between sporting participation and choice of sport and personality traits.
4. To what extent can sporting success be considered a product of personality traits?
5. Explain why mental toughness is considered an important concept but is so difficult to pin down.
6. Discuss the concept of attentional style.

7. What are the advantages of adopting an interactional approach to personality? Discuss the POMS as a measurement instrument appropriate to the interactional approach.

Further reading

- Clough P, Earle K & Sewell D (2002) Mental toughness: the concept and its measurement. In Cockerill I (ed) *Solutions in sport psychology*. London, Thomson Learning.
- Gill D (2000) *Psychological dynamics of sport*. Champagne, IL, Human Kinetics.
- *Journal of Applied Sport Psychology* Volume 12, Special Issue: *Profile of mood states*. March 2000.
- Kremer J & Scully D (1994) *Psychology in sport*. Hove, Taylor & Francis.
- Vealey RS (2002) Personality and sport behaviour. In Horn T (ed) *Advances in sport psychology*. Champagne, IL, Human Kinetics.

Personality development and sport 3

Learning objectives

By the end of this chapter you should able to:

- outline social learning theory as a basis for understanding the relationship between sport and personality development
- appreciate the range of social influences on the development of sport-related behaviour, including the family and wider culture
- discuss the relationship between gender and sport
- understand the debate concerning the possible positive and negative influences of sport on social development
- discuss psychodynamic theory as an alternative approach to understanding the relationship between sport and personality development, with particular reference to the pathological aspects of sporting participation.

In Chapter 2, we examined the relationship between personality characteristics and sporting behaviour. However, there is another way of looking at the relationship between sport and individual differences. Trait, narrow-band and interactional approaches to personality all emphasise the aspects of personality that are fairly stable across the lifespan and are at least partly influenced by genetic make-up. This chapter is based on developmental approaches to psychology and focuses on the relationship between experience and personality. This calls for a slightly different definition of personality (Engler, 1999). Rather than thinking in terms of breaking down personality to its components, developmental theories see the personality of the individual as the sum of their formative experiences.

Social learning theory

The social learning approach to psychology (developed by Albert Bandura in 1977) differs from trait and interactional approaches in that it sees individual differences in behaviour as resulting from different learning experiences. This means that what determines an individual's response to a situation is not so much their genetic make-up or the constraints of the particular situation, but instead how past experience has taught that person to act. Although social learning theory is not the only psychological approach that emphasises the role of past experience on personality, it is the most influential such theory in sport psychology.

Bandura (1977) proposed that learning of behaviour takes place in two main ways, operant conditioning and modelling. Operant conditioning involves learning by reinforcement. When we experiment with a new behaviour, there are four possible outcomes – positive reinforcement, negative reinforcement, a neutral response and punishment.

- In positive reinforcement, the behaviour is *rewarded*.
- Negative reinforcement involves *removal of an aversive stimulus* in response to the behaviour.
- A neutral response means that no positive or negative consequences result from the behaviour.
- Punishment involves introducing an unpleasant consequence or removing a pleasant one.

Clearly, if we try out a behaviour and something positive results, we are rewarded. The behaviour is thus said to be positively reinforced, and we learn that that is a 'good' or 'useful' behaviour and add it to our repertoire of behaviours. Similarly, if we commit a suspect behaviour and escape punishment, we are negatively reinforced, and are likely to repeat the behaviour. If, on the other hand, the behaviour does not achieve anything (neutral response), or if it results in something nasty happening to us (punishment), we are not likely to repeat it.

Modelling involves learning new behaviours by watching and copying the behaviour of others. Bandura has proposed that learning of behaviour takes place in the following four stages:

- *Attention*; we watch others behave in a certain way.
- *Retention*; we commit what we have watched to memory.
- *Reproduction*; we try out the behaviour ourselves.

- *Reinforcement*; we consider the consequences of the behaviour and decide whether or not to repeat it.

We do not have to experience reinforcement personally to learn from it. If we observe someone else's behaviour being rewarded, we can add that behaviour to our own repertoire. This is called *vicarious* reinforcement. We can similarly learn by seeing someone punished or escaping punishment for a behaviour.

An important factor in determining whether a particular behaviour is imitated is the nature of the model. Duck (1990) has suggested that the resemblance between the model and the observer may determine the effectiveness of that model; thus, same-sex models are more effect-ive than opposite-sex models. Other important attributes of effective models include their social status, social power and general likeability. Parents, teachers, high-status peers and celebrities, including top ath-letes, can all be potent models. The fact that professional athletes enjoy high social status and are thus role models for young people makes it important that they conduct themselves in a 'sporting' manner.

Applying social learning theory to sport

Social learning theory will crop up throughout this book. It provides at least a partial explanation of individual differences in attitudes, aggression and motivation. Two applications of social learning are particularly worth considering in this chapter: explaining how we acquire patterns of sport-related behaviour and explaining how we acquire a love of sport.

Patterns of sport-related behaviour

To social learning psychologists, personality is not something we are born with but rather a set of learned behaviour patterns. Some of these learned patterns can be quite specific to sport. Earlier in the chapter, we considered how we might explain why some people display very aggressive behaviour during sport, even though they do not appear aggressive in other situations. Social learning theory would explain this in terms of the individual's learning that aggression is the correct response to the sporting situation. This might mean that somehow that individual had received reinforcement for acting aggressively in the past, as for example, by scoring a point, or receiving a pat on the back or a comment of 'that's my boy' from a coach or parent after an aggressive act (Figure 3.1). In Bandura's model, this might be represented by the sequence shown in Box 3.1.

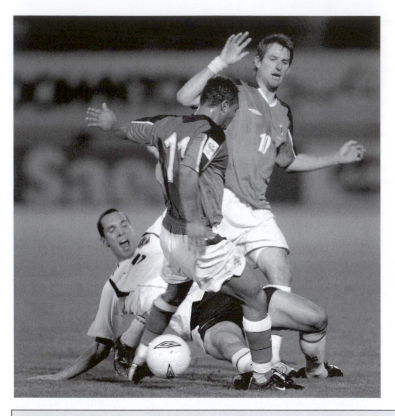

Figure 3.1 Children witnessing this behaviour may imitate it.
Copyright © Paul McErlane/Reuters/Corbis

Box 3.1 An example of social learning

- *Attention*; a child witnesses a very aggressive tackle while watching football on television.
- *Retention*; the knowledge of aggressive tackling is retained in memory.
- *Reproduction*; the next time the child is playing football, he copies the technique of aggressive tackling.
- *Reinforcement*; if the aggressive tackle receives negative reinforcement as by preventing a goal, or positive reinforcement in the form of receiving praise, it is likely to become part of the child's regular behaviour.

Athletes as role models

An important implication of the fact that children tend to copy the sport-related behaviour of adults is that any athlete in the public eye is a role model for children. Since the huge majority of sportspeople conduct themselves admirably, and regularly demonstrate to young people the importance of hard work, perseverance, cooperation and a 'sporting' attitude, the world of sport can give itself a collective pat on the back and acknowledge that it probably contributes very significantly to the healthy development of young people. Some sportspeople such as Jonathon Edwards and Kriss Akabusi provide particularly good role models by visiting local schools and conducting training sessions.

The other side of the coin is that, from a social learning viewpoint, it is important that poor behaviour by high-profile athletes is punished. If public figures in sport are seen to behave inappropriately and profit from doing so, children may receive vicarious reinforcement and copy the inappropriate behaviour. At the time of writing, there is particular concern over the behaviour of Premiership footballers. In 2005, Martin Ward, deputy leader of the Secondary Heads Association, which represents head teachers in England and Wales, went so far as to say that football should be shown after the 9 pm watershed because 'violence, verbal abuse, foul language, cheating and defiance of authority . . . occur much more frequently . . . in professional football, often without the player even being cautioned'. There have, however, been moves to amend the situation in football, and, recently, cases of poor behaviour have been promptly and severely punished. For example, in March 2005, Southampton's David Prutton was fined £6000 and banned for 10 matches after he refused to leave the pitch and threatened officials, on receiving a red card. In terms of social learning, Prutton's case was probably not the worst – he showed genuine remorse and was severely punished for his actions.

Reflective exercise

This will help develop your creative thinking. According to sport psychologist Ellis Cashmore, the world's most potent role model in the early 2000s is David Beckham. It has been suggested that Beckham, in contrast to previous leading footballers such as Paul Gascoigne, has been in many ways a good role model for young men. In particular, he provides a model of the 'new man'. In 2000, Beckham missed training at Manchester United in order to care for his sick son. The editor of *Dad* magazine has commented that Beckham's attitudes are making it easier for fathers to display love for their children publicly.

Figure 3.2 David Beckham. Copyright © Ian Hodgson/Reuters/Corbis

Most radically for a footballer, Beckham has welcomed his gay following.

1. On the basis of social learning theory, explain why David Beckham has become such a powerful role model.
2. Consider what other reasons there might be for Beckham's high profile.
3. According to social learning theory, what might be the effect of Beckham's alleged affair in spring 2004?

Acquiring love of sport

One very obvious question that sport psychologists have probably not asked enough is, 'Why, as a species, are we so obsessed with sport in the first place?' From a trait perspective, Eysenck et al (1982) proposed that people of a certain personality type are naturally attracted to sport. However, social learning theory can perhaps provide a better explanation, although it is probably not a complete answer. Children (perhaps especially boys) receive positive reinforcement from a very young age if they show interest and talent in sport. We also receive vicarious reinforcement every time we see an athlete win and enjoy the benefits of winning. It is important for Parents and coaches to remember that if they want young people to acquire a positive attitude toward sport, they should provide them with plenty of positive experiences of sport. Sport teachers also need to present themselves as the type of people all children, not just the athletic elite, can identify with. If, as has been sadly common in the past, PE teachers present themselves as brusque and unapproachable, providing reinforcement only for the talented few, they should not be surprised when those children who have been ignored do not go on to participate in sport.

Sources of influence on social development and sport

We are all constantly influenced by other people. Perhaps our most important influences are those we encounter when we are children. The term *socialisation* describes the process whereby people acquire the rules of behaviour and the systems of beliefs and attitudes that form part of life in their society. Probably the most important influence on our socialisation is the family. The term *primary socialisation* is used to mean socialisation by the family, especially by our parents. Other agents of socialisation include our friends and teachers, and, in the case of young athletes, our coaches and teammates. The influence of these others is known as *secondary socialisation*.

The influence of the family

Both everyday experience and research suggest that our experiences of family life exert a profound influence on our social development. Social learning theory emphasises the role of models in the family and sources of reinforcement. This can affect sport-ing behaviour in a number of ways. Most obviously, children are likely to identify with a family member and follow in their footsteps, participating in their sport (Figure 3.3).

Spectating with family members is also important because children can receive vicari-ous reinforcement when family members are heard to praise athletes. In fact the attention given to athletes when a family spectates together can be a vicarious reinforcer. Because sport is widely considered a socially valuable activity, it is also likely that children who imi-tate the sporting behaviour of athletes will receive direct positive reinforcement from praise from family members.

The role of families in developing attitudes to sport was investigated in a study by Jambor (1999). A total of 165 parents of children aged 5–10 years who did or did not participate in football were questioned on their beliefs and attitudes about sport. The parents of football players differed signifi-cantly from those of non-players, having more positive beliefs about sport, for example, in terms of health benefits, and being more likely to take part in sport themselves. Thus, it seems that modelling of sporting behaviour is one factor in children's participation, but that parental attitudes and beliefs also have an effect, independent of modelling.

Figure 3.3 Children imitate family role models. Copyright © Rick Gomez/Corbis

The influence of wider culture

A *culture* is a set of beliefs, practices, values and customs that are associated with a group of people. Although the term is commonly used in comparing the behaviour of different national and ethnic groups, a culture can exist in any group. Thus, a sporting team will develop their own culture. Cultural differences between ethnic and national groups have been extensively studied in psychology. Psy-chologists are interested in the similarities between cultural groups (these similarities are collectively known as *emic*) and differences between them (collectively known as *etic*). Culture operates at a wider level than the family, influencing *what* values, beliefs and customs we learn from the family through mechanisms such as social learning. Of course, we absorb culture outside the family as well, through interaction with peers and through the media.

An example of the way in which cultural beliefs can affect our sporting development is in our attributions of success and failure. Morgan et al (1996) compared black, Native American and white field and track athletes' perceptions about the influences on sporting success, and found significant cultural differences. The white athletes tended to see success as something unchangeable ('you've either got it or you haven't'). However, the black and Native American athletes placed much more emphasis on the importance of effort in achieving success.

The extent to which children are socialised toward sport depends to a large extent on the culture in which socialisation takes place. For example, Zaman (1998) has pointed out that Muslim women are excluded from almost all British sports, not due to any lack of desire to participate in physical activity, but rather because of a clash of cultures. The values of competitiveness, masculinity and confidence that dominate British sport are simply incompatible with Islamic feminine ideals. The Muslim *awarh* (modesty of dress) is also difficult to cater for in Anglicised sport settings.

Cultural differences in socialisation can also be seen in sport-related attitudes to things such as cooperation, competition, achievement and winning. Azuma (1987) identified Japanese children as socialised to be particularly respectful, cooperative and oriented toward achievement. All these characteristics probably serve to make Japanese children excellent team players and extremely coachable. By contrast, North American children, whilst also very oriented toward achievement, have been found in many studies to be less cooperative and respectful of authority. This has clear implications for coaching. Team building is a priority in Western sport, as cooperation and putting the team first cannot be taken for granted as they can be in a more collectivist culture.

Gender and sport

The term *gender* refers to the psychological as opposed to the biological aspects of being male and female. Biological *sex* differences have an obvious influence on sporting performance, but what is subtler and perhaps more interesting is the way in which issues of *gender* affect sporting behaviour. Our perceptions of what is appropriate masculine and feminine behaviour can have profound effects on our actions, and this is clearly important in sport. Typically, boys and girls are socialised into different patterns of behaviour. For example, girls are much more likely to be nagged at in childhood not to get dirty (Kremer & Scully, 1994). They also tend to have role models who maintain stereotypically feminine behaviour that does not normally involve wallowing in mud! (Figure 3.4). Clearly, this is likely to lessen the chances of girls' involvement in sports such as rugby and hockey that necessarily involve getting muddy. Girls are also likely to receive positive reinforcement for displaying the 'feminine' characteristics of passivity, submissiveness, dependency, low aggression and low need for achievement (Cox, 2001). Clearly, these qualities are not helpful in sport.

Figure 3.4 Feminine roles can be hard to reconcile with athleticism. Copyright © Brooke Fusani/Corbis

There are, then, good reasons why gender should affect sporting behaviour, but what does the research say? Miller & Levy (1996) surveyed 145 young women about their attitudes to femininity and sport. They found that most women were anxious about appearing feminine if they participated in sport, but that this anxiety tended to be less in a woman whose mother was also a sporting participant. Concerns about femininity and sport may begin in early adolescence. Hagger (1997) surveyed 9–11-year-old English children on their attitudes to sport and found that both boys and girls were overwhelmingly positive in their perceptions of sport, and no gender differences emerged. However, a recent French study suggests that gender identity does affect sporting participation. Guillet et al (2000) investigated whether gender role was associated with participation by girls in handball, regarded in France as a masculine sport. A total of 336 French girls aged 13–15 were classified as either feminine, masculine or androgynous (i.e. they had a balance of masculine and feminine characteristics) by a psychometric test called the Bem Sex Role Inventory. At the start of the study, all the participants played handball; however, they had the opportunity to drop it at school. Girls with a feminine identity were significantly more likely to drop handball than others.

Reflective exercise

This should help develop your critical and creative thinking.

The Hagger (1997) and Guillet et al (2000) studies found quite different conclusions. Hagger's results suggest no relationship between gender and sport, whereas Guillet suggests a strong relationship.

1. Identify as many differences as you can in the way the two studies were carried out. What are the limitations of each study?
2. Design the 'definitive' study that would give you the answer to the question, does gender affect participation in sport?

Some additional research has suggested that there can be difficulty in combining the roles of athlete and woman. In one study, Lantz & Schroeder (1999) assessed athletic identity with a self-rating inventory called the Athletic Identity Measurement Scale and the Bem Sex-Role Inventory in 173 male and 236 female athletes. Athletic identity was positively correlated with masculinity and negatively correlated with femininity. This suggests that athletic identity involves adopting 'masculine' characteristics and rejecting 'femininity'. Some sports can present particular difficulties to women. Grogan et al (2004) interviewed seven female bodybuilders and found evidence of a conflict between living in a culture that equates femininity with slimness and seeking a more muscular body type. The authors conclude that female bodybuilders find themselves in a balancing act between the values of the body-building community and society at large.

Modern sports and alternative gender roles

Most research has supported an association between participation in the traditional sports and the traditional masculine identity. However, in looking at less traditional sports, a more mixed picture has emerged. Beal (1996) investigated 41 American skateboarders, using a combination of participant observation and interviews. It emerged that skateboarders have a subculture quite distinct from that of more conventional sport. There was an emphasis on self-control, self-expression and open participation, rather than aggression and

Box 3.2 Media coverage of male and female athletes

A fascinating body of recent research has looked at the different ways in which men and women are portrayed in the media. In one recent study, Billings et al (2002) analysed the way commentators used language to discuss sporting performances by men and women. A total of 2367 lines of commentary from the 2000 American Collegiate Athletic Association Finals were examined. Significantly more time was spent discussing male than female athletes, and, while the men were commented on for their performance and athletic ability, women were primarily talked of for their personality, looks, decorum and background (Figure 3.5).

Figure 3.5 Female athletes are evaluated by commentators for looks and personality rather than performance. Copyright © Pete Saloutos/Corbis

Another study by Curry et al (2002) looked at coverage of sport in men's and women's magazines. In women's magazines, 65% of athletes were female, and 85% of those featured in men's magazines were male. Importantly, the coverage in men's magazines was much more likely to emphasise competition and aggression, whereas that in women's magazines predominantly emphasised cooperation and participation for pleasure. The results of both these studies are interesting in that they reveal the kinds of subtle messages being given out about the role of women in sport. In particular, both studies show how the athletic performance of women is played down.

conformity. Nonetheless, the skateboarders considered their sport to be masculine. A different picture emerged of snowboarders in a study by Anderson (2001). Using interviews, participant observation and content analysis of snowboarding magazines, Anderson found that snowboarders identified with other traditional masculine role models, were frequently aggressive and violent, and vigorously asserted their heterosexuality.

Sport as an influence on social development

It has been widely proposed that participation in sport, particularly by children, is in some way 'character building'. Ewing et al (2002) have suggested the following six ways in which taking part in sport might exert an influence on child development: fitness, social competence, physical competence, moral development, aggression and education. The evidence for the benefits of sport across these domains is highly mixed. On the one hand, sport does provide opportunities for young people to experience both cooperation and competition, and so to develop their social competence. On the other hand, there is a worrying body of evidence to suggest that athletes are more prejudiced and sexually aggressive than other people.

The 'character-building' argument

It is common to hear successful adults speak fondly of their childhood experiences of sport, and to attribute their success, at least in part, to having participated in sport while growing up. There may be some basis for this. Certainly, participants and spectators witness dedication, courage, discipline and perseverance on almost every sporting occasion. In addition, socially disadvantaged groups can benefit from seeing members of their community publicly succeeding in sport (Krane, 1998). In fact, the stereotypes held of minority ethnic groups by others may be changed for the good in response to their sporting success. However, this is not to say that sport is necessarily a positive influence on the lives of most or all young people. Whilst successful adults speak fondly about their sporting youth, we should perhaps not take this too seriously as evidence. Energetic, competitive people are likely to be successful both in sport *and* in their careers. This means that, although they may *believe* their success in business is related to sport, it is more likely that both their sporting and career success owe much to their personality. In addition, as Krane (1998) says, most research has focused on successful athletes, and we know almost nothing about the futures of those who have negative childhood experiences of sport.

Evidence for the benefits of sporting participation

It has proved to be fairly tricky to demonstrate much in the way of benefits for taking part in sport. One line of research has compared problem behaviours in young people who do and do not take part in sport. Kirkcaldy et al (2002) looked at 988 German adolescents, assessing their mental health, smoking, drinking, self-image and educational achievement. In all measures, those who regularly participated in sport came out better, emerging with better self-image and mental health, and smoking and drinking less. The authors suggested that sport facilitates meaningful discussion among young people, who can then tackle personal issues; thus, the sporting participation directly led to the superior mental state of participants. However, this interpretation is open to challenge.

Reflective exercise

This should help you develop your critical and creative thinking.
  Consider the Kirkcaldy et al (2002) study.

1. To what extent can the authors' beliefs that sport led to the better results in measures of mental health and health-related behaviour be justified?
2. Consider other possible factors that could have led to these findings.

Another way of looking at the relationship between taking part in sport and character development is to conduct experiments using sport as a tool to improve the development of young people. In one study, Hastie & Sharpe (1999) followed up the development of 20 Australian adolescents classified as 'at risk', who took part in 20 sessions of 'kangaroo ball'. Coaching particularly emphasised fair play. Significant improvements in compliance with teachers, interpersonal interaction and leadership were found after the programme. These findings are encouraging; however, there are limitations to the usefulness of studies like this. The style of coaching used in this study was designed to foster prosocial development, and may have been quite different from the PE teaching and coaching most young people encounter. Moreover, the participants in this study were not typical young people; therefore, we should be cautious about generalising results to young people as a whole.

Sport and the development of antisocial behaviour

If the research evidence for positive effects of sporting participation is rather thin on the ground, and the positive interpretations are open to challenge, there has been no shortage of studies of the potential negative impact of sport on development. There are, for example, many cases in which athletes model antisocial as well as prosocial behaviour. Waxmonsky & Beresin (2001) have highlighted the antisocial values modelled in professional wrestling. Wrestling in the entertainment form (as opposed to the purely sporting form) is characterised by a verbal intimidation and cheating directly opposed to 'sporting' values. If wrestling stars are indeed role models, their influence may be a negative one. Vicarious reinforcement through witnessing professional wrestlers win matches by cheating and intimidation may be a further negative influence on children's social behaviour.

There is evidence to suggest that sport may be associated with antisocial behaviour, including violence and intimidation, and with antisocial attitudes such as sexism and homophobia. Mixed results emerged in a recent study by Smith & Stewart (2003), in which male undergraduates were assessed for hostility to women and attitudes to rape. Athletes scored significantly higher in hostility to women, but were no more supportive of rape than students who did not take part in sport. In another study by Muir and Seitz (2004), in which rugby players were studied by participant and non-participant observation, considerable evidence of sexism and homophobia was found. A fascinating study by Craig (2000) suggests that sexual violence by athletes is expected. Students were given scenarios in which men, either athletes or non-athletes, battered women. The students' responses to the men's behaviour were analysed, and it emerged that the participants were much less harsh in their judgements of battering by athletes.

Thinking critically about the arguments

If the evidence linking sport to the development of prosocial behaviour can easily be picked apart, the same is true of the evidence for the antisport case. Although some sporting spectacles, such as professional wrestling, do lead to the modelling of antisocial behaviour, there is no direct evidence that watching them has a negative impact on viewers. It may also be that, although there is a relationship between athletic participation and unhealthy attitudes to women, it is not a simple one. It may be, for example, that there is an additional variable that is more common in athletes and in misogynists, meaning that samples of athletes contain more misogynists than matched groups of non-athletes, but that attitudes are no more extreme or antisocial amongst athletes taken as a whole. Evidence for this comes from Caron et al (1997), who assessed athletic participation, competitiveness, hostility to women and attitudes to rape in 104 male students aged 18–24. No overall difference in sexual aggression between participants and non-participants in sport emerged; however, it was found that highly competitive people were both more supportive of rape and more likely to participate in sport. This suggests that it is competitiveness rather than sporting participation per se that is linked to sexual aggression. Other studies (e.g. Dru, 2003) have supported the importance of this quality of *hypercompetitiveness* in explaining intolerance among some athletes. It is also worth considering the samples used in most of the research in this area, that is, undergraduate students. It may well be that hypercompetitive individuals are overrepresented among student samples of athletes simply because most students, including those who participate in sport before and after university, are simply too laid back to play sport while they are students!

The role of coaching

It seems, then, that, if we leave aside for a moment the limitations of the research, sport may exert both positive and negative influences on development. An important factor affecting the extent to which sport is a positive influence appears to be the values put across during teaching and coaching. In one study of the coach's role, Shields (1999) assessed the association between situation, pressure and coaching style and the frequency of intimidation and violence during basketball and football. Coaching style was the only factor associated with frequency of intimidation and violence, suggesting that the coach and the PE teacher have enormous power over the social behaviour of those in their charge.

The psychodynamic approach to personality development

The psychodynamic approach to personality development represents a radical departure from the sort of psychology usually favoured by sport psychologists. It is derived mainly from clinical case studies, and its main applications have been clinical. However, there is a small body of literature linking psychodynamic theory to sport. The general assumptions underlying the psychodynamic approach to psychology are shown in Box 3.3.

Putting these assumptions together, we can arrive at a simple definition of the psychodynamic approach as one which emphasises the importance of unconscious factors in our emotional state and hence our behaviour, and the role of early experience, particularly early relationships, in shaping those unconscious influences. The psychodynamic approach is heavily theoretical, the first and most important theory being that of Sigmund Freud. For reasons of space, only Freudian ideas and their relationship to sport are examined here.

> **Box 3.3** Assumptions of the psychodynamic approach. Adapted from Jarvis (2004)
>
> - **The primary importance of emotion.** In contrast to the emphasis in other psychological approaches to behaviour, thinking and reasoning, emotion is the primary focus of psychodynamic psychology.
> - **The continuity between childhood and adult experience.** Many characteristics of the adult personality, both normal and abnormal, can be traced to childhood experience.
> - **The significance of early relationships.** Our social and emotional development is powerfully affected by the quality of the relationships we have experienced. Relationships with parents are considered particularly important.
> - **The psychological significance of subjective experience.** Experiences such as dreams, fantasy and sense of identity are of particular interest to those adopting a psychodynamic approach to psychology.
> - **The influence of the unconscious mind.** The nature of the unconscious mind varies considerably in alternative theories, but all psychodynamic approaches share the assumption that we are influenced in some way by mental processes of which we are not normally aware.

Applications of Freudian theory

Freudian theory is vast and complex, and no attempt at a comprehensive review is made here (see Jarvis, 2000, for a quick overview and Jarvis (2004), for a detailed account). What we can do is to relate some of Freud's key ideas to sport. The most basic of Freud's ideas was the influence of the unconscious mind, which consists of sexual and aggressive instincts and early experiences. The unconscious exerts a subtle but constant influence on us, for example, through seeking secondary gain and sublimation.

Unconscious motivation and secondary gain

Sometimes we can be motivated to behave irrationally and against our conscious wishes in response to unconscious influences. The term *secondary gain* is given to the benefits of behaviours that we would not consciously opt for. Ferraro (1999a) has suggested that there are profound secondary gains in sporting defeat in the form of sympathy, and that awareness of these can lead to an unconscious desire to be defeated. Ferraro cites the example of the golfer Greg Norman, who received thousands of supportive letters and extremely positive press coverage when he lost the 1996 Masters after a 6-stroke lead.

Sublimation

Freud proposed a set of psychological defence mechanisms with which the mind protects itself from unpleasant emotional states. These include denial, in which we refuse to admit an unpleasant fact to ourselves, and repression, in which we forcibly forget a memory charged with negative emotion. Another defence of particular relevance to sport is *sublimation*, which takes place when we manage to displace our emotions into constructive rather than destructive activity. Freud cited sport, along with art, as a method of sublimation. Richards (1994) has emphasised the sublimation of aggressive instincts in football. Kicking is an aggressive act, and by kicking a ball what we are really doing is sublimating our instinct to kick each other into a safe and socially acceptable action.

Psychosexual development

Freud (1905) proposed three major stages of personality development in early childhood. These are critical in shaping the adult personality. Ferraro (1999b) has suggested links between each stage and the development of sport-related behaviour. In the oral stage (0–1 year), the infant is suckled and weaned, and its experiences are reflected in later personality characteristics such as dependence/independence and in oral behaviours such as smoking and eating. Ferraro suggests that the American tendency to take performance-enhancing drugs is rooted in cultural norms of early weaning that result in unsatisfied oral needs in the developing child. He supports this argument by comparison with Japan, in which weaning is more flexible and rates of drug taking are much lower. In the anal stage (1–3 years, dominated by potty-training), the developing child acquires attitudes to authority, control and perfectionism. These are all significant in sport. In the phallic stage (3–6 years), the child learns to master aggression and competitiveness in order to win the affection of its opposite-sex parent. It may be no coincidence that hypercompetitiveness, which in psychodynamic terms results from unresolved phallic issues, is associated with sexual violence (see p 49).

Narcissism

The term 'narcissism' comes from the legend of the Greek youth Narcissus, who fell in love with his own reflection (Rathvon & Holmstrom, 1996). *Primary narcissism* is a normal characteristic of infants (Freud, 1914). Mental energy is centred on the self rather than others, meaning that the infant is self-centred and does not have deep emotional attachments to others. Normally, as the child develops relationships, initially with the primary carer and later with other family members, narcissism declines. However, in response to poor early relationships, the child may go on to exhibit *pathological narcissism*. Highly narcissistic people can function well in situations where they need to form only shallow relationships, but have difficulty in forming deeper relationships. Their behaviour is also characterised by self-aggrandisement and fantasies of perfection or power. They are exploitative and typically demand special favours. Serious narcissism is associated with serious mental health problems, including schizophrenia and personality disorders.

Elman & McKelvie (2003) observed that American football players frequently display signs of narcissism on campus; for example, they expect not to have to queue. This fits the image of American footballers as physically impressive and their use of figure-enhancing padding. Thirty-six footballers, 33 other athletes and 43 non-athletes were administered a standard psychometric test called the Narcissistic Personality Inventory. As expected, the football players were indeed more narcissistic than other students.

Discussion of the psychodynamic approach

Freudian theory is very different in nature from most of the approaches used in sport psychology, and its speculative and heavily theoretical nature does not sit comfortably with many sport psychologists. Concepts such as sublimation, psychosexuality and narcissism are resistant to precise definition and measurement. Conducting empirical studies into Freudian ideas is thus notoriously difficult. However, this is not to say that the approach is without merit. The 'psychodynamic paradox', as it is sometimes called, is that, in spite of the limitations of the approach, there is definitely something in it. Unconscious influences, however we think of them, undoubtedly exist, and our understanding of personality would be incomplete without some reference to them (Jarvis, 2004). Certainly, when we are thinking about highly irrational behaviour, such as giving up a lead to lose a match or behaving dangerously, it is worth considering the influence of the unconscious mind.

On a practical level, Strean & Strean (1998) and Ferraro (1999a) have suggested that there is a place for psychodynamic therapy in helping athletes to cope with psychological problems rooted in the unconscious. However, this is not widely practised, and hence there is a lack of evidence of its effectiveness in the sporting context. As Giges (1998) says, applying psychodynamic techniques in working with athletes, without highly specialist training and supervision, is inappropriate. There is also some evidence that athletes resist attempts to 'put them on the couch'. As one international athlete said, 'If I am going to lie on my back for an hour then I expect to be enjoying myself' (quoted in Moran, 2004).

Reflective exercise

Practise your critical thinking on the psychodynamic approach to personality development. Consider in particular the following:

1. Is the theory based on a sound evidence base?
2. How testable and well supported by research are psychodynamic concepts?
3. Does the approach address aspects of the personality not adequately addressed by other psychological approaches?
4. Does the approach have practical applications?

Summary and conclusions

Although some aspects of personality are fairly stable and probably influenced by our genes, our behaviour is also influenced by our experiences. The most important theory within sport psychology on this influence of experience is Bandura's social learning theory, which explains learning in terms of modelling and reinforcement of behaviour. Social learning is important in understanding the development of sporting behaviour and in particular the influence of athletic role models. The family and culture at large are potent sources of influence on the development of sporting behaviour. Social learning theory is important in understanding how these influences operate. A radical alternative to social learning theory comes in the form of Freud's psychodynamic theory. This has been less influential in sport psychology, largely because of its heavy reliance on speculative theory. However, it is helpful in understanding the more irrational aspects of sporting behaviour. Gender and sport have a complex relationship. Some, though by no means all, research has found that gender role is associated with sporting participation, and that female athletes struggle to maintain both a feminine and athletic identity.

An important question for child and sport psychologists is the effect of sporting participation on social development. Although it is widely assumed that sport is 'character building', the evidence is actually highly mixed, and the character-building hypothesis is not particularly well supported. There is a large body of research linking sporting participation to sexism, aggression and homophobia. However, these findings may be explained by the existence of large numbers of hypercompetitive individuals in university sports teams, and they certainly do not constitute a reason to discourage children from taking part in sport. But it is well worth considering the style of coaching and teaching used with young athletes, as coaching style predicts the frequency of antisocial behaviour.

Self-assessment questions

1. Outline social learning theory and explain one way in which social learning is linked to sporting behaviour.
2. Explain how primary and secondary socialisation influence the development of sport-related behaviour.
3. Is there a relationship between gender identity and sporting participation? Use evidence to support your answer.
4. Discuss the idea that taking part in sport is 'character-building'.
5. How helpful is Freudian theory in understanding sporting behaviour?

Further reading

- Ellis CJ, Riley TL & Gordon B (2003) Talented female athletes: are they going for gold? *Journal of Secondary Gifted Education* 14, 229–242.
- Ewing ME, Gano-Overway LA, Branta CF & Seefeldt VD (2002) The role of sports in youth development. In Gatz M & Messner MA (eds) *Paradoxes of youth and sport*. Albany, NY, State University of New York Press.
- Ferraro T (1999) A psychoanalytic perspective on anxiety in athletes. *Athletic Insight* 5, np.
- Jarvis M (2004) *Psychodynamic psychology: classical theory and contemporary research*. London, Thomson Learning.
- LeUnes A & Nation JR (2002) *Sport psychology*. Pacific Grove, CA, Wadsworth.

Attitudes to sport 4

Learning objectives

By the end of this chapter, you should be able to:

- define attitudes and explain their structure and functions, with particular reference to the ego-defensive function of attitudes
- discuss ways of measuring attitudes, including the Thurstone, Likert and Osgood scales
- understand the factors affecting attitudes to sport
- use the theory of reasoned action and the theory of planned behaviour to understand the relationship between sporting attitudes and behaviour
- use the transtheoretical model to understand the problems of translating pro-sport attitudes into sporting participation
- discuss strategies to change attitudes to sport.

The social psychologist Elliott Aronson has defined an attitude as 'an enduring evaluation – positive or negative – of people, objects and ideas' (Aronson et al, 1994: p 287). We can pick out two important features of attitudes from this definition. First, attitudes are long-lasting. Once we have established a firm attitude to sport, we are likely to stick with it. Second, attitudes involve making judgements. Our attitudes to sport are likely to emerge as either distinctly positive or distinctly negative. Understanding attitudes is important to sport psychologists for a number of reasons. If parents and teachers, can understand how children acquire attitudes, they can use this understanding to try to ensure that as many young people as possible develop positive attitudes to sport. By understanding the link between attitudes and behaviour, we can try to help more people enjoy the medical and psychological benefits of both participation and spectatorship in sport. An understanding of the ways in which attitudes can be changed is valuable in helping us to increase sporting participation and motivate athletes.

The nature of attitudes

Pennington et al (1999) distinguished between two approaches to understanding attitudes. The functional approach looks at *why* we have attitudes, and how adopting particular attitudes can be helpful to us. The structural approach looks at what different factors make up attitudes.

Functions of attitudes

Smith et al (1964) suggested that having attitudes serves three main psychological purposes: the adaptive function, the knowledge function and the ego-defensive function. The adaptive function of attitudes involves the usefulness of certain attitudes in helping us achieve our goals. For example, one way in which we might 'get in' with a desirable crowd is to share their interest in sport in general or in a particular sport. This is not to say that people regularly and cynically change their attitudes in order to gain favour (although some people may do so on occasion). It is more likely that, without being aware of it, we are influenced in our attitudes by our awareness of how much good or harm certain attitudes can do us.

The knowledge function of attitudes refers to the fact that having attitudes makes the world a simpler and more predictable place. It also means we can save ourselves 'mental energy' that would otherwise have to be spent analysing every person and situation we come across. For example, we might have a universally positive view of sport, regardless of the nature of different sports and the contexts in which sport takes place. Such an attitude then frees us from the complex business of making moral judgements about details such as safety and politics.

The ego-defensive (or *self*-defensive) function of attitudes concerns the fact that we can adopt attitudes to help protect ourselves from difficult or painful feelings. For example, one way children might defend themselves against the feelings of humiliation they have experienced in PE lessons is to adopt a strongly negative attitude to all sport. People whose pride has suffered by a defeat in sport might similarly adopt a defensive attitude: 'I'm not bothered – I'm sick of basketball anyway.' Teachers, coaches and parents must recognise how people use attitudes to make themselves feel better. We should not take people too seriously if they say they are giving up their sport after one bad game. If, on the other hand, a player adopts an enduring negative attitude after a bad experience, we may wish to intervene to alter this attitude.

Of course, the defensive function of attitudes does not always lead to negative attitudes to sport and sport psychology. In a study amusingly entitled 'Death can be good for your health', Arndt et al (2003) examined the relationship between encountering reminders of one's own mortality and attitudes to exercise. Regardless of their current fitness or sporting participation, participants reminded of their mortality experienced a shift in attitudes in favour of regular exercise. Presumably, this was defensive, a pro-sport attitude being used to deny the reality of death.

Structure of attitudes

The structural approach to attitudes looks at the different components that make up our attitudes. It is generally agreed that there are three aspects to our attitudes, the cognitive dimension, the affective dimension and the behavioural dimension.

- The cognitive dimension of attitudes concerns our *beliefs*.
- The affective dimension of attitudes concerns our *feelings* (the term 'affective' means emotional).
- The behavioural dimension of attitudes concerns our *actions*.

Our beliefs are often stereotyped. We might, for example, hold stereo-typical views about those who favour particular sports. Stereotypes are beliefs that exaggerate the similarities of all members in a group and minimise the differences between members of the group. Thus, we might believe that all rugby players drink too much or that all football fans are violent. We also hold beliefs about the benefits of exercise and sport. Such beliefs are likely to have a strong effect on our sport and exercise behaviour.

It seems likely that our feelings about sport result at least in part from our beliefs. For example, if we believe that rugby players are always drunk or that football fans are all violent, we are likely to feel repulsed or frightened by them. We are also likely to have strong feelings about exercise and sport in general and about par-ticular sports. Research has shown that the amount and type of information about a sport that are given to students can affect their feelings about that sport. In general, the more we know about a sport, the more positive we feel about it. Theodorakis (1992) found that by increasing the level of technical information given to stu-dents on a skiing course, it was possible to make them feel more positive about skiing. The relationship between beliefs and feelings and sport and exercise behaviour will be examined later in this chapter.

Reflective exercise

Practise your critical thinking. It is often assumed that emotional and behavioural responses are a product of our beliefs. Test this idea by thinking about boxing, a sport that most of us have a strong attitude toward, either positive or negative (Figure 4.1).

1. Identify the cognitive, affective and behavioural components of your attitude.
2. What do you think causes your emotional response to boxing and your boxing-related behaviour? Is it simply a question of beliefs or are other factors at work?

Measuring attitudes

We can measure attitudes directly by asking people questions or ask-ing them to respond to statements that describe beliefs, feeling or behaviours associated with the topic we are interested in. There are

**Figure 4.1** Boxing arouses strong attitudes. Copyright © Gary Kufner/Corbis

other, indirect ways of measuring attitudes (such as measuring physiological change or responses to ambiguous pictures), but sport psychologists tend to rely more on direct measures. Direct measurement of attitudes is done in three main ways: Likert scales, semantic differential scales and Thurstone scales.

Likert scales

Likert (1932) developed the simplest and what has become the most common way of measuring attitudes. We start by producing an equal number of positive and negative statements concerning whatever we are measuring attitudes to. These statements can concern beliefs, feelings and behaviours. Then people are asked to respond to the statements, usually on a 5-point scale, ranging from (SA) 'strongly agree' to 'strongly disagree' (SD). Examples of statements measuring attitudes to boxing are shown in Box 4.2.

Box 4.2 Likert scale items measuring attitudes to boxing

	SA	A	?	D	SD
1. Boxing causes brain damage.	[ ]	[ ]	[ ]	[ ]	[ ]
2. I watch boxing matches on TV.	[ ]	[ ]	[ ]	[ ]	[ ]
3. I find boxing exciting.	[ ]	[ ]	[ ]	[ ]	[ ]

Item 1 refers to a belief, item 2 to a behaviour and item 3 to an emotion. Thus, cognitive, affective and behavioural dimensions are all included. This is worth considering in designing one's own Likert scales. Note also that item 1 is a negative statement whilst the other two are positive statements. This is important because some people have a tendency to agree with most items (the yea-sayer effect) or generally to disagree (the nay-sayer effect). In order to score this type of test, we need to give all the positive statements values of 1–5 or 0–4, 5 (or 4) being the most positive. For the negative statements, we must reverse this, giving them values of 5–1 (or 4–0). Each person who fills in the test can then be given a score for each item and finally an overall score, which shows how positive or negative his or her attitude is overall.

Semantic differential scales

Osgood et al (1957) developed an alternative procedure for direct measurement of attitudes, the semantic differential scale. To prepare such a scale, we first think of a number of words with opposite meanings that are applicable to describing the subject of the test. There are seven points between each pair of words. The respondents' task is to select a point between the two extremes that best describes how they feel. Kenyon (1968) developed a semantic differential scale called the Attitudes Toward Physical Activity (ATPA) to measure how positively people feel about sport and exercise. The ATPA uses eight pairs of words opposite in meaning, referring to various types of physical activity and various functions of physical activity. Some items from the ATPA are shown in Box 4.3.

Box 4.3 Semantic differential items from the ATPA

(a) Sport as a social experience

good	1 2 3 4 5 6 7	bad
pleasant	1 2 3 4 5 6 7	unpleasant
wise	1 2 3 4 5 6 7	foolish

For example, in the three items above, someone with a positive attitude to sport as a social experience would be expected to select numbers nearer 1 than 7 for each word pair. The ATPA has been commonly used as a measure of attitudes to sport in sport psychology research.

Thurstone scales

Thurstone & Chave (1929) developed a complex system of attitude measurement. Thurstone scales resemble Likert scales in that they appear as a series of statements to which respondents choose a response based on how closely they agree with the statement. However, Thurstone believed that it was important that we should know just *how* positive or negative each statement in a scale is, not just whether it is positive or negative. This is achieved by having a panel of at least 50–100 judges rate each statement for positivity or negativity. The advantage of this is that when we add up someone's scores, we can weight very positive and very negative statements more heavily than only mildly positive statements. Thus, to return to the example of boxing, if someone replied 'strongly agree' to the statement, *There should be an immediate world ban on boxing*, it would represent a more negative view than the same response to the statement, *Boxing can be dangerous*.

Although, in principle, Thurstone scales should be more valid than Likert scales because of the weighting of items, in practice, few researchers are willing to go to the extra effort needed to compile this type of scale. As Oppenheim (1992) pointed out, Likert scales generally produce much the same results as Thurstone scales with a fraction of the preparation time.

Reflective exercise

Practise your creative thinking.

1. Pick a sporting issue, such as the danger of boxing, or the importance of sport to children's development.
2. Construct an attitude scale using the Likert format, and come up with 5–10 statements, comprising both positive and negative statements.

The formation of attitudes to sport

How do we form the attitudes we hold to sport? Think about your own sporting attitudes for a moment. You may remember early positive or negative experiences that shaped your attitudes. You might be able to point to family members or teachers that were a strong influence on you. Did you take up a sport to impress someone attractive or get into the in-crowd, and then find you liked the sport? You may feel that you are just the type of person that is naturally attracted to sport, or you may not. Actually, research has linked all these factors to the development of attitudes.

Personality, genes and attitudes

Eysenck (1982) proposed that people high in extroversion and psychoticism (see Chapter 2 for a discussion) tend to have pro-sport attitudes. To trait theorists such as Eysenck, personality is primarily determined by genetic factors. It is certainly conceivable that genes may influence sporting attitudes. This is not to say that there is a gene for liking sport, but, if some aspects of personality are inherited, it may be that we can inherit a *predisposition* to developing certain kinds of attitude. There is indeed some evidence that our genetic make-up may predispose us to generally positive or negative attitudes to sport. Waller et al (1990) found that separated identical twins (who are genetically identical) have more similar views on a variety of topics than separated fraternal twins (who share 50% of their genes). This study implies that genes play some role in affecting our attitudes. However, we should remember that there are serious difficulties in conducting studies with separated twins – we never know for sure whether similarities between separated twins are due to similarities in genetics or environment. Actually, it is probable that our childhood environment is more important than our genes in influencing the development of our attitudes.

Social learning of attitudes

As we discussed in Chapter 3, children tend to observe and imitate the behaviour of their role models. Thus, children are likely to adopt the attitudes to sport they see in their parents. Children also receive powerful reinforcers in response to the attitudes they express from a very early age. Social learning can help explain attitudes to both participation and spectating. We can easily imagine a scenario where a boy observes his father intently watching a football match and cheering when one team scores. The boy would be likely to copy the father's behaviour. It is also extremely likely that the father would respond to this by praising the boy and explaining the finer points of the match – thus reinforcing the behaviour. Bandura's four-stage model of this process is shown in Figure 4.2.

You may be thinking that this is a shamefully politically incorrect example – what about girls' attitudes to sport? Actually, this was a deliberate ruse to make you think about how boys and girls might be exposed to different learning experiences. Imagine that in the above scenario, instead of the son, the young daughter of a football fan cheered at the football. It is unlikely that she would receive the same positive reinforcers as her male counterpart. She might well be ignored – or, worse, punished. In our culture, there are fewer opportunities for girls than boys to learn the pleasure of sport spectatorship. The problem of gender differences in attitudes to sport spectatorship was highlighted during the 1998 World Cup, when the disparity between some men's and women's attitudes to watching football became so polarised that the term 'World Cup widows' was coined, and Relate Marriage Guidance had to issue advice on how to maintain a relationship between two partners with different attitudes to watching football!

Figure 4.2 Social learning of a child's attitude to football.

Parental involvement

The extent to which parents actively get involved in children's sporting activities can affect their attitudes to sport. At one extreme, parents who do not acknowledge children's achievements are clearly not giving them appropriate reinforcement. At the other extreme, it may be possible for parents to become overinvolved. This was supported by a study by Stein et al (1999), who surveyed 42 13–14-year-olds who played soccer, volleyball or American football. Most respondents said that their parents were moderately involved and that this was appropriate. Both very low and very high levels of involvement were associated with reduced satisfaction with sport and increased stress levels.

Desire for health and physique enhancement

Currently, there is increasing social pressure on people of all ages and both sexes to maintain a particular body type that is characterised by low fat mass and high muscle mass. This is a paradoxical situation for psychologists. On the one hand, there is genuine concern about the rapidly rising rates of child and adult obesity and the accompanying health problems. Thus, we may argue that society is right to pressure people to use sport and exercise to manage their weight and fitness. On the other hand, the evidence of rising rates of eating problems suggests that too much emphasis on the importance of sport in weight management can have serious, negative psychological consequences. This was underlined by a study (Burak & Burckes-Miller, 2000) in which 371 children aged 10–15 were assessed for their exercise and sporting activity, attitudes to their weight and other weight-control strategies. Nearly half believed they were too fat. A significant minority used extreme weight-control strategies, such as fasting, vomiting and taking slimming pills, as well as exercise.

Attitudes to competition

Social learning theory is useful in understanding how we acquire our attitudes to competition. There has been much discussion in the last few years of British attitudes to competition. On the one hand, it has been pointed out that the British may be less motivated to win than other cultures because of the philosophy, 'it's not the winning that counts, but the taking part'. On the other hand, concern has also been expressed that too much emphasis on competition prevents many children from learning to enjoy sport. One of the most comprehensive surveys of attitudes to sport, the Miller Lite Report (1983), found that 86% of American parents surveyed thought that PE teachers place too much emphasis on competition. Gervis (1991) pointed out that problems can arise when early training overemphasises the importance of winning. This can be at least partially understood in terms of social learning theory. If reinforcement is provided only for winners, then, by definition, it is provided for half the participants in team games, and much fewer in individual sports. With most participants failing to receive positive reinforcement, it is unlikely that they will maintain their interest in sport. Box 4.4 gives examples of some ways in which positive reinforcement can be used by teachers and coaches to encourage positive attitudes to sport in all children.

There appear to be differences between athletes and non-athletes in attitudes to competition. Finkenberg & Moode (1996) surveyed 164 university students on their attitudes to sport, half of these being participants in sport at university level. Athletes placed more emphasis on the importance of competition in sport than did the control group, along with opportunities for social status and career enhancement. Non-participants in sport were positive about sport but saw its purpose more in terms of enhanced self-esteem and character development.

Reflective exercise

Practise your critical thinking on your own PE lessons.

1. Did you generally receive plenty of positive reinforcement?
2. Do you think that you received most reinforcement for your successes, or for your participation and effort?

Attitudes to sport and sporting behaviour

As Gill (2000) says, we are interested in attitudes in sport psychology, not so much for their own sake, as for their influence on sporting behaviour. Therefore, a very important issue concerns the extent to which attitudes can be used to predict behaviour. Early psychological research seemed to show that there was little relationship between attitudes and behaviour, but our current thinking is that attitudes *can* effectively predict behaviour, but only if we also have access to certain other information.

The theory of reasoned action

Ajzen & Fishbein (1980) have produced a model of the link between attitudes and behaviour that has proved popular in sport psychology. This is called the theory of reasoned action (TRA). A simple version of

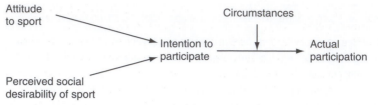

Figure 4.3 Applying the theory of reasoned action to explaining participation in sport.

the TRA is shown in Figure 4.3, as used to explain participation in sport.

In the TRA, two factors determine individuals' *intention* to take part in sport: their general attitude to sport and how socially desirable they consider sport to be. Therefore, before we even intend to participate in sport, we need to have positive feelings and beliefs about sport *and* we need to see sport as a socially desirable activity. Of course, the intention to participate does not necessarily lead to the behaviour. Other circumstances may still interfere. For example, we might be particularly busy or plagued by a recurring injury.

The theory of planned behaviour

Ajzen (1985) introduced a modification to the theory of reasoned action, creating an offshoot known as the *theory of planned behaviour* (TPB). The idea was that, although the TRA is effective in predicting how people would behave in situations where they have full control over their actions and can behave entirely voluntarily, it is less useful in situations where behaviour is highly constrained by circumstances. The theory of planned behaviour gets around this by introducing a further variable, *perceived behavioural control*, which influences intentions. As in the TRA, there is a strong link between intention and action; however, we formulate the intention to act in a certain way only when we perceive that we have control over our behaviour.

Discussion

Sport psychologists widely support the TRA and TPB as explanations of the relationship between attitudes to sport and sporting behaviour. Gill (1986) had students survey 68 people on their attitudes to jogging. They then asked the participants how many times per week they jogged (as a measure of behaviour). A moderate relationship ($r = 0.44$) was found between attitude to jogging and frequency of jogging. However, as the TRA would predict, a much stronger correlation ($r = 0.81$) emerged between *intention to jog* and frequency of jogging. A study by Wankel et al (1994) suggested that the TPB predicts participation more accurately than the TRA. Data from over 3000 Canadians taken from a national survey of well-being were analysed, looking at measures of exercise, perceived behavioural control and social norms. Attitudes to sport and perceived behavioural control were more predictive of taking part in sport than social desirability, supporting the TPB as opposed to the TRA. In another study by the same research group, Mummery & Wankel (1999) found that both perceived behavioural control and social desirability affected attitudes to participation in adolescent swimmers. Both a recent meta-analysis (Hagger et al, 2002) and a qualitative review (Culos-Reed et al, 2001) of studies on the TRA and TPB have confirmed that research has supported the idea that the TPB is a superior explanation.

There are important lessons to be learned from the body of research on the link between attitudes and behaviour in sport. To understand what factors affect the decision to take part in sport, we need to know subjects' perception of its social desirability and their beliefs about their own opportunity to participate. Both of these perceptions may be inaccurate, and one way to persuade more people to take part in sport may be to tackle these inaccurate beliefs.

The transtheoretical model (TTM)

The TTM was originally produced by Prochaska & DiClemente (1983) in order to understand better why some smokers succeeded in giving up without professional help. Marcus & Simkin (1993) applied it to understanding the process whereby people take up and maintain sport/exercise behaviour. The term 'transtheoretical' refers to the fact that the model comprises elements from several psychological theories. According to the TTM, people go through five stages before they regularly participate in sport. These are shown in Box 4.5.

Box 4.5 Stages in taking up sport

1. **Precontemplation**: people have no intention to exercise.
2. **Contemplation**: they have an intention to take up a physical activity.
3. **Preparation**: they begin irregular or infrequent exercise.
4. **Action**: they engage fully in short-term participation.
5. **Maintenance**: they maintain regular participation.

Each stage is defined by a different relationship between intentionality and behaviour. This makes the model dynamic and gives it an advantage over the TRA and TPB, which assume a static relationship between intentions and action. Of course, people do not simply pass through the five stages and end up with maintenance. They may relapse a number of times at different points for a number of reasons, ranging from injury to the seasonal nature of their chosen sport. A simple example is the person who takes up jogging in the summer but relapses to preparation or even contemplation when the nights draw in and jogging becomes a considerably colder and wetter experience! The model explains why some people undergo such relapses in terms of *self-efficacy* (discussed in detail on p 147). Briefly, self-efficacy is our perception of our own competence in an activity. The more competent we perceive ourselves to be, the more likely we are to maintain the physical activity. This has an important practical application; we can encourage people who have recently taken up a sport to maintain it in the face of new barriers, such as injury, weather or a change in working or family patterns that makes training less convenient, by building their confidence in their ability.

During the progress through the five stages, an individual may use a variety of strategies to encourage the continued shift from inactivity to activity. These include making use of social support, as in cultivating friendships with athletes who tend to socialise in sporting contexts. Another approach is *stimulus control*. This involves removing oneself from situations that encourage inactivity and instead planning events such as skiing or cycling holidays that will inevitably mean taking part in sport and that will provide incentives to training. Individuals may also deliberately expose themselves to information on the health benefits of sporting participation (this is called *consciousness raising*) or the risks of inactivity (this is called *dramatic relief*).

On any occasion, influenced by their self-efficacy beliefs and activity strategies, individuals are faced with a choice of whether to proceed with sporting activity. This involves a cost-benefit analysis in which they weigh the advantages of training this evening (I'll see my friends, I'll feel better about myself, or I'll sleep better after some exercise) against the cons (I'll have to walk there in the cold, I'll miss the last in the series of *Buffy*, or there's pizza and beer in the fridge). The influence of the pro arguments should increase as the individual progresses through the five stages (Figure 4.4).

Discussion

The TTM is intuitively appealing; that is, it has good *face validity*. It acknowledges the dynamic nature of attitudes, intentions and behaviours, and it incorporates well-validated ideas such as self-efficacy and cost-benefit analysis. On a practical level, it opens up the possibility of stage-specific interventions to encourage people to take up sport, and a small body of research has provided some support for this approach (Peterson & Aldana, 1999). On the other hand, although the model explains the difficulty of reconciling positive attitudes to sport with active participation in inactive people, it has little to say about those whose attitudes, intentions and sporting behaviour have always been consistent with one another.

Changing people's attitudes to sport

There are a number of theoretical approaches to attitude change. Perhaps the most famous and influential theories of how attitudes change are cognitive dissonance theory, proposed by Festinger (1957), and Bem's self-perception theory.

Figure 4.4 There is always a decision-making process involved in choosing to participate in sport.

Cognitive dissonance

Cognitive dissonance is the unpleasant sensation we experience when an attitude we hold comes into conflict with a current situation or intention. For example, we might believe that it is very important to work out at least three times a week to maintain our fitness, but we might not be able to work out for the next week, perhaps because we are going on holiday or working particularly hard. The belief and the intention are not compatible, and we experience dissonance. We can deal with this dissonance in two ways: either by changing the behaviour, that is, decide to work out after all, or by changing the attitude. We might use one of a number of rationalisations to change our attitude, as shown in Box 4.6.

Box 4.6 Rationalisations to relieve cognitive dissonance

- It won't matter just for 1 week, especially at my age.
- Too much working out was making me muscle-bound anyway.
- I can't stand people who spend all their time in the gym.
- I've missed weeks before and it hasn't done me any harm.

Thus, cognitive dissonance explains how we can change our attitudes in response to new situations. We can also use techniques based on cognitive dissonance deliberately to influence people's attitudes. Gill (1986) mentioned a PE teacher who used dissonance to alter boys' negative attitudes to skipping as an exercise and a feminine activity. The teacher gave them a number of facts that were incompatible with their attitude, such as the fact that boxers skip because skipping is one of the toughest and best exercises. Faced with these facts, the boys experienced cognitive dissonance and responded by changing their attitudes to skipping.

Cognitive dissonance theory provides a way of understanding the ways in which we persuade ourselves to forego healthy behaviour such as regular training. Once we understand how we do this, we are much less likely to con ourselves. Cognitive dissonance also provides us with a technique for persuading others to indulge in behaviour they see as socially undesirable. Looking back to Azjen & Fishbein's theory, we can see that, as beliefs about social desirability are one of the main influences on our behaviour, techniques to alter these are extremely valuable.

Self-perception theory

A radically different approach to attitude change was proposed by Bem (1967), who proposed that our attitudes are determined by our behaviour. Bem used the example, 'Since I eat brown bread, I must like brown bread.' The implication of this is that we can change our own attitudes to sport for the better if we participate more, and we can change the attitudes of others if we can persuade them to participate. Clearly, if people hold strong antisport attitudes, it is unlikely that we will succeed in persuading them to participate. However, encouraging participation in those who are not hostile to sport, but who have got out of the habit, may well produce significant alteration of their attitudes. Workplace football teams, community sports initiatives and fun runs can all persuade people to participate in sport and hence develop more pro-sport attitudes.

There is empirical support for the idea that changing sporting behaviour will affect sporting attitudes. Sidney et al (1983) measured the attitudes of 78 Canadian adults over 60 years old. The participants then took part in 14 weeks of endurance training. The ATPA was then administered again, and scores for each person were compared to those gathered before the training programme. The attitudes of those who trained the most were found to have become more positive after the training programme, whilst the attitudes of those who trained least became more negative.

Clearly, self-perception theory can be applied fairly easily to change the attitudes of large numbers of people, via community and work-based sporting activities. Of course, there are two provisos to bear in mind when using this approach. Firstly, regular participation in sport is much more likely to change attitudes than a one-off event. Secondly, participation must be an enjoyable experience.

Summary and conclusions

An understanding of attitudes can help us to develop positive attitudes to sport in children and also help change attitudes for the better in adults. Research has also suggested some fascinating possibilities; for example, athletes' attitudes to sport psychology may be defensive in nature. The most important influence on our attitudes to sport comes from direct experience and observation. It is therefore essential that we give children positive experiences of sport, and encourage and reward their efforts. People's attitudes to sport are closely related to their participation in sport. The TRA and TPB have proved useful in predicting people's sporting behaviour according to their attitudes to sport and the perceived social desirability of sport. The TTM provides a useful explanation of the process inactive individuals go through to reconcile their attitudes and behaviour. It has proved possible to change people's attitudes to sport, even quite late in life. Cognitive dissonance and self-perception theories have proved particularly useful in changing attitudes to sport.

Self-assessment questions

1. Explain one way in which the functional approach to attitudes has proved useful in sport psychology.
2. Compare two approaches to measuring attitudes.
3. What sorts of factors affect attitudes to sport?
4. Compare the TRA and the TTM as explanations of the relationship between attitudes to sport and sporting participation.
5. How can attitudes to sport be changed?

Further reading

- Gill DL (2000) *Psychological dynamics of sport*. Champagne, IL, Human Kinetics.
- Hayes N (2000) *Foundations of psychology*. London, Thomson Learning.
- Pennington DC, Gillen K & Hill P (1999) *Essential social psychology*. Oxford, Oxford University Press.

Aggression and sport 5

Learning objectives

By the end of this chapter you should able to:

- define aggression and understand the distinctions between hostile and instrumental aggression and between sanctioned and unsanctioned aggression
- discuss research into the relationship between aggression and performance
- describe and evaluate theories of aggression, with particular reference to instinct theories, social learning and the frustration–aggression hypothesis
- be aware of the range of factors affecting individual differences in sporting aggression
- consider the relationship between sporting participation and spectating, and aggression
- identify strategies for the reduction of aggression in sport.

As a society, we have a certain ambivalence about aggression in sport. On the one hand, as Russell (1993) has pointed out, sport is perhaps the only peacetime setting in which we not only tolerate but actively encourage and enjoy aggressive behaviour. In the notoriously violent ice hockey, violence clearly sells, attendance at matches being positively correlated with frequency of violent acts (Jones et al, 1993). On the other hand, there is a moral panic regarding football hooliganism, and in recent years there have been a string of high-profile court cases in which athletes have pursued cases against others who deliberately injured them. One reason for this apparent ambivalence is that we tend to see aggression very differently in different situations. Before we proceed any further, it is perhaps useful to look more closely at how we should define aggression.

Defining aggression

It is perhaps easiest to begin by saying what aggression is *not*. Aggression is not competitiveness, nor is it anger. Competitiveness is an attitude; anger is an emotion. Whilst anger and competitiveness may both contribute to aggression, aggression itself is a *behaviour*. Aggression, by definition, involves actively *doing something unpleasant to someone*. Aggressive behaviour may come in many forms, ranging from verbal abuse – designed to cause psychological harm – to physical violence. It is generally agreed that all aggression involves the intent to cause harm in some form; thus, behaviour which accidentally harms someone is not aggression. Putting these factors together, a simple working definition of aggression would be something like this: 'Behaviour of any kind that is carried out with the intention of harming another person.'

Hostile aggression, instrumental aggression and assertiveness

Whilst this simple definition may suffice when describing aggression in most situations, things are more complex in sport. Clearly, when we perform a rugby tackle or a karate kick, we do so in the knowledge that we are inflicting certain discomfort on the other athlete, and that there is some risk of causing injury. This raises the difficult question, are behaviours which involve hurting another person within the rules of the sport truly aggressive? Baron (1977) addressed this issue in his influential distinction between hostile and instrumental aggression.

- *Hostile* aggression takes place when the primary intention of the behaviour is to harm the other player. This type of aggression is accompanied by anger, and the underlying wish is to see the victim suffer.
- *Instrumental* aggression takes place when the behaviour is clearly likely to cause harm, but its *intention* is to achieve a different aim, such as to score a point or prevent the opposition from scoring a goal.

Husman & Silva (1984) have made the further distinction between aggression and assertiveness. Assertiveness involves the type of behaviour that might *appear* aggressive, but which does not result in harming an opponent. In many sports, for example, we might choose at certain times to charge directly toward an opponent, perhaps with an accompanying cry, but without any intention of making contact.

The classic example of this is rushing the net in tennis. Thirer (1994) pointed out that physical contact can be assertive rather than aggressive, provided the intention is to gain dominance over opponents rather than to injure them. Thus, footballers can shoulder-barge one another while tackling, but, provided the intention is to obtain the ball rather than to injure, this is assertive rather than aggressive behaviour.

In contact sports, we generally accept a degree of instrumental aggression, although in no sport is it acceptable to inflict serious damage on an opponent for the sake of gaining or saving a point. There is normally an elaborate set of rules in contact sports to make sure that moderate levels of instrumental aggression are permitted, whereas serious instrumental aggression and hostile aggression are not. Thus, although one footballer pushing another off balance would be unlikely to receive a card from the referee, high rugby tackles and low punches in combat sports, which are judged likely to cause serious harm, are banned. Even in ultimate fighting (Figure 5.1), designed so as to have the minimum interference of rules, certain moves are banned.

As Tenenbaum et al (1997) pointed out, spectators as well as athletes can display both hostile and instrumental aggression. A crowd may hurl objects and abuse at players. If they do so with the aim of distracting the opposing team and so giving their own team an advantage, this constitutes instrumental aggression. If, however, it is done in anger and with the intention of harming opposing players, the same behaviour would be classed as hostile aggression.

Figure 5.1 The greater the potential for serious injury, the more elaborate are the rules for preventing it. Copyright © Les Stone/Corbis

Sanctioned and unsanctioned aggression

Apter (1993) has pointed out that there is often a set of unofficial rules, as well as official rules, governing what aggressive behaviours are acceptable. Thus, a footballer committing a professional foul to avoid conceding a goal is committing *sanctioned aggression*; that is, instrumental aggression that, whilst not within the official rules, is accepted as normal even though it would be punished. The case of combat sports raises particular problems for making a clear distinction between hostile and instrumental aggression, as the whole aim of the sport is to cause some degree of harm. Here, the distinction between sanctioned and unsanctioned aggression is perhaps a clearer one. We would probably all accept that boxers might lose their temper and try to hurt opponents, as by clashing heads in a clinch, and this would be sanctioned even if the fighter clearly breached the rules. However, striking at neck or groin is acknowledged to be extremely dangerous and would thus be unsanctioned.

Reflective exercise

This should help you refine your critical thinking.

1. For each of the following sporting examples, all based on real-life events, decide whether the incident involves hostile aggression, instrumental aggression or assertiveness:

    a. During a test match, bouncers are bowled in line with the batsman's body.
    b. During a heavyweight title fight, a boxer bites off part of his opponent's ear.
    c. A footballer consistently tackles over the ball, studs first.
    d. A tennis player hits a forehand smash that glances off her opponent's calf.

2. For each of the above examples, consider whether the behaviour would be *sanctioned*.

The link between aggression and performance

It is widely believed that the use of aggression wins games. The baseball coach Leo Durocher famously said, 'Nice guys finish last.' In Tutko & Ogilvie's (1966) athletic motivation inventory (see p 20), aggression was one of the 10 personality traits believed to be associated with athletic success. Of course, we should bear in mind the distinction between hostile aggression, instrumental aggression and assertiveness. It may be that the conventional wisdom supporting the value of aggression may in fact be supporting assertive behaviour rather than aggression. Young (1993) has noted the increase in unsanctioned violence in contact sports in recent years, and proposed that this is a direct result of increased professionalisation and the resulting financial incentives to win. There have been high-profile incidents in which the introduction of new and aggressive techniques appears to have enhanced performance. See, for example, Box 5.1, which details cricket's 'bodyline' controversy. However, this is not to say that aggression necessarily enhances performance.

Box 5.1 The 'bodyline' controversy

The term 'bodyline' refers to a cricket technique in which the ball is bowled to the leg stump such that it bounces toward the body of the batsman. On the leg side, fielders close in to make a close cordon. This means that the batsman is faced with the choice of getting out of the way of the ball or hitting it awkwardly to the leg side, with a high probability of being caught out. The technique, known originally as 'fast leg theory', was devised by Douglas Jardine, who became the England cricket captain after England's disastrous defeat by Australia in the 1930 Test Series. In the 1932–3 Test Series, it was put to work with devastating effect, and the term 'bodyline' was coined by the Australian press. England won the Ashes 4–1, and Don Bradman, Australia's highest scoring batsman, had his average score halved. There was, however, a high price to pay. The Australian crowd were so incensed when wicketkeeper Bert Oldfield suffered a fractured skull that police had to be deployed in force to protect the England team. The Australians accused the English of unsportsmanlike behaviour, and, in protest, the England team threatened to withdraw from the remaining two matches. This assumed the status of an international incident, as both governments got involved. It was resolved only when the Australian prime minister, mindful of Australia's dependence on trade with the UK, prevailed on the Australian board to withdraw the accusation of unsportsmanlike behaviour. In 1934, the rules of cricket were changed, giving umpires the power to intervene if bowlers aimed the ball at batsmen.

Surprisingly, there has been relatively little research on the link between aggression and results, and almost all published research has involved ice hockey. Results regarding the link between aggression and success in ice hockey are equivocal. McCarthy & Kelly (1978) found a positive relationship between the time taken for penalties (a

Figure 5.2 Although (American) ice hockey is notoriously violent, there is no clear link between aggression and success. Copyright © Christine Muschi/Reuters/Corbis

measure of a team's aggression) and number of goals scored. However, Wankel (1973) compared the penalty times of winning and losing ice hockey teams and found no difference. Since ice hockey is such an aggressive sport, if no clear results emerge here, it is unlikely that aggression would be associated with success in other sports. Of course, the situation and the reason for the aggression would make a difference to whether it was helpful (Gill, 2000). Whilst the willingness to perform a professional foul would probably benefit a team, the anger associated with hostile aggression would probably be unproductive, harming concentration and decision making.

Of course, much depends on the sport. Some sports, in particular combat sports, are inherently aggressive, and points are awarded in some martial arts contests for aggression. The sort of psyching up used for at least some combat sports can be intensely aggressive. The legendary bare-knuckle boxer Lenny McLean put it eloquently: 'What I have to do is hate – and I mean really HATE. From the top of my head right down to my ankles. The man in front of me has interfered with my wife, he's interfered with my kids. Bastard' (McLean, 1998: p 86).

Reflective exercise

This should help develop your creative thinking.

 Currently, there is very little useful research on the relationship between aggression and success. How would you go about researching this issue? Consider the following in particular:

1. What sport or sports would you focus on?
2. How would you measure aggression?
3. How would you measure sporting success?

Theories of aggression

A number of psychological theories aim to explain the origins and triggers of human aggression. Within sport psychology, three broad approaches have been particularly influential: instinct theories, social learning theory and the frustration–aggression hypothesis.

Instinct theories

In psychology, the term 'instinct' is used slightly more precisely than in ordinary conversation. An instinct is an *innate* tendency to behave in a certain way. By 'innate', we mean that the behaviour is influenced by our genetic make-up and is therefore present at birth, as opposed to learned. A number of psychological theories see aggression as instinctive and, at least to some extent, inevitable. Sigmund Freud (1919) proposed that we are born with two opposing instincts, the life instinct and the death instinct. Our death instinct leads us to be aggressive. Freud proposed that although the instinct for aggression is always with us, we can to some extent exert conscious control over it. Thus, aggressive behaviour is not always inevitable. Some contemporary writers influenced by Freud have viewed sport in general as a healthy way of expressing our death instinct. For example, Richards (1994) looked at the importance we attach to kicking in expressing our aggressive tendencies, as in phrases such as 'putting the boot in' and 'a kick in the teeth'. Richards suggested that football is particularly important in sublimating our aggressive instincts (channelling them constructively). For this reason, Richards describes football as a civilising influence.

Another psychological approach that sees aggression as instinctive is that of ethology. From the ethological perspective, Lorenz (1966) proposed that humans have evolved a 'fighting instinct'. Evolution takes place through natural selection; therefore, aggression must, historically at least, have been a survival trait, that is, a characteristic that increases the likelihood of survival. Like Freud, Lorenz saw human aggression as inevitable but manageable. Lorenz saw sport as serving the social function of channelling human destructive instincts constructively. We shall return to the issue of the effects of sport on aggression later in the chapter.

Discussion

The issue of whether aggression is instinctive or whether we have to learn it remains an ongoing controversy in psychology. There is a lack of direct evidence for or against an aggressive instinct, and we have to look to indirect support. If aggression were *universal*, that would be strong evidence of an instinctive basis. Lore & Schultz have (1993) pointed out that all vertebrates display aggression; thus, it must be a survival trait, as suggested by Lorenz. However, cross-cultural studies have found wide variation in human aggression (Baron & Richardson 1992). There appear to be human cultures, such as that of the Arapesh of New Guinea, where there is very little aggression by European and American standards. This suggests that there must be external influences as well as an instinctive component in aggression.

Social learning theory

In a radical alternative to instinct theory, Bandura (1973) proposed that all human aggression, like other social behaviour, is learnt by imitation and reinforcement. Bandura (1965) famously demonstrated that children copy adults behaving aggressively in his 'bobo doll experiment' (Figure 5.3). Children observed an adult beating a large inflatable doll. They tended to imitate the behaviour and also beat the bobo doll. When children were rewarded or witnessed the adult being rewarded for beating the doll, their level of aggression increased.

Clearly, there are instances where children can witness aggression in sport, and there are a number of ways in which aggression can be reinforced. An act of aggression might result directly in scoring or preventing the opposition from doing so. Watchers might cheer; the coach and parents might praise the aggressive child. Children may also witness highly assertive acts and incorrectly imitate them in an

aggressive form. To a child with little technical knowledge of football, it is difficult to distinguish between an assertive shoulder-barge and an aggressive push.

Figure 5.3 Bandura's famous bobo doll study. Reproduced by kind permission of Professor Albert Bandura.

Baron & Byrne (2002) suggest the following four aspects of aggression that can be explained by learning: how to be aggressive, who is an appropriate target of aggression, what actions require an aggressive response and in what situations aggression is appropriate. Thus, by observation, we might learn how to commit a foul, whom we can 'legitimately' foul, what they have to do to warrant a foul and under what circumstances a foul is the best response.

Because social learning theorists propose that there is nothing inevitable about aggression, but that it results from learning, it follows that we should be able to shape young athletes' aggression by the proper application of reinforcement and punishment. The alert teacher or coach can make sure that, whilst assertive behaviour is properly rewarded, aggression is not. We will return to the use of social learning to reduce aggression later in the chapter.

Discussion

There is no doubt that children imitate adult behaviour and that rewards will increase the probability of aggressive behaviour's being repeated. However, what is much more controversial is the claim that social learning is a *complete* explanation of human aggression. One question you might ask is, 'If every generation copies aggression from the previous generation, how did it happen in the first place?' This is not an easy question to answer. Animal studies have shown that animals reared alone, without any opportunity to learn aggression from others, still display aggression. This shows that, in some species at least, aggression does not require social learning. Baron & Byrne's four aspects of learned aggression explain well the importance of learning in aggression. Nonetheless, we could see these as simply learning how and when to express our instinct for aggression. Social learning theory fails to account for findings (discussed on p 86) that, despite providing models of how to act aggressively, martial arts training reduces rather than increases aggressive behaviour.

The frustration–aggression hypothesis

This approach, first suggested by Dollard et al (1939), sees the most important factors in aggression as the characteristics of the situation. Dollard et al proposed that, although we have an innate aggressive drive, aggressive behaviour is elicited by *frustration*; that is, when we are frustrated we respond with aggressive behaviour. In the original version of the frustration–aggression hypothesis, frustration was seen as *always* leading to aggression, and *all* aggression was seen to be due to frustration.

Berkowitz (1989), who produced a more sophisticated version of the frustration–aggression hypothesis, proposed that frustration leads to anger rather than directly to aggression. More anger is generated if the frustration is unexpected or seen as unfair. Anger may lead to aggression, but because we can apply our higher mental processes, such as thinking and reasoning, we do not *necessarily* respond to frustration with aggression. We may do so, however, if our anger is great enough or if, for some reason, we cannot think logically at that moment.

Discussion

Frustration is just one of several causes of aggression. Like instinct theory, and social learning theory, it is a partial but incomplete explanation of human aggression. Although the frustration–aggression hypothesis is not particularly influential in social psychology (Baron & Byrne 2002), it is useful to sport psychologists because sport can involve so much frustration that, even if frustration is a relatively minor cause of aggression in general, it is probably one of the major contributors to sporting aggression. Bakker et al (1990) found that aggression increases when a team is losing, particularly when the game is of great importance, presumably in response to the frustration of the situation. Reducing the aggression associated with frustration will be examined later in the chapter.

Individual differences in sporting aggression

A number of factors affect how aggressive individual athletes are. These include gender, motivational factors and the extent of their emotional identification with their team.

Gender

Research conducted in a variety of situations has found that, in general, women are less physically aggressive than men. A number of studies have shown that, in keeping with this principle, female athletes are less supportive of aggressive behaviour than male athletes. In one study, Tucker & Parks (2001) assessed the attitudes of 162 top-level American university athletes to aggression by a standard questionnaire, the Sport Behaviour Inventory. Overall, women were more negative about the role of aggression in sport. This was especially true of those who participated in non-contact sports. This is particularly interesting because it suggests that men and women have different influences on their attitudes, men being more affected by gender role expectations and women by the norms of their sport.

Reflective exercise

Practise your critical thinking on the Tucker & Parks study.

1. Is the sample large enough and is it representative of athletes as a whole?
2. Was a good range of sports covered?
3. How valid are the measures used?
4. Do the results correspond with other findings on gender and aggression?
5. Is the study useful in identifying something new and interesting?

Identification with team

In team sports, research suggests that athletes who have a particularly strong identification with their team are more willing to behave aggressively toward opposition team members. Most research has looked at instrumental aggression, that is, that aimed at gaining competitive advantage rather than deliberately hurting an opponent. However, a recent study by Wann et al (2003) suggests that hostile aggression is also affected by team identification. A total of 175 university students were questioned about the extent to which they identified with their team and what aggressive acts they would consider committing. As expected, those who were highly identified with their team were more willing to consider hostile aggression toward opponents. The effect was greater for males than females, and (fortunately!) it was greater for minor acts of hostile aggression. Thus, highly identified men were very likely to consider tripping an opponent, but few were willing to consider murder.

Daniel Wann's research extends to the effects of team identification on the behaviour of spectators. Wann et al (1999) questioned 88 sports fans on their team identification, general willingness to commit murder and willingness to injure a member of an opposing team. There was no relationship between team identification and willingness to murder, suggesting that being strongly identified with a team does not simply make one a more aggressive person in general. However, highly identified fans were more willing anonymously to injure a member of an opposing team.

Box 5.2 Team identification and attitudes to war analogies in sport

Figure 5.4 9/11 triggered a reaction against war analogies. Copyright © Rob Howard/Corbis

One of the ways we often talk about sport, particularly contact sport, is to use analogies from war. Thus, we may talk about a 'massacre', refer to a highly aggressive team as 'taking no prisoners' or describe a losing team as 'getting fragged' (an American term literally meaning to be murdered by a hand grenade). After the terrorist attacks of 9/11, many sporting figures protested against the use of these terms. In a study by End et al (2003), sports fans were questioned about their team identification and their views on war analogies in sport. As expected, those highly identified with their team were more approving of war analogies. This supports the findings of studies such as those of Daniel Wann and colleagues that show a link between aggression and team identification.

Motivational style

It seems that our motives for participating in sport have an impact on how aggressive we become during play. Research has focused particularly on goal orientation, a subject dealt with in detail in Chapter 8 (p 142). Briefly, athletes tend to have either a task orientation or an ego orientation. Task-oriented athletes judge their success relative to their past efforts and deal well with adversity. Ego-oriented athletes judge their performance according to their success against others and are much more likely to cheat in the face of adversity. An ego orientation is associated with aggression, presumably what matters because to an ego-oriented athlete is the result, not how it is achieved. A study of 240 handball players by Rascle et al (1998) supported the association between ego orientation and the tendency to indulge in instrumental aggression. Similar results were found in a study of elite ice hockey players (Dunn & Dunn, 1999).

Situational factors affecting aggression

Although individuals do vary in their tendency toward aggression, we are all influenced in aggression – and indeed in all social behaviour – by the situation in which we find ourselves. A number of factors in our physical environment, including temperature, noise and crowding, all affect aggression. The circumstances in which a match takes place can also be important; thus, frequency of play and league position can have an effect.

The physical environment

There is little doubt that the probability of aggressive behaviour changes with ambient temperature. Anderson et al (1995) suggest that there is a simple linear relationship between temperature and aggression; that is, the higher the temperature, the higher the levels of aggression. Evidence for this comes from a study by Reifman et al (1991), in which archived data from the 1986–8 US baseball seasons were analysed. A positive correlation emerged between temperature and the number of batters hit by pitchers in each game. In non-sporting contexts, evidence suggests that crowding and noise levels are also associated with increased aggression. However, there is a lack of research within sporting contexts.

Game circumstances

The circumstances in which a match is played appear to affect the likelihood of aggression. For example, league leaders tend to indulge in aggression less frequently than those trailing them. Englehardt (1995) analysed 4000 game summaries from the US ice hockey league and found that the higher the team was in the league, the lower the number of penalties. Widmeyer & McGuire (1997) analysed game statistics for 840 US ice hockey matches. Intradivisional matches, in which teams play each other up to eight times, were compared to interdivisional matches, in which teams meet only three or four times. Significantly more aggressive incidents occurred in intradivisional matches, suggesting that the more frequently teams meet, the more aggressive are the matches.

Reflective exercise

Practise your critical thinking by reflecting on theories of aggression and research into factors affecting aggression.

1. Which strikes you as more useful in understanding aggression, theory or research?
2. Why do you think psychology retains both theory and research?

The $64,000 question – does sport increase or reduce aggression?

Instinct theories imply that, in general, sport serves to reduce aggression in society, because it gives us a legitimate way to express our aggressive instincts. The frustration–aggression hypothesis also supports the idea that sport is beneficial because it gives us a release for our frustrations. Most of us would agree that, if we are frustrated and in a bad mood, we tend to feel better if we exercise. Sport may also reduce aggression by helping us acquire self-discipline. From a social learning perspective, however, we run the risk of learning new aggressive behaviours if we indulge in 'aggressive sports'.

The martial arts give us one way of directly testing these contrasting views. If the social learning approach is correct, we would expect the learning of aggressive repertoires of behaviour in martial arts training to increase levels of aggression. Research has shown quite the reverse, however; martial arts training appears to reduce aggression (Figure 5.5). Daniels & Thornton (1990) assessed karateka for aggression, using a test called the Buss-Durkee Hostility Inventory. They found that there was a negative relationship between assaultive hostility (reported tendency to respond with physical violence) and length of training ($r = -0.64$).

The problem with using martial arts training to investigate the relationship between sport and aggression is that martial arts instructors tend to differ substantially in their philosophy and training methods from other coaches, and so we cannot extrapolate from martial arts to other sports. Evidence that this makes a difference comes from a recent study by Lakes & Hoyt (2004), in which 193 American 5–10-year-olds were allocated either standard PE lessons or tae kwon do sessions at school. After 3 months, the tae kwon do group showed significantly more improvement in their prosocial behaviour as well as better concentration and persistence. An alternative approach to examining the relationship between sport and aggression is to compare aggression in athletes and non-athletes. A recent study by Lemieux et al (2002) compared aggression in 86 university athletes and 86 matched non-athletes. Although physical size was associated with aggression, there was no difference between participants in sport and non-participants.

Figure 5.5 Martial arts training tends to reduce aggression. Copyright © Jim Arbogast/Corbis

Effects on spectators

Whilst some research cautiously supports the view that at least some sports help reduce aggression in participants, the reverse seems to be true for spectators. Given the problem of football violence, this should perhaps not surprise us. Arms et al (1979) measured the hostility of spectators after they watched aggressive sports (wrestling and ice hockey) and a non-aggressive sport (swimming). They found increased hostility in those who had watched the aggressive sports, but not in those watching the non-aggressive sports. Phillips (1986) tracked the rates of murder in the USA and found that, in the weeks following heavyweight title fights, rates of murder increased. The characteristics of murder victims appeared to be related to the losing fighter; when a white boxer lost, more white men were murdered, and when a black boxer lost, more black men were murdered.

All the main theories of aggression could explain these effects. Instinct theorists would say that watching the aggressive sport aroused the aggressive instincts of the spectators but did not allow them a means of expressing their aggression. Frustration–aggression theorists could point to the frustration of having to watch the game and not be able to help one's own team. Social learning theorists might identify the modelling of aggressive behaviours by the athletes as the main factor in the increased hostility of spectators.

Interestingly, although there is no evidence to suggest that watching aggressive sport reduces aggression in spectators, it appears that this is in fact a common belief, and that such beliefs may influence spectating habits. Wann et al (1999) gave questionnaires to 109 students to assess their sporting preferences and beliefs about aggression. Those who believed that watching sport is cathartic, that is, it helps discharge pent-up aggression, were more likely than others to watch aggressive sport.

The reduction of aggression

There are a number of strategies that can be used to help reduce aggression in athletes. These approaches can be variously applied to preventing young athletes from developing aggressive behaviour in the first place and curtailing aggressive behaviour in those prone to it.

Punishment

Punishment can be an effective tool in tackling athletic aggression. The effects of punishment are most easily understood in the context of social learning theory. The aggressive athlete can learn through punishment that the consequences of aggression are negative. This is clearly most effective if punishment is implemented early in life – before the young athlete has received positive reinforcement for aggressive behaviour. Punishment can also serve as a deterrent. In social learning terms, the witnesses to punishment learn vicariously that aggression does not pay. To be effective, punishment needs to be prompt, severe enough to outweigh the benefits of the aggression and consistent. An example of prompt, severe punishment is football's red card. If this is to be seen as inevitable, it is important that referees apply the sanction consistently.

Catharsis

Both instinct theories and the frustration–aggression hypothesis imply that 'getting it out of your system', or catharsis, will reduce the need for aggression. Sport itself is cathartic; therefore, we would expect that prolonged and hard training will reduce aggression. Baron & Byrne (2002) suggest that vigorous exercise can reduce aggression because it reduces both physical tension and feelings of anger. Although catharsis undoubtedly does reduce aggression, there are two serious limitations of its usefulness. Firstly, the effects are very short-term. If we start brooding again about what made us angry a few hours after exercise, we are likely to get angry all over again! Secondly, exercise in general is less satisfying and therefore less cathartic than hitting the person you are angry with!

Role modelling

If children can learn aggressive behaviour from watching aggressive adults, it follows that if we expose children exclusively to appropriate, non-aggressive role models, we can, to some extent at least, prevent them from developing an aggressive repertoire of behaviour. This approach underlines the importance of the teacher or coach as a role model. Unfortunately, it is almost inevitable that children will observe other athletes acting aggressively. Tenenbaum et al (1997) suggested that the media are irresponsible in over-covering and sensationalising violent incidents in sport. Certainly, unless we prevent children from spectating altogether – something that would probably kill their love of sport – it is impossible to prevent children from encountering aggressive role models.

Contracting

One way of tackling aggression in persistent offenders is by the use of psychological contracts. Athletes signing a contract are committing themselves to eliminate certain behaviours. The terms of each contract are negotiated between the individual athlete and coach or psychologist, but the contract will always specify what behaviours are to be eliminated under what circumstances. Leith (1991) suggests that a simple contract should include specification of the behaviour to be eliminated, punishment for breaching the contract, rewards for sticking to the contract, the names and signatures of both parties, and the date.

Anger-management groups

We all experience anger, and anger per se is not a bad thing, but it can lead to hostile aggression. If athletes often become angry and that anger is consistently manifested in aggressive behaviour, they may benefit from anger-management groups. An anger-management group is a type of therapy group, in which anger is explored and mental strategies for better coping with anger are taught. Some groups – from the psychoanalytic tradition – emphasise exploration of the individual's anger, whilst more cognitive-behaviourally oriented groups emphasise the learning of strategies to control anger.

Summary and conclusions

Aggression is behaviour intended to cause physical or psychological harm to another person. We can classify aggression as hostile or instrumental in intent, and as sanctioned or unsanctioned according to its acceptability. Whilst instrumental aggression under certain circumstances may help performance, hostile aggression is generally agreed to be detrimental to performance. There are three main theories of the origins of aggression in sport. Instinct theory suggests that humans are innately aggressive. Social learning theory suggests, by contrast, that we learn to be aggressive from others. The frustration–aggression hypothesis suggests that we become aggressive in response to frustration. It seems likely that there is an element of truth in each of these theories. A complementary approach to theorising about the origins of aggression in general has been to examine the factors affecting individual differences in aggression. There are a number of such factors, such as gender, motivational style and the extent to which members identify on an emotional level with their team.

One important practical aspect of research into sporting aggression has concerned whether participating in and watching sport has an effect on levels of aggression. There is no firm evidence to suggest that taking part in sport in general has any effect on aggression; however, there is evidence to suggest that spectating, contrary to public opinion, may increase aggression. Another practical application of research has been in strategies to reduce aggression. A number of strategies have been found to be moderately effective in reducing aggression by individual athletes.

Self-assessment questions

1. Distinguish between hostile and instrumental aggression, and between sanctioned and unsanctioned aggression.
2. Discuss the link between sporting aggression and success.
3. Critically compare two theories of aggression.
4. Discuss two or more factors affecting individual levels of aggression.
5. How can aggression be reduced?

Further reading

- Baron R & Byrne D (2002) *Social psychology, the study of human interaction*. Boston, MA, Allyn & Bacon.
- Conroy DE, Silva JM, Newcomer RR, Walker BW & Johnson MS (2001) Personal and participatory socialisers of the perceived legitimacy of aggressive behaviour in sport. *Aggressive Behaviour* 27, 405–418.
- Cox R (2001) *Sport psychology, concepts and applications*. Boston, MA, McGraw-Hill.
- Frith D (2002) *Bodyline autopsy*. Australia, ABC Books.
- Kerr J (1997) *Motivation and emotion in sport*. Hove, Psychology Press.
- LeUnes A & Nation JR (2002) *Sport psychology*. Pacific Grove, CA, Wadsworth.

Social factors in sporting performance 6

Groups and teams

As social animals, we spend a considerable amount of our time in groups. A group has been defined by Moorhead and Griffin (1998) as 'two or more persons who interact with one another such that each person influences and is influenced by each other person' (p 291). A team is more than just a group. Moorhead & Griffin define a team as 'a small number of people with complementary skills who are committed to a common purpose, common performance goals, and an approach for which they hold themselves mutually accountable' (p 293). A team in the broader sense is not *necessarily* a group, because the members of a team can be working for a common aim without ever coming into contact with one another. For example, the British Olympic Team is clearly devoted to a common purpose, but it is not necessarily a group, because its members *could* fulfil their team roles without swimmers, boxers and long-distance runners ever meeting and directly influencing one another. Usually, however, when we refer to a team in sport psychology we are also referring to a group of people who play together and have a powerful influence on each other. For this reason, the terms *group* and *team* are sometimes used interchangeably.

Group formation

Merely placing a collection of individuals together does not in itself create a group or a team. Tuckman & Jensen (1977) suggested that when groups come together they go through five distinct stages. In the first, *forming* stage, the group members get to know each other, and basic rules for the conduct of group members are established. In the second, *storming* stage, members compete for status in the group, and group members take on different roles. In the third, *norming* stage, the group settles down, and group members develop attachments to each other and to the group. In the fourth, *performing* stage, the group members become oriented toward the task they have come together for, and begin to achieve their goals. In the final, *adjourning* stage, the task of the group has been accomplished, and it drifts apart. As Sutton (1994) points out, although this model of group formation is useful, not all groups operate in this manner. For example, in football, unless a new team is being started, it is unusual for a group to form in the way described by Tuckman & Jensen (1977) because new players join the team at different intervals. For an individual player joining an *existing* team, things are likely to be rather different.

Group cohesion

The word cohesion literally means *sticking together*. Festinger et al (1950) defined group cohesion as the sum of the forces that influence members in whether to remain part of a group. A highly cohesive group is likely to be more united and committed to success than a group low in cohesion. It is often said that a team is more than just the sum of the individual players. This is because the cohesiveness of a team can be just as important as the talent of individual team members. If you are a follower of football or rugby, you might have noticed that, in certain seasons, teams composed of brilliant individual performers collectively underperform. This is probably due to the fact that the team members have somehow failed to 'gel' together. This is an example of lack of cohesion.

Elements of group cohesion

Widmeyer et al (1985) distinguished between two different aspects of team cohesion. Each member of a team has a view of the team as a unit (this is known as the members' *group integration*) and of every individual within it (this is called the *individual attractions*). The members may also have different perceptions of the team and its members as regards their sporting performance and their social interactions. In other words, you can think of your team-mates quite differently as individuals and as a team, and as people and co-competitors. We might, for example, see them as socially unpleasant both individually and collectively but as effective co-competitors. Carron et al (1985) devised a psychometric test, the Group Environment Questionnaire (GEQ), which can be used to measure team cohesiveness. The GEQ considers group integration and individual attractions, and both the task achievement and the social life of a team. Items from the GEQ are shown in Box 6.1.

Box 6.1 Items from the Group Environment Questionnaire

Strongly agree 1 2 3 4 5 6 7 8 9 Strongly disagree

1. Our team is united in trying to reach [ ][ ][ ][ ][ ][ ][ ][ ][ ] its goals of performance.
2. Members of our team would rather go [ ][ ][ ][ ][ ][ ][ ][ ][ ] out separately than as a team.
3. I'm not happy with the amount of [ ][ ][ ][ ][ ][ ][ ][ ][ ] playing time I get.
4. Some of my best friends are on this [ ][ ][ ][ ][ ][ ][ ][ ][ ] team.

Factors affecting team cohesion

In a recent UK study, Holt & Sparkes (2001) studied a university football team over the course of one season. Data were gathered by means of observation and interviews. It was concluded that the following four factors affect team cohesion: a clear role for each member of the team, willingness to make personal sacrifices for the good of the team, quality of communication between team members and shared goals for the team as a whole. An additional factor may relate to coaching style. Turman (2003) looked at a range of coaching techniques and attempted to relate these to team cohesiveness. It emerged that use of embarrassment, ridicule and *inequity*, that is, talking down to athletes, has a negative impact on cohesiveness, while athlete-directed technical assistance, motivational speeches and team prayers all had positive effects.

Thinking more broadly, Carron (1993) identified four types of factors that affect the cohesiveness of a team. *Situational factors* include the physical environment in which the team meets and the size of the group. *Individual factors* refer to the characteristics of the athletes that make up the teams. For example, the satisfaction of individuals in being in the team can have a powerful influence on cohesiveness. The third type of factor is *leadership*. Team coaches, captains and managers have a role in helping to make the team cohesive. *Team factors* include past shared successes, communication between members and having collective goals.

Cohesiveness and performance

Numerous studies have shown that there is a relationship between team cohesiveness and success; that is, more successful teams tend to have greater cohesion. In one study, Gould et al (1999) interviewed athletes and coaches from the US Olympic teams in a range of sports, assessing a number of factors including team cohesion. It was found that teams with low cohesiveness were more likely to underperform. There is a logical problem of studies like this, however; they do not tell us whether the teams became more successful *because* they were already more cohesive, or whether, instead, they *became* highly cohesive because of their shared success. Actually, it is quite possible that both of these relationships hold true. Slater & Sewell (1994) measured team cohesion in 60 university hockey players, representing three male and three female teams, early in, midway in and at the end of the season. The researchers were able to see how early cohesion related to later success and how early success related to later cohesion. It was found that, whilst early success was related to later cohesion, the stronger relationship was between early cohesiveness and later success.

Interestingly, not all studies have supported the relationship between cohesiveness and performance. In one experiment, Grieve et al (2000) randomly assigned 222 male university student basketball players to three-person basketball teams, and manipulated the interactions of each team in order to create either high or low levels of team cohesiveness. Each team was then assessed for cohesiveness, given a series of games and then assessed again for cohesiveness. In this study, there was no relationship between early cohesiveness and later performance; however, successful early performance was associated with high levels of cohesiveness at the end of the games. This suggests that cohesiveness does not influence performance but that performance *does* influence cohesiveness.

Reflective exercise

This should help to develop your critical and creative thinking. The studies of Slater & Sewell (1994) and Grieve et al (2000) point to rather different conclusions.

1. Identify as many differences as possible between the two studies. Consider why they might have arrived at different conclusions.
2. Based on these existing studies, design a study of your own to investigate the relationship between cohesion and performance.

Developing team cohesion

Making a group of individuals into an effective team is an important part of a coach's task, particularly in highly individualist cultures such as Britain and the USA, where we do not tend to be taught as children to put the greater good of our groups above our individual needs. Strategies to develop team cohesion are known as *team building*. Carron et al (1997) offer a four-point model for team building, which aims to increase team distinctiveness, for example, by training attire; to increase social cohesiveness, for example, by social events; to clarify team goals, for example, by having collaborative 'goal of the day' sessions; and to improve team communication, for example, by holding regular meetings. Their principles are summarised in Box 6.2.

Team building has been tested in a number of experimental studies, but the results have been equivocal. Moran (2004) suggests that one reason for this is that team building can improve cohesiveness only if the team lacks it in the first place. Thus, studies on already cohesive teams encounter a ceiling effect and have little impact.

Social facilitation

We have already discussed how being in a strongly cohesive team appears to improve the performance of team members. There are

> **Box 6.2** Principles of team building. After Carron et al (1997)
>
> - Each player should be acquainted with the responsibilities of other team members.
> - The coach should learn something personal about each team member, and use it to gain cooperation.
> - Develop pride in the sub-teams within larger teams, such as the defence in a football team.
> - Involve players in decision making to make them feel that the team belongs to them.
> - Set the team goals and celebrate when they are attained.
> - Teach team members their responsibilities and convince them of their individual importance.
> - Allow team members to have disagreements.
> - Prevent the formation of cliques within the team, by giving every member opportunities to perform and avoiding scapegoating.
> - Use routines in practice designed to teach team members how dependent they are on each other.
> - Highlight the positive aspects of play, even when the team is on a losing streak.

several other ways in which the presence of other people can affect our behaviour and performance. Under some circumstances, the presence of other people, such as competitors, enhances our performance. However, under other circumstances, our effort and our ability to make decisions can be adversely affected by others, leading to poor performance. The term 'social facilitation' describes the ways in which our performance can be affected by the presence of others.

Co-action and audience effects

Co-action effects occur when other people are carrying out the same task alongside us, as in a race, or when training with friends or teammates. One of the earliest studies in sport psychology, by Triplett (1898), found that children asked to wind fishing reels did so faster when in the presence of other children also winding fishing reels. Triplett also found that cyclists who trained with another cyclist practised at faster speeds than those training alone.

Audience effects occur when we are being watched. A study of audience effects was carried out by Michaels et al (1982). Researchers observed pool players in a college student union and selected above-average and below-average players (Figure 6.1). First those selected

Figure 6.1 The effect of being watched on pool players will depend on their level of expertise. Copyright © Joyce Choo/Corbis

were watched, and the percentage of successful shots was recorded. Four researchers then walked up to the tables of the selected players and watched the rest of their game. It was found that the audience had the opposite effect on the below-average and above-average players. The players identified as below average in ability played worse in the presence of an audience, whilst those identified as above average played better when watched. Not all recent studies have replicated the findings of the Michaels et al study. Geisler & Leith (1997) tested the effect of an audience on penalty taking in 40 Canadian ex-university soccer players. There was no difference in the number of goals scored when alone or with an audience.

The personality of the athlete may also affect the relationship between audience and performance. Graydon & Murphy (1995) assessed the personality of students with the EPI (see p 15 for details), and identified 10 extroverts and 10 introverts. These 20 were given the task of serving a table tennis ball into a grid. In one condition, they did this alone and in another condition they did it in front of an audience. The extroverts performed better in front of an audience, whereas the introverts did better alone.

The home advantage effect

An important application of research into audience effects is in understanding the effects of playing in home and away matches. The home advantage effect (HAE) operates when performance is enhanced by the presence of a large supportive home audience. This is an extremely powerful effect. In football's World Cup, for example, no team other than Brazil has even won the competition when playing outside its own continent. Interestingly, it appears that audience effects increase as the size of the audience increases. Nevill & Cann (1998) examined the size of crowds in home-win games in the English and Scottish football leagues in 1985–96, finding that the HAE was greatest when crowds were large and least when crowds were small.

Explanations for audience and co-action effects

Drive theory

Zajonc (1965) proposed that the presence of others affects performance because it directly raises arousal levels. Drive theory proposes that heightened arousal produces a better performance when the task is simple and/or the performer is an expert. Heightened arousal produces a worse performance, however, when the task is complex or the performer is a novice. Therefore, it follows that the presence of others will lead to a better performance for expert athletes but a worse performance for novices.

The Michaels et al (1982) study described above strongly supports drive theory. Expert pool players performed better and novices worse

> **Box 6.3** The home disadvantage effect (HDE)
>
> The HAE is well known and well understood. However, what is much less well understood are the circumstances under which it is reduced and even sometimes reversed. The home disadvantage effect (HDE) is a much less obvious phenomenon than the advantage effect. It seems that when teams are working under particular pressure, the presence of a large audience can work against them. In an American study, Wright et al (1995) demonstrated the existence of the HDE in an analysis of ice hockey scores in home and away games. In low-pressure matches, teams performed better when playing at home; however, in high-pressure matches, such as a crucial championship game, they played better away. A recent UK example of the HDE was Sheffield Wednesday's 2001–2 season, in which they won considerably more games away than at home. So what might cause the HDE? One explanation is that when teams are less sure of themselves, as when they have been playing badly or when defeat has dire consequences, they perceive the audience to be critically evaluating them. By contrast, in low-pressure situations, the fans can afford to be unconditionally supportive. A related explanation comes from Baumeister & Steinhilber (1994), who suggest that the presence of a supportive audience can serve to shift athletes' attention inward so that, rather than focusing on the game, they focus on their own actions. This means that skills that would normally be practised automatically become conscious and are therefore performed less efficiently. This is related to the phenomenon of 'choking' (discussed on p 126). Kremer & Scully (1994) discuss this in relation to the famously supportive atmosphere at Cardiff Arms Park. It has commonly been assumed that the effect of the passionate and highly knowledgeable Welsh crowd on Welsh performance is a positive one. However, it may be that both the passion and the expertise of the Welsh crowd contribute to self-attention by the Welsh team and hence increased errors.

when the researchers provided an audience for their game. Aronson et al (1994) reviewed studies and concluded that there was overwhelming evidence for drive theory in that performance consistently improved in experts and declined in novices in numerous studies. However, a weakness of Zajonc's application of drive theory is that he failed to explain *why* the presence of others should lead to increased arousal and how individuals might differ in their reactions to the presence of others.

Evaluation-apprehension theory

Cottrell (1968) offered an alternative to Zajonc's drive theory to explain *why* the presence of others might lead to increased arousal. In evaluation-apprehension theory, the presence of others causes an increase in our arousal because we feel that we are about to be *evaluated*. If we are competent in the task to be observed, we are likely to feel confident, and the effect of the observer on performance will be confidence. If we are novices, however, the anxiety that results from the belief that we are about to be judged and found wanting increases our arousal levels and so spoils our performance.

Cottrell (1968) discovered that the more expert the observer of athletes, the greater the decline in the performance of non-expert performers. This supports the idea that it is fear of being judged that leads to increased arousal and poor performance. You can imagine, for example, that if you found yourself watched by a panel of England team selectors, your arousal level would be higher than if observed by a group of friends! However, whilst evaluation apprehension is almost certainly one cause of arousal in the presence of others, it may not be the *only* factor.

Negative effects of team membership

Social loafing

In the 1880s, the French engineer Ringelmann discovered that when a group of men pulled together on a rope, each pulled considerably less hard than when pulling alone. When eight men were pulling, each man averaged half the effort he put in when pulling alone. This effect, known as *social loafing*, has since been demonstrated in a variety of settings, including team sports.

In view of this effect, an obvious question to ask is, 'How do we know whether, in a given situation, social facilitation or social loafing will occur?' Aronson et al (1994) identified two factors that affect which response takes place: the complexity of the task and the possibility of observers successfully seeing how much effort you make. If your individual efforts can be evaluated easily, you will tend to be highly aroused, and therefore you are likely to do better on simple tasks and worse on complex tasks. If people cannot tell to look at you how hard you are trying, your arousal levels will tend to be lower, and therefore you should do worse at simple tasks and better at complex tasks.

This identifiability effect has been demonstrated in a study by Swain (1996), in which 96 15-year-old boys ran a 30-metre sprint under three conditions. In the first condition, they ran individually; in the second, they ran in teams, but each boy's time was recorded. In the third condition, they ran in teams, but only the team time was recorded, and therefore each boy's own performance was not identifiable. Overall, the boys ran slower in the third condition; however, this masked considerable individual differences in the boys. It emerged that *goal orientation* (see p 85 for a detailed discussion) was the major factor – task-oriented boys ran equally fast in the three conditions, but ego-oriented boys slowed down when they believed their individual times were not being measured.

Other factors apart from goal orientation may affect on social loafing behaviour. Heuze & Brunel (2003) conducted an experiment in which students threw darts under four conditions. In one condition, they had no opposition. In the other three conditions, fictitious opponents were created who were either inferior, equal or superior in standard. Performance was best against an opponent of equal standard and worst against a superior opponent. This suggests that we tend to indulge in social loafing in situations where we are not expected to succeed, but less so when expectations of us are higher.

Reflective exercise

Practise your creative thinking on the phenomenon of social loafing. Based on the studies above, draw up a list of the factors that might increase and decrease the likelihood of social loafing.

Groupthink

The presence of others affects us in many ways, not just in our arousal levels and efforts. One other way in which we differ when alone or in a group is in the way we make decisions. Janis (1982) identified the phenomenon of groupthink, which occurs when group cohesion is so great that it prevents group members, from voicing opinions that go against the majority. Groupthink can cause serious problems for teams, because the entire team can become so focused on a particular goal that important considerations of practicality and safety are abandoned. Janis (1982) described the symptoms of groupthink. The group feels that it cannot make a wrong decision, and that fate will support it. Group members decide not to 'rock the boat' by arguing with the majority. Those who do argue are made to conform, or ignored.

Searle (1996) suggested that groupthink might have contributed to the loss of six climbers on K2 in 1995. Three combined teams of climbers continued to press on toward the summit, despite clearly dangerous and worsening conditions, resulting in the deaths of six climbers. One of the survivors was quoted as saying, 'The most

dangerous thing about groups is that everyone hands over responsibility for themselves to someone else.' It appears that, because of the
desire to complete the climb, the group went into groupthink and
ignored the danger.

Leadership

Leadership has been defined by Moorhead and Griffin (1998) as 'the
use of noncoercive influence to direct and coordinate the activities of
group members to meet a goal' (p 352). Leadership may be informal or
formal. When we appoint a team coach and a captain, we know that
they have formal leadership roles. However, other team members
might also take on informal roles in which they influence and inspire
others. For many years, psychologists have been concerned with who
becomes leaders and how they carry out their role. In the remainder of
this chapter, we shall examine both of these issues.

Leadership style

There is more than one way to lead people. An early but still influential distinction is that between authoritarian, laissez-faire and democratic styles of leadership (Lewin et al 1939). The *authoritarian* leader
makes decisions alone and expects unquestioning obedience from the
group. This approach has advantages and disadvantages in sport. The
main advantage is that team members can still be directed toward
purposeful action when they are exhausted, stressed and disil-
lusioned. However, authoritarian leadership has its costs. Other
group members are often denied what would be useful input to decision making, and, in the absence of the leader, the members may have
difficulty in motivating themselves.

By contrast, the *laissez-faire* leader leaves group members to get on
with the task at hand without interference. Such leaders may assist
individuals, but do not attempt to organise or motivate the group as a
whole. Whilst being a member of a group with laissez-faire leadership
might allow you to explore your talents without being unnecessarily
restricted, leaders who can operate *only* in a laissez-faire manner often
fail to motivate groups to achieve their potential or cope with crises.

Lewin's third category, the *democratic* leader, can be seen as a half-
way house between authoritarian and laissez-faire styles. The democratic leader takes decisions and enforces them, but decisions always
take account of the views of the rest of the group. Democratic leadership can cause difficulties when very rapid decision making is
required in an emergency, but in most cases this is the most successful

style of leadership. Lewin has offered a useful approach to understanding how leaders may operate. This does not mean, however, that a leader can operate in only one way. Lewin believed that each style of leadership works in different situations, and that the best leaders can use all three styles as appropriate.

Theories of leadership

Trait theories

Early psychological approaches to leadership emphasised the importance of being a certain type of person, that is, having certain *personality traits* (see Chapter 2), in order to be a good leader. This great-person approach depends on three main assumptions. Firstly, all successful leaders have certain personality traits in common. Secondly, the rest of us 'mere mortals' do not share the characteristics of great leaders. Thirdly, the traits that make someone a leader in one situation will also enable that person to lead successfully in quite different situations. Researchers have attempted for many years to find out what traits make a good leader. Although there appears to be no set of personality traits that are necessary to be a leader, there are certain characteristics that are found in a large number of successful leaders, and which appear to be helpful in leading others. Kirkpatrick & Locke (1991) identified the following eight characteristics associated with successful leadership: drive (ambition and persistence), honesty, motivation to lead, self-confidence, intelligence, expertise in the purpose of the group, creativity (imagination and originality) and flexibility. Kirkpatrick & Locke concluded that 'leaders do not have to be great men or women by being intellectual geniuses or omniscient prophets, but they do need to have the "right stuff" and this stuff is not equally present in all people' (1991: p 58).

The trait approach has failed to identify a combination of personality traits that will invariably lead to a person's becoming a successful leader. However, it has been quite successful in the more modest aim of identifying characteristics that are likely to be *helpful* to leaders. Looking at Kirkpatrick & Locke's list of characteristics associated with successful leadership, you can see how it might be useful to bear these in mind when choosing a leader, such as a team captain. If someone you are considering as captain lacks a number of these attributes, it is perhaps unlikely that they will turn out to be a good choice. The main problem with the trait approach is that it neglects the importance of the *situation* in which the leader is operating. Different leaders do best in different circumstances. In the next theory we shall look at, Fiedler has aimed to explain how leaders might be matched to their particular task.

Fiedler's contingency theory

According to contingency theory, the success of leadership depends on the characteristics of leaders *and* the situation in which they are leading. Fiedler (1967) identified two categories of leader, those who are task-oriented, that is, their main preoccupation is the *task* of the group, and those who are person-oriented, that is, their main pre-occupation is the *members* of the group. Fiedler distinguished task-oriented and person-oriented leaders by asking them, by means of a questionnaire, about their least effective team member or, to use Fiedler's terms, *least-preferred co-worker* (LPC). Those who hold the LPC in low esteem are assumed to be task-oriented, because they are thinking first of the likelihood of accomplishing their task while handicapped by the ineffective team member. Those who hold the LPC in high esteem are assumed to be person-oriented, because they value the team member despite their lack of contribution to achieving the task at hand.

Fiedler proposed that task-oriented and person-oriented leaders are effective under different circumstances. Under very favourable or very unfavourable circumstances, task-oriented leaders get better results. Favourable conditions occur when there is a clearly defined task and good leader–group relations, and the leader has the power to enforce his or her decisions. Under moderately favourable conditions, person-oriented leaders are more effective.

Fiedler has contributed to our understanding of leadership by showing how the personality of leaders and the situation in which they are leading are both important to how successful leadership is. Cox (2001) has pointed out that there are a number of cases in sport that demonstrate how leaders with particular personalities have been very successful under some circumstances and unsuccessful in others. You have only to look at the changing fortunes of British football managers to see the validity of this principle! However, more questionable are the *specifics* of Fiedler's theory. Gill (2000) reviewed research into the effects of situation and leader personality in sport teams and concluded that results were inconclusive.

The coach and athlete: a special case of leadership

Athletes spend much time with their coaches, and rely on them for information, direction, feedback and support. All these factors require trust – advice and direction will be better followed and feedback better received in the context of a good relationship. But what exactly do we mean by a good relationship? Based on an understanding of research into relationships in general, Jowett & Cockerill (2002) suggest that the coach–athlete relationship can be understood in terms of three key variables: closeness, co-orientation and complementarity.

- *Closeness* is the emotional aspects of the relationship, referring to the attachment between coach and athlete.
- *Co-orientation* is the cognitive aspect of the relationship, referring to the commonality of knowledge, views and concerns between coach and athlete.
- *Complementarity* is the behavioural aspect of the relationship, referring to the interpersonal behaviour between coach and athlete, in particular their effective cooperation.

In a series of case studies and a study of 12 Olympic athletes, Sophia Jowett and colleagues (Jowett & Meek, 2000a, 2000b; Jowett & Cockerill, 2001) have studied the closeness, co-orientation and complementarity of athlete–coach pairs. In all cases, athletes placed great emphasis on closeness, reporting that their own motivation and confidence were tied up with their experience of being cared for, liked, trusted and respected by their coaches. A particular issue thrown up by Jowett's studies is that of *dual-role relationships*, in which the coach and athlete have an additional relationship, such as parent and child or husband and wife. Two such relationships are summarised in Box 6.4.

Box 6.4 Two examples of dual-role coach–athlete relationships. After Jowett & Cockerill (2002)

1. **Mary and Andy**: Mary coached her son Andy in athletics. Their relationship in mid-childhood was very close and successful, Andy achieving a high national ranking. However, as an adolescent, Andy began to resent his mother's constant presence and at times appeared to lose all interest in athletics. Although they remained close, incompatibilities were emerging in co-orientation and complementarity.
2. **Peter and Sarah**: Peter coached his wife Sarah in athletics from the time they married. Although they shared the goal of Sarah's making the Olympic team, and both reported mutual trust, conflicts emerged around their home life. Peter's belief that some aspects of Sarah's preparation could be best achieved at home led to her feeling that he was unduly controlling. In this case, the problem was with complementarity; in spite of their closeness and shared aims, Peter's behaviour was perceived as inappropriate.

Ryan & Deci (2000) suggest that athletes need to feel competent, related to others and autonomous (independent). The problem with dual-role relationships is that autonomy is difficult to attain. One way of resolving this type of difficulty, which can of course occur even in the absence of dual roles, is improved communication. Once both parties understand the nature of their differences, it is more likely that a mutually satisfactory path can be taken. There is a range of techniques for improving communication (see Anshel 1994, for a review).

Coaching as decision making

Chelladurai (1993) points out that all coaching activities involve decision making, and he suggests that we can understand the leadership displayed by coaches in terms of their style of decision making. The main focus of the model is on understanding when athletes will actively participate in team decision making. Within this model, decision making is affected by the following seven factors:

- Time pressure: when decisions have to be made very quickly, the coach often has to make them without athlete participation. Less urgent decisions are more likely to involve athletes.
- Decision importance: when problems can be resolved by several options athlete participation is more likely. When there is a single correct answer (such as which goalkeeper to use), the coach is more likely to make the decision singly.
- Information location: whoever possesses the necessary information is likely to take a role in decision making. When the coach is the only person in possession of all the facts, they are likely to make a decision single-handed; otherwise athletes with specialist knowledge are likely to be consulted.
- Problem complexity: the more complex the problem, the more likely it is that only the coach will possess all the information necessary to make the decision; therefore, he is more likely to do so without participation by athletes.
- Group acceptance: a coach is likely to make a unilateral decision either when it will be fully accepted by the team or when its acceptance is not of primary importance. For example, a popular footballer playing his last professional game may tire early. In this case, the coach/manager might wish to substitute a younger, fitter player. However, the decision will also take account of the fact that it might be resented by team-mates and might lower team morale and concentration for the remainder of the match.

- Coach's power: coaches may exert power over athletes by means of reward, punishment, the authority of their position, the admiration of athletes, and their superior knowledge and experience. The greater their power, the more likely they are to make unilateral decisions.
- Group integration: the more integrated a team, the more likely its members are to participate in decision making. The term *integration* refers to the extent to which the team members have good interpersonal relationships and equal status.

Influenced by these seven factors, the coach adopts one of three decision-making styles. In the *autocratic* style, the coach makes the final decision unilaterally. Alternatively, the *participative* style involves the full participation of athletes, the coach simply functioning as a group member. Finally, the *delegative* style involves delegating decision making to one or more athletes.

Box 6.5 Relationships *between* leaders: the captain and the coach

Traditional theories of leadership assume that a team has a single undisputed leader. In reality, athletes are often led by more than one person. For example, a team will have a captain, a manager and perhaps, depending on the management structure, a separate coach. Disunity between these leadership figures can lead to morale problems in the team. As Sven-Goran Eriksson (2002) puts it, 'a bad atmosphere can spread quickly, particularly if one of the leaders of opinion in the team represents negative thinking – the captain for instance' (p 116). Interestingly, however, some highly successful captain–manager relationships have been stormy; for example, Sir Alex Ferguson and David Beckham at Manchester United. Although Ferguson and Beckham have kept their dressing-room interchanges largely secret, it is widely believed that they frequently clashed; for example, over Beckham's marriage. Their strained relationship was brought to a head in February 2003 when, after losing to Arsenal in the FA Cup, Ferguson kicked a stray football boot in the dressing room and it hit Beckham in the face, leaving him in need of two butterfly stitches. Even stormier perhaps was the relationship between Irish football manager Mick McCarthy and captain Roy Keane. This came to a head in the 2002 World Cup finals, when Keane publicly criticised the organisation and management of the Irish team. McCarthy responded by dismissing Keane and sending him home. This was in keeping with the belief that disunity must be dealt with instantly to preserve morale. Ireland's good performance after the incident lends weight to the belief and McCarthy's decision.

Summary and conclusions

Other people constantly influence us. This is very much part of the experience of being a member of a social species, and it is unsurprising that these social influences extend to sporting behaviour. Our behaviour and sporting performance are influenced in several ways by our membership of groups and teams. Team cohesiveness, that is, the extent to which the individuals in our team 'gel' together, appears to be one influence on our performance, although research findings are inconsistent. The presence of others, whether as competitors, spectators or team-mates, can have a variety of *social facilitation* effects, that is, effects, both positive and negative, on our performance.

In addition to social facilitation effects, there are purely negative influences of team membership in the form of social loafing and groupthink. Psychological research has illuminated the circumstances in which these phenomena are most common. Leaders can have a profound effect on the way teams behave and perform. There are a range of leadership styles, and it seems that different types of leader are effective under different circumstances. However, generally, certain personality traits seem to be helpful in effective leadership. A special case of leadership particularly important in sport is the coach–athlete relationship. Where the emotional, cognitive and behavioural aspects of the relationship are mutually acceptable, harmony and high levels of motivation and self-confidence should result.

Self-assessment questions

1. Define a team. How does a team differ from a group?
2. Identify two factors that affect team cohesion.
3. To what extent does evidence support the idea that a team's cohesiveness affects its performance?
4. What is meant by the term 'social facilitation'? Explain how social facilitation is linked to home advantage and disadvantage effects.
5. What factors affect the likelihood of social loafing?
6. What makes a good leader?
7. Why might an athlete and coach not get on?

Further reading

- Baron R & Byrne D (2002) *Social psychology*. New York, Allyn & Bacon.

- Chelladurai P (1993) Styles of decision-making in coaching. In Williams JM (ed) *Applied sport psychology*. Mountain View, CA, Mayfield.
- Cox R (2001) *Sport psychology: concepts and applications*. Boston, MA, WBC McGraw-Hill.
- Jowett S & Cockerill I (2002) Incompatibility in the coach–athlete relationship. In Cockerill I (ed) *Solutions in sport psychology*. London, Thomson Learning.
- Moran A (2004) *Sport and exercise psychology*. London, Routledge.
- Scully D (2002) 'The team just hasn't gelled'. In Cockerill I (ed) *Solutions in sport psychology*. London, Thomson Learning.
- Swain A (1996) Social loafing and identifiability: the mediating role of achievement goal orientation. *Research Quarterly for Exercise and Sport* 67, 337–351.

Arousal, anxiety and sporting performance

7

Learning objectives

By the end of this chapter, you should be able to:

- define key terms including arousal, anxiety and stress
- distinguish between state and trait anxiety and between cognitive and somatic anxiety
- understand the influences on arousal and anxiety, including both situational and individual factors
- describe and evaluate theories of the relationship between arousal and performance, including drive theory and the inverted-U hypothesis
- describe and evaluate theories of the relationship between anxiety and performance, including catastrophe theory and zones of optimal functioning
- discuss a range of stress-management techniques that can be applied to athletes, with particular reference to goal setting and imagery.

Common sense tells us that there are important links between sport and arousal, anxiety and stress. Sport normally involves competition, which in turn tends to induce anxiety, characterised by an increase in arousal. You may have had the experience of performing better than you expected when anxious, or, alternatively, you might have had the less fortunate experience of making mistakes under pressure. Sport psychologists have been concerned with understanding what factors affect arousal, anxiety and stress; how these affect athletic perform-ance; and how we can learn to regulate our arousal and anxiety in order to improve our performance. As Jones (1991) has pointed out, at the top sporting levels (at least in many sports), there is very little difference in the skill levels of the participants. It is thus often the ability to handle anxiety and stress that separates the winner and loser. Before going any further, it is important to understand exactly what psychologists mean by the terms 'arousal', 'anxiety' and 'stress'.

Definitions of arousal, anxiety and stress

Arousal may be defined as 'a general physiological and psychological activation varying on a continuum from deep sleep to intense excitement' (Gould & Krane, 1992). When we are bored, relaxed or asleep, we are in a state of low arousal. When excited, angry or anxious, we are in a state of high arousal. You can see from this that being in a state of high or low arousal is not *in itself* necessarily a pleasant or unpleasant experience. On the other hand, *anxiety* is by definition an unpleasant sensation. Weinberg & Gould (1995) have offered the following definition of anxiety: 'a negative emotional state with feelings of nervousness, worry and apprehension associated with activation or arousal of the body' (p 264). We can thus think of anxiety as an unpleasant state of high arousal.

The term *stress* has a broader meaning than anxiety. Stress is the process whereby an individual perceives a threat and responds with a series of psychological and physiological changes, including increased arousal and the experience of anxiety. We tend to experience stress when we meet demands that are difficult to meet, but which carry serious consequences if we fail to meet them. If stress is long-term, or *chronic*, it can cause serious harm to both physical and mental health. Whilst it is quite normal – and as we shall see quite beneficial – to experience some anxiety before competing, athletes should not feel constantly anxious and see themselves as facing insurmountable odds.

Cognitive and somatic anxiety

Martens et al (1990) distinguished between two aspects of anxiety. When we are anxious, we experience the physiological changes associated with high arousal, including increased heart rate and blood pressure, 'butterflies' in the stomach, faster breathing and flushed face. These effects are similar (though not identical) to the physiological effects of excitement and anger. We call the experience of physiological changes associated with anxiety *somatic anxiety* (from the Greek *soma* meaning body).

We can measure somatic anxiety directly by physiological means, or indirectly by self-rating inventories. Direct physiological measures include urinalysis, galvanic skin response (GSR) and blood pressure testing. Elevated levels of certain hormones released when we are anxious (such as adrenalin) can be detected in urine. We also tend to sweat more when anxious. This can be detected by a GSR meter, which measures the electrical conductivity of the skin – the more we sweat, the better conductor our skin becomes. Our blood pressure also increases when we are anxious, and this can be measured by a sphygmomanometer. There are two major problems with these physiological measures of anxiety. Firstly, as we vary quite a lot in our normal physiological levels, all individuals studied would have to have physiological measures taken over time to establish their levels with and without anxiety. Secondly, physiological measures require laboratory equipment and are difficult to administer in the field. Self-rating inventories can be used to measure somatic anxiety indirectly. We shall examine two such questionnaires, the SCAT and the CSAI–2, later in this chapter.

At the same time as we experience somatic anxiety, we may also experience *cognitive anxiety*. Cognitive anxiety refers to the anxious thoughts that accompany somatic anxiety. Anxious thinking involves worries, self-doubts and images of losing and humiliation. A number of studies have examined how cognitive anxiety and somatic anxiety change before a sporting event. Swain & Jones (1993) followed 49 field and track athletes, measuring both the frequency and intensity of their cognitive and somatic anxiety on four occasions (2 days, 1 day, 2 hours and 30 minutes) prior to an important competition. They found that both cognitive and somatic anxiety increased before the event, the most dramatic increase being in the frequency of anxious thinking immediately before competition.

Once competition begins, it is commonly believed that somatic anxiety declines sharply, whilst cognitive anxiety fluctuates, depending on how the event is going. Therefore, many researchers have proposed that errors during performance are due to cognitive anxiety, and not somatic anxiety. Cox (1998) proposed that cognitive anxiety is negatively related to performance – as cognitive anxiety increases, performance declines. However, in the Swain & Jones (1993) study, several athletes reported that they needed a degree of cognitive anxiety in order to perform well. Since it is very difficult to measure cognitive anxiety *during* sport, we can estimate the frequency and intensity of anxious thinking only whilst athletes are performing.

Of course, it is important to consider the demands of different sports. Hanton et al (2000) examined self-reported cognitive and somatic anxiety in 50 rugby league players and 50 target rifle shooters.

There were no differences in the extent of anxiety between the two groups of athletes or between their perceptions of the effect of cognitive anxiety on performance. However, rugby players were more likely to report that somatic anxiety had a positive impact on their performance, and shooters were more likely to say it had a negative impact. Studies like these are important because they show that it is important to make a distinction between somatic and cognitive anxiety. Later in this chapter, the relationships between cognitive and somatic anxiety and performance are examined in some detail.

Reflective exercise

This should help develop your creative thinking. Design a study to assess in what sports performance is enhanced by somatic anxiety and in which it is experienced as debilitating. Consider the following:

1. What sports might you investigate?
2. What do you expect to find?
3. How will you assess somatic anxiety?
4. How will you assess its effect on performance?

State and trait anxiety

Another important distinction was made by Spielberger (1966) between state and trait anxiety. *Trait anxiety* refers to anxiety as an aspect of personality. A person high in trait anxiety will be frequently anxious, almost irrespective of the situation. Recall Chapter 2 in which we looked at Hans Eysenck's trait theory of personality. Eysenck believed that some people are generally more anxious and moody than others because they are genetically programmed to react more to potential threats in their environment. Martens et al (1977) developed a self-rating inventory called the Sport Competition Anxiety Test (SCAT), designed to measure trait anxiety related to sport. Items from SCAT are shown in Box 7.1.

The items in Box 7.1 obviously refer to both cognitive and somatic anxiety. A serious problem with the SCAT is that, although it was intended to measure the *trait* of anxiety in sporting situations, because items refer to how the individual feels before competing, it is likely that it actually measures *state anxiety* rather than trait anxiety. However, some contemporary research still uses the SCAT. For example, Cunningham (2000) used the SCAT to look at the relationship between anxiety and golfing performance in 80 students. Moderate SCAT scores were associated with good performance and high SCAT scores with poor performance.

State anxiety refers to the emotional state of anxiety (cognitive and somatic), typically experienced prior to and during competition. Martens et al (1990) have produced an updated questionnaire, the Competitive State Anxiety Inventory–2 (CSAI–2), based on the SCAT, which seeks to measure state anxiety before competition. Items from the CSAI–2 are shown in Box 7.2.

During the 1990s, the CSAI–2 became the most widely accepted research tool for measuring competitive anxiety. It includes three subscales measuring cognitive anxiety (e.g. items 1 and 3), somatic anxiety (e.g. items 2 and 5) and self-confidence (e.g. item 4). The Swain & Jones (1993) study discussed earlier in the chapter used the CSAI–2 as the measure of pre-competitive anxiety. However, the CSAI–2 has recently been criticised, both for its phrasing and for its usefulness. Some items (such as item 1 above) use the word 'concerned'. It is likely that all athletes are concerned about imminent competitions, so the answers probably do not tell us much about the athlete's anxiety. Collins (1998) has launched a particularly vigorous attack on research using the CSAI–2, saying that it is not a good predictor of performance and that it tells us little about the processes involved in the relationship between anxiety and performance. A meta-analysis of 29 studies linking CSAI–2 scores to performance (Craft et al, 2003) found only weak correlations between items measuring cognitive anxiety, somatic anxiety and self-confidence, suggesting that it is a conceptual error to combine them in a measure of state anxiety.

Factors inducing anxiety and stress

How anxious we feel at any time is a product of both our individual psychological make-up and the characteristics of the situation we find ourselves in. Therefore, when looking at why someone is anxious, we need to take into account both situational and individual factors.

Situational factors

Event importance

The more important a sporting event is, the more stressful we are likely to find it. It is probably true to say, for example, that most footballers would find themselves more anxious competing in the World Cup than in a 'friendly'. However, we must remember that it is the importance of the event *to the individual* that counts. This does not necessarily depend on the status of the competition. For example, athletes who know they are being watched by talent scouts, or perhaps by their family for the first time, may feel particularly anxious. Marchant et al (1998) carried out an experiment in which event importance was artificially set up. Pairs of golfers competed for either three new balls (low importance) or a new pair of golfing shoes (high importance). As expected, those competing for the new shoes experienced more anxiety than those competing for golf balls.

Expectations

It seems likely that both high and low expectations can be linked to anxiety. In the 2004 European Championships, it was said by many that England had to cope with very high expectations that they would win. It seems likely that in the end this contributed to their downfall. By contrast the winners, Greece, as first-time qualifiers, had far less pressure on them to succeed. Individuals as well as teams can be adversely affected by the pressure of high expectations. Too much pressure from teachers, coaches and family can add tremendously to competitive anxiety. Of course, the opposite can also hold true. Hall & Kerr (1998) studied 111 fencers, assessing anxiety and ability beliefs. There was a strong relationship between ability beliefs and anxiety, those with low expectations of their performance experiencing more anxiety.

Individual factors

Trait anxiety

Some people are prone to suffer more anxiety than others, whatever the situation. This can be explained by genetics (see Eysenck's theory, Chapter 2), but also by experience. Social learning theorists might explain trait anxiety as having been learned from adults in childhood. The psychodynamic view emphasises the importance of early family relationships, and the fact that those who experience early trauma or family disruption may afterward suffer chronic anxiety. Individuals high in trait anxiety are likely to see competition as particularly stressful. In the Marchant et al (1998) study of anxiety in golfers (see above), trait anxiety, as well as event importance, was a significant predictor of state anxiety.

Performance concerns

One way in which we vary as athletes is the manner in which we are concerned about our performance. Of course, it is essential for our motivation that we show some concern in this direction; however, too much in the way of perfectionism or concern over our image as opposed to our achievement is associated with high anxiety. Hall et al (1998) found that high levels of perfectionism were associated with cognitive anxiety in secondary school runners. Wilson & Eklund (1998) examined the importance of self-presentational concern in 199 American university-level athletes, who were assessed for somatic and cognitive anxiety and their concerns over their image. Concerns over appearing untalented, non-composed, fatigued and unattractive were all related to cognitive, though not somatic anxiety.

Locus of control

Locus of control describes the extent to which we believe that we are in control of our lives. The concept was developed by Rotter (1966). Research in a number of contexts has found that individuals low in locus of control are generally more vulnerable to anxiety and stress. There is a range of psychometric tests available to assess locus of control. Items from one such test are shown in Box 7.3.

Box 7.3 items from a locus of control scale		
1. I usually get what I want in life.	☐ True	☐ False
2. I need to be kept informed about news events.	☐ True	☐ False
3. I never know where I stand with other people.	☐ True	☐ False
4. I do not really believe in luck or chance.	☐ True	☐ False
5. I think that I could easily win a lottery.	☐ True	☐ False

Ntoumanis & Jones (1998) investigated the relationship between locus of control and competitive anxiety in 83 university- and county-level athletes (45 men, 38 women), using the CSAI–2 and a standard measure of locus of control. Interestingly, locus of control was not associated with somatic or cognitive anxiety levels; however, there was a relationship with how the athletes saw anxiety. Those with an internal locus saw anxiety as *facilitative*, that is, likely to improve their performance, whereas those with an external locus of control tended to see it as *debilitative*, that is, bad for their performance.

Reflective exercise

Practise your critical thinking on the Ntoumanis & Jones study. Consider in particular the following:

1. Is the sample sufficiently large and representative? Consider gender and performance level.
2. Have standard measures been used to record the results?
3. Has the study discovered something new or with important practical applications?

The relationship between arousal and performance

Drive theory

Drive theory was proposed by Hull (1943). The theory itself is complex, but its application to sporting performance is relatively simple.

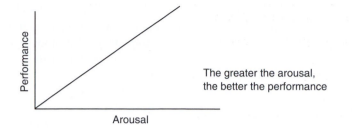

The greater the arousal,
the better the performance

Figure 7.1 Drive theory of the relationship between arousal and performance for expert performers.

According to drive theory, three factors influence performance: complexity of task, arousal and learned habits. The greater the arousal, the more likely we are to adopt the dominant response to a situation, that is, our habit. Provided the task is *a simple one* and our dominant response is *the correct one*, the higher is our arousal, the better will be our performance; that is, performance = arousal × habit. This is shown in Figure 7.1.

If, however, the task is a complex one or the dominant response is not correct, arousal will inhibit performance. Because arousal level is greater in competition than in practice, and increases according to the importance of the competition, drive theory predicts that the best performances take place in high-importance competition. Drive theory also predicts, however, that, because expert performers are likely to have correct habits and novices bad habits, novices are more likely to make mistakes under pressure. Empirical support for this idea can be found in Chapter 6, which deals with audience effects (see p 98). An important application of this principle is that if novices are to acquire better skills, they need to practise under conditions of low arousal, that is, with minimal spectators and minimal competition.

Drive theory has proved extremely useful in explaining why experts do better in competition and novices are more likely to crack under pressure. It has also given us an insight into how to optimise athletes' arousal during training. However, drive theory fails to explain instances where even expert athletes become *too* aroused and make errors. It also fails to take account of the *type* of arousal experienced or psychological factors that may accompany arousal, such as cognitive anxiety.

Inverted-U hypothesis

By the 1970s, psychologists were dissatisfied with drive theory and had turned to the inverted-U approach to explain the relationship between arousal and performance. The inverted-U hypothesis was originated by Yerkes & Dodson (1908). The idea is that for every task

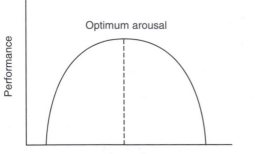

Figure 7.2 The inverted-U hypothesis of arousal and performance.

there is an optimum level of arousal. Performance peaks at this level and drops off above and below it. This is shown in Figure 7.2.

The optimum level of arousal for a task depends on the complexity of the skill required to carry out that task. For a complex task involving fine motor skills, such as potting a ball in snooker, low levels of arousal are preferable. For gross tasks such as weightlifting, the optimum arousal level is much higher. Support for the inverted-U hypothesis comes from athletes' reports of what factors they believe affect their performance. Thelwell & Maynard (2000) questioned 198 county-level English cricketers about what they considered to be the most important variables affecting their performance. Optimum level of arousal emerged in the top four factors affecting both batsmen and bowlers (the others being self-confidence, a pre-match routine and following a performance plan).

Like drive theory, the inverted-U hypothesis has important applications in sport psychology. By looking at how fine the motor skills required for a particular sport are, we can then seek to optimise the arousal levels of competitors in that sport. Thus, we may recommend relaxation procedures to lower the arousal levels of darts and snooker players whilst recommending 'psyching up' exercises for weightlifters and rugby players. Unlike drive theory, the inverted-U hypothesis can easily explain why expert performers sometimes make errors under pressure. However, like drive theory, the inverted-U hypothesis fails to take account of the nature of the arousal or the effects of psychological factors, such as cognitive anxiety, on performance.

The relationship between anxiety and performance

In recent years, the emphasis in sport psychology has shifted away from study of simple arousal in favour of looking at the more complex phenomena of anxiety. There are three particularly influential theories seeking to explain the relationship between anxiety and sporting performance: the catastrophe model, zones of optimal functioning and reversal theory.

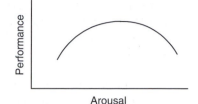
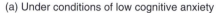
(a) Under conditions of low cognitive anxiety

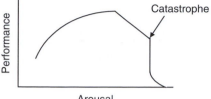
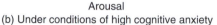
(b) Under conditions of high cognitive anxiety

The catastrophe model

Fazey & Hardy (1988) rejected the assumption of the inverted-U hypothesis that a small change in arousal will bring about a small change in performance. Instead, they pointed out that when athletes are experiencing high cognitive anxiety (that is, they are worried), a small increase in arousal beyond the optimum level can cause a massive fall in performance. Figure 7.3 shows the relationship between arousal and performance under conditions of low and high cognitive anxiety.

Under conditions of low cognitive anxiety, that is, when the athlete is not particularly worried, the inverted-U hypothesis holds true. However, when cognitive anxiety is high, there comes a point just above the optimum level of arousal where performance drops off sharply. This represents a performance catastrophe.

The catastrophe model has proved difficult to test directly. However, a study by Hardy et al (1994) does support the idea that athletes' best and worst performances occur under conditions of high cognitive anxiety, and that under high cognitive anxiety performance drops off quickly after the optimum arousal level. Eight experienced crown-green bowlers were asked to bowl three balls at a jack on two consecutive days. On one day, before bowling, they were given neutral instructions designed to create low cognitive anxiety, and on the other day they were given 'threatening' instructions designed to raise their cognitive anxiety. The CSAI–2 was administered to confirm that cognitive anxiety was indeed higher after the 'threatening' instructions. To increase physiological arousal, the participants were given shuttle runs to perform and their heart rates were monitored. The results are shown in Figure 7.4

It is clear from Figure 7.2 that under conditions of low cognitive anxiety the results showed a weak inverted U, whereas under high cognitive anxiety performance peaked considerably higher but then dropped off quickly. This supports the catastrophe model.

The catastrophe model is more complex than the inverted-U

Figure 7.3 Fazey & Hardy's catastrophe model of the relationship between anxiety and performance.

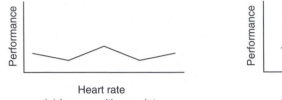

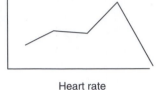

Heart rate
(a) Low cognitive anxiety

Heart rate
(b) High cognitive anxiety

Figure 7.4 The relationship between arousal and bowls performance under low and high cognitive anxiety. From Hardy et al (1994).

hypothesis and offers a more sophisticated understanding of the relationship between arousal and performance. The major practical application of the model is in showing that cognitive anxiety is not necessarily an enemy of performance, but under certain circumstances is beneficial (Hardy 1996). This fits in with the results of interviews by Jones et al (1993), who found that many athletes reported that they performed best when worried. There has, however, been criticism of the model. Gill (1992) has suggested that it is essentially too complex to be entirely testable.

Zones of optimal functioning

Hanin (1986) criticised other theories of the relationship between anxiety and performance on the basis that they underemphasised individual differences in our responses to anxiety. When Hanin measured the pre-competitive anxiety scores of 46 elite female rowers (Hanin, 1986), he found a very wide variety of scores (mean score 44, range 26–67). Given the comparable success of these athletes, this variety of anxiety levels suggested that there was a variety of different responses to anxiety. Instead of proposing a general relationship between anxiety and performance, Hanin suggested that each athlete has their own preferred level of anxiety and that their performance would suffer if their anxiety went below or above their preferred level. The athlete's preferred anxiety level is called the individual zone of optimal functioning (IZOF). Figure 7.5 illustrates the differences athletes have in their preferred level of anxiety.

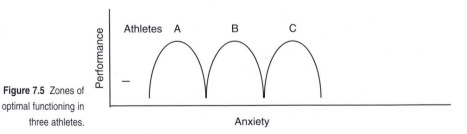

Figure 7.5 Zones of optimal functioning in three athletes.

In Figure 7.5, it is clear that athlete A has a low preferred level of anxiety. We might therefore refer to them as having a low IZOF. Athlete B has a medium IZOF and athlete C a high IZOF. In general, athletes competing in team sports have a lower IZOF than competitors in individual events (Randle & Weinberg, 1997). Athlete A is therefore typical of a team player and athlete C more typical of an individual athlete.

The IZOF approach has clear applications for athletes. By knowing your own ideal level of anxiety for competition, you can monitor your current level and decide whether you need to relax or get more psyched up. Some athletes learn to monitor their heartbeat in order to tell whether they are below, in or above their zone. It is also useful for coaches and teachers to know individuals' IZOF. You might, for example, choose not to use psyching up procedures prior to a competition if you are working with athletes who have a low IZOF and therefore prefer a lower level of anxiety.

There is some support for the idea that athletes do best when at the level of anxiety they prefer. Inlay et al (1993) investigated anxiety levels in field and track athletes across seven competitions and found that, of athletes assessed as being in their IZOF, 63% performed well and 31% performed badly. This provides moderate support for the IZOF theory. However, there are problems with this and similar studies. Pre-competition anxiety was assessed after the event rather than before. This means that there is some doubt as to the accuracy of measurement. More recently, Russell & Cox (2000) assessed IZOF in 55 American university basketball and football players by measuring their positive and negative emotions during performance. Performances were also assessed. Like those in the Inlay et al study, athletes judged to be in their IZOF because they reported positive rather than negative emotions performed better but only moderately so. This suggests that the IZOF is a valid idea but that it is only moderately important.

Randle & Weinberg (1997) used the CSAI–2 to assess cognitive and somatic anxiety of 13 college-level female softball players and relate these to performance. No difference emerged between performance when in or out of the IZOF; thus, this study did not support the idea of zones of optimal functioning. A further problem was highlighted in a study of Italian rugby players (D'Urso et al, 2002). It was found that the players' preferred level of arousal fluctuated considerably within individuals as well as between individuals. Thus, the IZOF varies as a function of situation as well as person. Despite these problems, however, Hanin's approach has many practical applications and is popular with athletes, coaches and sport psychologists.

Box 7.4 Choking

Choking is a phenomenon in which performance is suddenly and severely impaired by intense anxiety. It is most problematic in sports requiring fine motor skills such as golf, snooker, tennis and darts. Performers as notable as John McEnroe, Ian Woosnam and Eric Bristow have been sufferers. Golfers call choking 'the yips'. It tends to occur in high-pressure situations, but can easily become a habit. Athletes report that when choking occurs they experience rapid heartbeat, shakes, butter-flies in the stomach, racing thoughts and panic. Often, there are unintentional muscular movements or tension becomes so great that a movement cannot be completed. As Moran (2004) says, choking is particularly interesting to psycholo-gists because it represents a paradox. Sport psychologists spend considerable time trying to understand motivation in order to persuade athletes to increase their efforts, but choking occurs precisely because the athlete is trying *too* hard.

Choking is generally regarded as an anxiety problem. Influenced by drive theory (see p 120), Baumeister (1984) suggests that our ability to perform fine motor skills is affected by the pressure of the situation because self-consciousness leads the performer to make a conscious effort to carry out a task that is already mastered and so would normally be carried out automatically. Effectively, this means that the athlete has unlearned how to perform the tech-nique. In keeping with this idea, Baumeister notes that choking does not generally take place in sports requiring physical effort rather than precision. An alternative to Baumeister's approach comes from Eysenck & Calvo (1992), in the form of processing-efficiency theory. This suggests that when we become highly anxious we invest extra effort in our performance. In the short term, this appears to yield results; however, it can quickly reach a point where the effort becomes too great and is withdrawn. It is this rapid withdrawal of effort that leads to the rapid drop-off in performance.

Stress management

Regardless of which theories of arousal and anxiety we would consider to be the most correct or useful, there is no doubting the fact that athletes' performance can be seriously affected by their levels of arousal and anxiety. There are a number of psychological techniques for regulating arousal and anxiety that can be applied to sport psychology. We can divide these techniques into three main approaches. Relaxation techniques are designed to reduce the athlete's arousal levels. Cognitive-behavioural techniques are designed to improve the confidence of the athlete and reduce cognitive anxiety. Imagery can be used in a number of ways, both to increase confidence and reduce arousal and anxiety.

Relaxation techniques

Relaxation means to reduce the body's arousal level. There are a number of ways in which we can learn to relax better. Two important ways of achieving relaxation are biofeedback and progressive muscle relaxation.

Biofeedback

One reason why we are not good at regulating our arousal levels consciously is that we have no accurate way of perceiving how aroused we are. The indicators of arousal, such as heart rate, blood pressure and skin temperature, are all very difficult for us to judge. The principle behind biofeedback is that if we can receive accurate information about our arousal level we can learn to control it consciously. The simplest way to tell how aroused you are is to measure your skin temperature with a biodot, a small disc that changes colour according to the temperature of your skin. The more relaxed you are, the higher your skin temperature will be. By seeing the dot colour change as you relax and tense, you can gradually learn to relax or tense at will. Other simple ways of monitoring arousal include measuring the number of heartbeats per minute with a stethoscope and counting the number of breaths per minute. Of course, as we all have slightly different heart rates, breathing rates and skin temperature, it is necessary before attempting biofeedback to establish what our individual levels are when we are relaxed and when we are tense.

There is a wealth of evidence supporting the effectiveness of biofeedback in aiding relaxation. There is also some evidence for its effectiveness in improving performance. Petruzello et al (1991) reviewed studies relating biofeedback to performance and concluded that there was strong support for the idea that biofeedback by measurements of heart and breathing rate is effective in improving performance. A note of caution needs to be sounded at this point. While relaxation procedures such as biofeedback are effective in reducing arousal and aiding performance in over-aroused athletes, they should not be used without knowing that the athlete *is* over-aroused. There is little point in reducing the arousal of a relaxed athlete – you will merely send them to sleep!

Progressive muscle relaxation (PMR)

PMR was the first of the modern relaxation techniques. Jacobson (1929) proposed that, by relaxing each group of voluntary muscles, we can induce relaxation in the involuntary muscles as well. He developed a technique whereby each group of voluntary muscles is relaxed in turn. In the modern version of PMR, four sections of the body are relaxed in turn. These are the arms; face, neck, shoulders and upper back; stomach and lower back; and the hips and legs. Participants are taught to tense each muscle group before relaxing it, helping them to appreciate the difference in sensation between tense and relaxed muscles. A training session lasts about 30 minutes. Once athletes have mastered the techniques of PMR they can induce relaxation much more quickly. An extract from a PMR training session (adapted from Harris & Williams, 1993) is shown in Box 7.5.

Box 7.5 An example of progressive muscle relaxation training

'As we progress through each muscle group, you will first tense for approximately 5–7 seconds and then relax for 30–40 seconds. Do not start the tensing until I say "NOW". Continue to tense until I say "Okay".'

'Begin with tensing the muscles in the dominant hand and lower arm by making a tight fist NOW. Feel the tension in the hand, over the knuckles, and up into the lower arm. . . . Okay, relax by simply letting go of the tension. Notice the difference between tension and relaxation. . . . Make another fist NOW. Okay, relax. Just let the relaxation happen; don't put out any effort.'

As with biofeedback, numerous studies have shown that PMR is effective in inducing relaxation. However, Cox (1998) reported finding no studies showing that PMR alone improved performance, although several studies showed that PMR combined with other techniques was successful in enhancing performance.

Cognitive-behavioural techniques

Cognitive-behavioural techniques for stress management, although only recently developed by psychologists, are rooted in the writings of the first-century philosopher Epictetus, who wrote that people are disturbed not so much by things as by the views they take of them. The principle behind cognitive approaches to stress management is that if we can make athletes perceive events as less threatening, they will not respond to them with the same anxiety. There are many forms of cognitive-behavioural therapy that can be applied to controlling competitive anxiety. In Chapter 7, which concerns motivation in sport, we shall discuss attribution training and self-efficacy theory. These are cognitive-behavioural approaches that help to increase confidence and reduce anxiety. Another approach of particular importance in sport psychology is Locke & Latham's (1985) goal-setting theory.

Goal-setting theory

Over the last decade, the goal-setting approach has become popular in industry and education as well as in sport. The idea behind goal-setting theory is that, faced with the broad, general aims of whatever we are trying to achieve, we are likely to feel overwhelmed, demotivated and anxious. By breaking down the general goal to a number of smaller and more specific goals, we can make what we are trying to achieve appear less intimidating and more achievable. Thus, goal-setting theory is both a theory of motivation and stress management.

A rugby back might wish to improve his game. However, this broad aim is difficult to achieve because there are so many aspects to the game of rugby, and because the size of the task is so daunting that it creates anxiety. According to goal-setting theory, players should first identify one or two specific aspects of their game to work on. They should then set themselves small manageable goals for improvement. For example, the players might identify their tackling as an area to improve. They could then set themselves the highly specific task of successfully bringing down opponents 75% of the time in the next game, and increasing this to an average of 80% by the end of the season.

There are two types of goal that can be set in sport. In the above example, the rugby back has set a performance goal, that is, to improve an area of his performance. The alternative is to set an outcome goal. An outcome goal would involve winning contests as opposed to improving personal performance. This can create problems, as winning is not entirely in the control of the athlete. If athletes set themselves an outcome goal of winning a match and vastly improved their performance, but were then beaten by stronger or more experienced opponents, they would probably be needlessly demotivated. This illustrates that goal setting is no panacea, but must be carefully thought out to be effective. Cox (1998) offered some guidelines for effective goal setting, as shown in Box 7.6.

Box 7.6 Guidelines for effective goal setting

1. Specific goals are better than general goals.
2. Goals should be measurable.
3. Difficult goals are better than easy goals.
4. Short-term goals can be useful in achieving longer-term goals.
5. Performance goals are better than outcome goals.
6. Goals should be written down and closely monitored.
7. Goals must be accepted by the athlete.

Broadly, research has supported the usefulness of goal setting in improving performance. However, researchers have been divided on the importance of specific rather than general goals, and that of difficult rather than easy goals. Weinberg et al (1987) conducted an experiment on the impact of goal setting on sit-up performance and found no difference in the performance of participants given moderate or difficult goals and those told to 'do their best'. This would appear to contradict goal-setting theory. However, 83% of participants in the 'do your best' condition reported that they had set themselves goals. Thus, success in this condition could be attributed to goal setting. Weinberg & Weigand (1993) reviewed goal-setting research and concluded that most studies had found that goal setting by an instructor had led to better performance than informal self-setting of goals.

Goal setting has been applied to teams as well as individuals. Johnson et al (1997) randomly allocated 36 novice bowls players to different goal-setting conditions. One group was told to 'do your best'. The second group was set individual goals. The third group was set group goals. After 5 weeks, the three groups were assessed on their performance, and those in the group-goals condition were found to be performing significantly better than the other groups. Interestingly, performance was no better in the individual-goals group than the 'do your best' group. These findings suggest that somehow teams respond powerfully to goal setting, perhaps by increasing communication and cooperation.

Athletes and coaches rate goal setting as an important strategy. Weinberg et al (2000) surveyed 328 Olympic athletes on their use of goal setting, and found overwhelming support for the technique. All those surveyed used goal setting and reported it to be highly effective. The three most important goals reported were improving performance, winning and having fun. Weinberg et al (2001) followed this up by investigating coaches' perceptions of goal setting. Fourteen American high-school coaches were interviewed and reported extensive use of goal setting. They believed that the purpose of goals was to provide structure and focus, and that goals should be both negotiated with athletes and dictated by coaches. Long- and short-term goals were set. This is interesting in that research has found that the most effective goals are short-term and negotiated with athletes – clearly, many coaches do not subscribe to these principles.

Imagery techniques

The golfer Jack Nicklaus once said that a good shot is 50% due to the golfer's mental picture of what the shot should be like. The use of the 'mind's eye', or imagery, is considered important both in stress

Figure 7.6 Jack Nicklaus places tremendous emphasis on imagery. Copyright © Bettmann/Corbis

management and in focusing athletes on their task. Imagery can be used in various ways to aid relaxation and focusing. Sport psychologists distinguish between *external imagery*, in which athletes picture themselves from outside performing, and *internal imagery*, in which they view themselves performing from inside their own body. A good example of internal imagery is in the mental rehearsal of sporting techniques.

Mental rehearsal

Most of us that have participated in sport have, perhaps before a match, mentally rehearsed some of the actions that will be required during the contest. Mental practice of techniques does not necessarily involve imagery – we can mentally rehearse a tennis serve without visualising a tennis court and opponent in front of us. However, many athletes find that visualisation of themselves carrying out techniques is particularly helpful.

Mental rehearsal probably works for a number of reasons. The *psychoneuromuscular* theory emphasises the importance of 'muscle memory'. When we imagine carrying out a sporting technique, the nervous system and muscles react in a similar manner to that expected if we were actually carrying out the technique. This means that imagery helps us to learn and practise techniques. Another reason mental rehearsal works is that it desensitises us to the anxiety of competitive situations. The more we are exposed to things that cause us anxiety – whether in real life or in our imagination – the less anxiety they cause.

Vealey & Walter (1993) have described the use of imagery by the Soviet Union Olympic Team in the 1976 games. The team, who had never seen the Montreal stadium sites, were given photographs of the various sites so that when they could visualise themselves performing

Figure 7.7 Visualising a stadium before competition may reduce anxiety. Copyright © William Taufic/Corbis

at those sites. This may have helped the Soviet team to be less affected by the new environment when they encountered it.

Numerous studies have shown that mental rehearsal involving imagery is effective in enhancing performance. Grouios (1992) reviewed studies and concluded that mental rehearsal is more effective than no practice although less effective than real-life practice. In general, it appears that imagery is of most use to elite performers rather than novices and to those skilled in imagery.

Summary and conclusions

Arousal, anxiety and stress are distinct though related concepts. Anxiety is a complex issue, and it is important to distinguish between state and trait and between cognitive and somatic anxiety. Arousal and anxiety can affect sporting performance, although some of these relationships are complex, and are mediated by the situation, the sport and the individual characteristics of the athlete. There are two major theories of the relationship between arousal and performance. Drive theory suggests that the greater the arousal, the better the performance. The inverted-U hypothesis, by contrast, suggests that an optimum level of arousal and performance will decline above or below this. Both theories have important applications.

In recent years, the research emphasis has shifted to study of the relationship between anxiety and performance. Two theories have emerged as particularly influential. Catastrophe theory suggests that, under conditions of low cognitive anxiety, the inverted-U hypothesis holds true. However, under conditions of high cognitive anxiety, performance drops off sharply just after the optimum level of arousal has been reached. Hanin proposed that every athlete has their own zone of optimal functioning, the level of anxiety at which they perform best. This tends to be higher for individual than team sports. There are now a number of effective stress-management techniques that can be applied to sport psychology. These include relaxation procedures, such as biofeedback and progressive muscle relaxation, and cognitive-behavioural techniques such as goal-setting and imagery techniques.

Self-assessment questions

1. Distinguish between cognitive and somatic anxiety.
2. Describe how cognitive anxiety affects performance.
3. How can anxiety be measured?

4. What kinds of factors determine the amount of anxiety an athlete experiences?
5. Explain how drive theory can be used to understand the relationship between arousal and performance.
6. Compare two theories of the relationship between anxiety and performance.
7. Evaluate the use of goal setting in sport.

Further reading

- Cohen A, Pargman D & Tenenbaum G (2003) Critical elaboration and empirical investigation of the cusp catastrophe model: a lesson for practitioners. *Journal of Applied Sport Psychology* 15, 144–159.
- Cox R (2001) *Sport psychology: concepts and applications*. Boston, MA, McGraw-Hill.
- Moran A (2004) *Sport and exercise psychology: a critical introduction*. London, Routledge.
- Mullins J (1993) Victory in sight. *New Scientist Supplement*. October, 4–9.
- Williams J (ed) (1993) *Applied sport psychology*. Toronto, Mayfield.

Motivation and sport 8

Learning objectives

By the end of this chapter, you should be able to:

- appreciate the distinction between intrinsic and extrinsic motivation and discuss the usefulness of the additive principle
- describe and evaluate Maslow's hierarchy of needs as an explanation of sporting motivation
- understand the importance of achievement motivation, with particular reference to Nicholls' theory of achievement orientations
- outline attribution theory with particular reference to the work of Bernard Weiner, and assess the usefulness of attribution therapy
- discuss self-efficacy as a factor in sporting motivation
- explain the phenomenon of counterfactual thinking and explain its importance in sport
- consider that there may be pathological aspects of motivation for sport.

One of the fundamental questions about human nature that psychologists need to answer is, 'Why do we do things?' We could simply answer, 'because I want to', 'because I need to', or even 'because I just do'. However, although all these statements are useful starting points, psychologists are not satisfied with these answers, and seek to uncover the reasons *underlying* our experiences of wanting to, needing to or 'just doing' things. In this chapter, we can examine some basic types of human motivation, theories about specific motivators and research findings concerning what motivates us to participate and succeed in sport. A useful starting point is to examine intrinsic and extrinsic motivation.

Intrinsic and extrinsic motivation

An important distinction in types of human motives is that between extrinsic and intrinsic motivation. *Extrinsic* motivation results from external rewards. *Intrinsic* motivation comes from within the person. Both extrinsic and intrinsic motives are important in sport, and sport psychologists can work with both extrinsic and intrinsic motives to improve the performance of the individual. Intrinsic motives for taking part in sport include excitement, fun, love of action and the chance to demonstrate and improve our skills – in short, all the reasons that we *enjoy* sport. Later in this chapter, we will discuss some techniques designed to increase intrinsic motivation. The reason these can be used so effectively to motivate athletes is that they directly affect our intrinsic motivation. Extrinsic motives can come in the form of trophies, prizes and less tangible rewards such as praise and status.

Although there has been an enormous amount of research into how motivation can be improved in those already participating in sport, rather fewer studies have examined what motivates people to choose to take up sport. Ashford et al (1993) interviewed 336 adults at a community sports centre in Leicester about why they participated in sport, and what they enjoyed about it. Four main motivations emerged, physical well-being, psychological well-being, improvement of performance and *assertive achievement*, the last meaning to accomplish personal challenges and to gain status. Age and gender significantly affected motivation. Older people were more motivated by psychological well-being than younger people. Men were more motivated by assertive achievement than women. These motives are all intrinsic rather than extrinsic, lending support to the idea that most people come to sport for reasons of intrinsic motivation.

Of course, children's motives for taking part in sport may be different from those of adults. Daley and O'Gara (1998) investigated the motives of 145 children in a British secondary school for taking part in non-compulsory sport, using a questionnaire called the Participation Motivation Inventory (PMI). As in the Ashford et al study, the motives for sport participation differed according to gender and age. Between 11 and 15 years, intrinsic factors were more important and extrinsic factors less so. Girls emerged as more motivated by team affiliation and achievement than boys.

Given that intrinsic motivation is so important, a key aim of research has been to identify influences on intrinsic motivation. One recent study by Amorose & Horn (2001) assessed 72 American athletes on their intrinsic motivation at the beginning and end of their first year of college-level participation. They were asked about how much time they spent on training, the nature of their coaching and whether they had sport scholarships. The behaviour of coaches had the strongest effect on intrinsic motivation. Students whose coaches spent more time on technical instruction tended to display significant increases in their intrinsic motivation during the year. By contrast, those whose coaches threw their weight about experienced a decline in intrinsic motivation.

The additive principle

Generally, we tend to come to sport motivated more by intrinsic than extrinsic factors. However, extrinsic motivators have been used in an attempt to boost intrinsic motivation. The *additive principle* states that athletes low in intrinsic motivation can have their motivation boosted by adding some extrinsic motivation. However, this common-sense approach has not been well supported by research. There are numerous case studies of athletes whose performance sharply declined as soon as they received lucrative contracts (Cox, 2001).

Psychologists are always a little wary of case studies as evidence, but there are other ways of investigating the additive principle. One approach is to compare the motivation of athletes competing for pleasure and those competing for other reasons. Fortier et al (1995) compared the intrinsic motivation levels of Canadian athletes who participated for recreation with those involved in collegiate competition. The collegiate athletes, who were highly focused on the goal of winning, showed less intrinsic motivation than those participating for pleasure. An alternative approach to researching the additive principle is to follow up athletes after changes in their circumstances. In one such study, Sturman & Thibodeau (2001) followed the progress of 33 US baseball professionals for two seasons before and two seasons after they signed new contracts that substantially increased their income. Although there were substantial individual differences, performance typically dropped off after signing the contract.

One way in which extrinsic motivators can be used successfully to boost intrinsic motivation is in the grading systems of the Eastern martial arts, usually symbolised by a coloured belt or sash (Figure 8.1). Contrary to popular belief, such belts are not an ancient tradition, but a relatively recent innovation in the martial arts. They are designed to provide regular tangible rewards for students' achievements, with the aim of motivating them to continue.

Theories of motivation

Maslow's theory of needs

Maslow (1954) developed a theory of human motivation that aimed to explain all the types of human need and rank them in the order people seek to satisfy them. Maslow's hierarchy of needs is shown in Figure 8.2.

The idea behind the hierarchy of needs is that we ascend the hierarchy, satisfying each motive in turn. Our first priority is to satisfy our *physiological needs*, such as food and warmth, because we cannot live without these. Only when these needs have been satisfied do we seek out *safety*. Once we are safe, the next thing we need to worry about is our *social needs*, that is, to belong to a group and have relationships with others. When our social needs are satisfied, *esteem needs* become paramount. To satisfy them, we need to achieve, to become competent and to be recognised as so. Once this has been achieved, our focus will shift to satisfying our *intellectual needs*, which include understanding and knowledge. Next in Maslow's hierarchy above intellectual needs come *aesthetic*

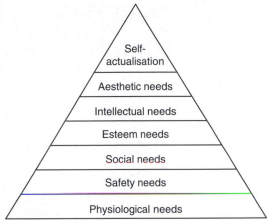

Figure 8.2 Maslow's hierarchy of needs.

needs, that is, the need for beauty, order and balance. The final human need identified by Maslow is for *self-actualisation*, that is, to find personal fulfilment and achieve one's potential.

According to Maslow, we are all striving to ascend the hierarchy of needs, but very few of us achieve self-actualisation. Sport, however, does provide a possible path to self-actualisation. Athletes who rise to the very top of their field, holding world records and championship titles, could be said to be self-actualised in that they have fulfilled their dreams and their potential. On the other hand, we should be careful not to equate self-actualisation with success. There are numerous sporting celebrities who, despite rising to the top of their chosen sport and appearing to fulfil their potential, have clearly not found personal fulfilment and have, by contrast, 'gone off the rails'.

Reflective exercise

This should help develop your critical thinking skills.

a. Using a spider diagram, brainstorm as many reasons as you can think of for doing sport.
b. Fit all these reasons into Maslow's hierarchy of needs, as shown in Figure 8.3.
c. At what level in the hierarchy are most of your reasons for sporting participation?
d. Most people's responses tend to be around the social and esteem levels. Why do you think this might be, and whose responses might tend to be higher up the hierarchy?

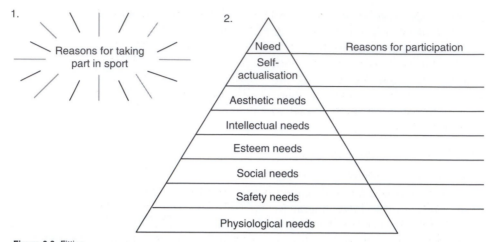

Figure 8.3 Fitting reasons for sport participation into the hierarchy of needs.

Maslow's theory has been enormously influential. Most importantly, he has opened our eyes to the *range* of human needs. If you have carried out the exercise above, you have probably seen that you have multiple reasons for participating in sport, and that your reasons are grouped above the physiological and safety needs. If you are motivated principally by physiological and safety needs (say, for example, if you are homeless and starving), it is unlikely that you would be able to raise much motivation to take part in sport. Sport is an excellent way of providing us with esteem and social needs. For some, it may also provide a path to self-actualisation.

Despite the usefulness of Maslow's work, his prediction that we are all motivated by these needs and that everybody seeks to satisfy them in the same order is suspect, particularly when we look at elite athletes who have put success ahead of other considerations. Saul (1993) has pointed out that 65% of ballet dancers have chronic injuries and suggested that they have sacrificed physiological needs in pursuit of aesthetic needs. This is perhaps an extreme example, but it illustrates that sometimes aiming for higher needs means not satisfying the more basic needs – contrary to Maslow's theory.

Achievement motivation

The link between the wish to achieve and sporting success is an obvious one. A strong wish to succeed in your chosen sport will be a huge asset in determining how hard you train and how hard you try in competition. All participation in sport involves achievement, regardless of whether you regard competition as important. You are in fact probably more likely to boost your performance by setting yourself goals of personal achievement, such as 80% of first serves in, 90% of penalties in the net, rather than goals of victory (see section on goal setting in Chapter 5). Some psychologists see the drive to achieve as innate, whereas others see it as acquired by experience. Some believe that the most important factor is to achieve success, whereas others emphasise the motive of avoiding failure. The most influential theory of achievement motivation comes from McClelland et al (1953) and Atkinson (1964).

The McClelland–Atkinson theory of need achievement

The aim of the McClelland–Atkinson theory was to explain why some individuals are more motivated to achieve than others. The athlete's intrinsic motivation is seen as the motive to achieve. Acting against this intrinsic motivation, however, is the motive to avoid failure. When faced with a task such as sport, we face an *approach–avoidance conflict*. We are motivated to approach and take part by our desire to succeed, but we are also motivated to avoid taking part by our desire to avoid failure. Our individual decision to participate in sport is determined by the relative strength of these two factors. This is shown in the following equation:

> achievement motivation = desire to succeed – fear of failure.

To McClelland and Atkinson, achievement motivation is a personality trait. For some of us, the desire to succeed far outweighs the fear of failure, and we are said to be high in achievement motivation. For others, the fear of failure is the more important factor, and they would be said to be low in achievement motivation. This personality trait is not the only factor that affects motivation. The situation is also important, specifically the *probability of success* and the *incentive for success*. Thus, even if athletes are low in achievement motivation, if the probability of success is high, and the rewards for success are great, they are likely to be motivated.

Gill (2000) reviewed research on choice of high- and low-difficulty tasks and concluded that there is much support for the prediction by the theory that high achievers seek out difficult tasks and low achievers prefer easier tasks. However, the theory does not reliably predict sporting *performance*. Of course, this does not mean that the theory is worthless. As Cox (2001) says, the value of measuring achievement motivation is not to predict performance, but to predict long-term patterns of motivation.

Achievement orientations

The most influential and researched approach to motivation in sport psychology, as well as in other arenas such as educational psychology, is Nicholls' (1984) theory of goal or achievement orientations. Nicholls makes the important distinction between two styles of achievement motivation, task orientation and ego orientation. These appear during different stages of psychological development. They result from the ways in which athletes explain their perceived ability. *Task orientation* appears at 2–6 years of age. Children at this stage tend to judge their sporting competence on the basis of how well they performed the task at the last attempt. Crucially, their judgements of their performance are strongly influenced by their effort; that is, if they try hard, they think they have done well. However, a change takes place in the way children come to view their sporting competence at around 6 years. *Ego-oriented* children base their judgement of their competence on their success relative to their peers.

As adults, we have access to information about both our past performances and the performances of others to judge our competence. Task and ego orientations are not mutually exclusive and can exist in the same person. However, some athletes prefer to rely on past performance whilst others prefer to look at performance relative to others. Athletes can be classified as *task-oriented* or *ego-oriented* according to these preferences. Table 8.1 compares the characteristics of task and ego-oriented athletes.

Both task and ego motives can be helpful to the athlete. However, as we can see from Table 8.1, a task orientation has the advantage of greater persistence in the face of adversity. One way in which sport psychologists can enhance athletic motivation is to help athletes develop a healthy blend of task and ego orientations. In a recent study of golfers, Steinberg et al (2001) compared the progress of 72 novice golfers who were assigned to one of four training conditions. In the first condition, training focused purely on competition; in the second, it was based purely on task mastery; in the third, there was a balance between mastery and competition; and in the fourth, there was no systematic orientation toward tasks or competition. After 6 weeks,

	Task-oriented	**Ego-oriented**
Criterion for judging success	Past personal performances	Comparison with others
Judged cause of success	Practice and skill development	Chance and natural ability
Response to difficulty/failure	Persistence	Cheating

Table 8.1 Comparison of task- and ego-oriented athletes

only the group with combined training orientations had significantly improved their performance.

Mastery and performance environments

Particular environments seem to foster task and ego orientations. A *mastery environment* can be defined as one in which there is a focus on the mastery of skills. This is associated with promotion of a task orientation. By contrast, the emphasis in a *performance environment* is on comparison of the individual abilities. In training, the latter can disadvantage low-ability participants, who simply experience the humiliation of comparison with more skilled athletes in response to their efforts. It is widely agreed that a task-oriented training environment is preferable to an ego-oriented environment (European Federation of Sport Psychology, 1996). Ames (1992) has suggested the TARGET system for ensuring that a training environment is task oriented. TARGET is shown in Box 8.1.

Box 8.1 The TARGET approach to creating a mastery environment

Tasks: a variety of challenging tasks in which players set process goals.
Authority: players play an active role in decision making.
Recognition: recognise individual progress.
Grouping: use mixed-ability groups.
Evaluation: evaluation should be based on personal progress and should be by self and peers.
Time: allow time for practice of technique as well as competition.

An interesting contrast is that between the environments in which martial arts are practised. Wing chun is taught in an extremely task-oriented environment with close attention to perfecting technique and without competition. By contrast, the emphasis in tae kwondo is very much on competition (Figure 8.4).

There is a similar division amongst the grappling styles. Gernigon & Le Bars (2000) compared achievement orientation in French practitioners of judo and aikido, the former being more of a competitive sport and the latter a highly traditional art. Task orientation was greater in aikidoka whilst ego orientation was dominant in judoka. The disparity was wider in more experienced practitioners.

Of course, once we are in competition, our environment is inevitably oriented to performance, and this appears to affect the orientation of competitors. Pensgaard (1999) tracked the orientations of the

Figure 8.4 Martial arts differ in the use of a predominantly task- or ego-oriented environment. (Left) World contest for the Taekwondo Olympic Games Qualification. Copyright © Christophe Paucellier/ Photo & Co./Corbis. (Right) Wing Chun. Alan Gibson (right) performs Bong sau against Lee Morrison's attack.

Norwegian women's soccer team throughout the 1996 Olympic Games. As we might expect, given the emphasis on medals at the Olympics, task orientation declined and ego orientation increased throughout the games.

Reflective exercise

Practise your creative thinking from what you have read about task and ego orientations. Design a training programme for your own sport. Consider how you will use task and ego incentives to motivate trainees.

Attribution theory

Because we have a desire to understand the world around us, we have a powerful tendency to make *attributions* about the causes of events and behaviour. This means that we come to a conclusion about *why* something happened or *why* someone behaved or performed in a certain way. We make attributions about our own behaviour and about the behaviour of those around us, *whether or not we have the evidence to arrive at accurate conclusions*. In this chapter, we are chiefly concerned with the attributions we make about ourselves.

Internal and external attributions

Broadly, we can make two types of attribution, *internal* and *external*. Internal attributions place the responsibility for behaviour or performance with the individual, whereas external attributions place the reasons in the situation. Consider the following example. A college rugby team has just returned home after their first match, having lost 72–0. They have the unenviable task of explaining the score to others. They make a number of internal or external attributions to explain

Internal	External
We are just no good	The referee was biased
We didn't try hard enough	The crowd was on their side
I let the team down	They have played together many more times than we

why they lost so badly. Examples of these attributions are shown in Table 8.2.

Table 8.2 shows various attempts to make sense of the catastrophic result. The players adopting the internal attributions are blaming themselves, whereas those adopting the external attributions are blaming other characteristics of the situation. As you can imagine, after a humiliating defeat, most of us would tend to adopt external attributions and blame other factors, whereas after a success most of us tend to adopt an internal position and take the credit. This phenomenon is known as *self-serving bias*.

Whether we make internal or external attributions appears to be related to self-esteem; hence, this can affect performance. Biddle and Hill (1992) conducted a study in which 58 sixth-form and university students fenced, all for the first time. The outcome of each match was manipulated by the experimenters so that some participants consistently won and others consistently lost. After a series of matches, the attributions and emotional states of the participants were measured. Statistical analysis of the results showed that the attributions made by the students to explain the results were strongly related to the

Figure 8.5 Fencing self-efficacy is affected by winning and losing. Copyright © Reuters/Corbis

emotions they experienced, particularly in those participants who consistently lost. This shows that the main predictor of self-esteem in losers is the perception of why they lost.

Reflective exercise

Practise your critical thinking on the Biddle & Hill study above. Consider the following:

1. How large and how representative is the sample?
2. Are results likely to generalise to other sports?
3. Is the situation realistic? In what ways is it artificial and how might this affect the results?
4. What practical applications do the results have?

Weiner's model of attribution

Weiner (1992) produced a model of self-attribution based on two factors, whether an internal or external attribution is made, and whether this attribution is stable over time or varies from one situation to another. The relationship between attribution and stability is shown in Figure 8.6.

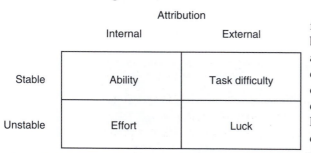

	Attribution	
	Internal	External
Stable	Ability	Task difficulty
Unstable	Effort	Luck

Figure 8.6 Weiner's model of attribution.

If we consistently succeed or fail, our attributions are likely to be stable. This means that we are likely to attribute the outcome to either our ability or the difficulty of the task. Because of self-serving bias, it is more likely that we will attribute success to ability and failure to task difficulty. If our results are less consistent, we will probably attribute them to effort or luck. Again, self-serving bias means that we are likely to attribute success to effort and failure to bad luck.

Weiner's model gives us a starting point to work with athletes to correct their attributions. We may wish to shift the attributions of lazy athletes toward the unstable-internal position so that they realise more effort is needed. We may also wish to shift the attributions of depressed athletes away from a stable-internal position, so that they cease to blame their lack of ability. This is examined further below when we look at the idea of learned helplessness. Altering an athlete's attributional state is called reattribution training, and is a form of cognitive therapy. An example of the use of attributional therapy comes from Orbach et al (1999), who investigated the effectiveness of attribution training with 35 inexperienced tennis players. They were given false feedback over four training sessions, in order to lead them to attribute successes to internal factors. As hoped, the players changed their attributions in response to the feedback, and these changes led to improved self-esteem and performance.

Self-efficacy

The term 'self-esteem' has already come up in this chapter, appearing to be important in the link between attributions and performance. Bandura (1982) has introduced the related but distinct concept of *self-efficacy*. Self-esteem refers to how we *feel* about ourselves, and it is generally stable across a range of situations. Self-efficacy, by contrast, refers to what we *believe* about our abilities. Unlike self-esteem, self-efficacy is situation specific. For example, if you are a natural athlete, but have some difficulty in getting to grips with sport psychology, your self-efficacy will probably be considerably greater on the field than in the classroom. Schunk (1991) has suggested four sources of information that we draw upon in order to arrive at our academic self-efficacy. These are shown in Box 8.2.

Box 8.2 Influences on self-efficacy

- **Previous experience**: athletes who have previously succeeded in particular tasks will generally tend to have higher self-efficacy for related tasks.
- **Direct persuasion**: poor self-efficacy beliefs are open to challenge. A persuasive coach can convince athletes of their ability to carry out tasks.
- **Observational learning**: we tend to pick up on the self-efficacy of fellow athletes. When peers of previously comparable ability or success express their positive beliefs about their ability to perform a task, this suggests that we should also be capable of doing so.
- **Physiological cues**: we constantly experience our physiological state and use this as a source of information about our current emotional state. If, for example, we notice the signs of anxiety while carrying out a task, we may attribute this to personal difficulty with the task, leading to reduced self-efficacy. If, on the other hand, we are relaxed while doing something, we may interpret this in terms of the ease with which that task comes to us.

Self-efficacy can exert a powerful effect on performance. As Bandura (1990) put it, 'once extraordinary performances are shown to be doable, they become commonplace' (p 29). Bandura proposed that self-efficacy could be boosted by successful performance, verbal persuasion and feedback about performance. Wells et al (1993) set out to test whether self-efficacy could be affected by feedback, and whether changes in self-efficacy could affect performance on a weightlifting task. Three groups of students were randomly assigned to three groups. Two of the groups were misled about the weight they were successfully lifting. One group, termed the 'light group', lifted less weight than they believed. A 'heavy group' lifted more than they believed. The third group received accurate information about how much they were lifting. The 'light group', who had received false feedback designed to boost their self-efficacy, were able, in a later trial, to lift more than they had originally. This finding underlines the importance of giving positive feedback to athletes – even if you exaggerate a little about how well they are doing!

There is little doubt that self-efficacy is a valid construct. It can be measured, and studies such as that by Wells et al (1993) have demonstrated that it can be manipulated, as predicted by Bandura, in order to improve performance. For a coach or teacher, self-efficacy is a useful idea to bear in mind during training. It is, however, a weaker predictor of success than previous performance. Krane et al (1996) looked at self-efficacy in wrestlers, and found that it was most important as a predictor of victory when competitors were evenly matched. Like other psychological factors, self-efficacy may make all the difference at very high levels, when competitors are probably physically well matched.

Counterfactual thinking

Sometimes our attributions about sporting successes and failures can be quite unrealistic. This type of thinking is called *counterfactual thinking* (CFT) because it runs counter to the facts of the situation. On occasion, our general tendency to make attributions about the causes of events can lead us to think about past events, over which we no longer have any control. Thus, athletes who have underachieved can waste time 'torturing' themselves about what might have happened had they approached things differently or not made an error. This is called *upward* CFT. The opposite phenomenon also occurs, and we might indulge in thinking excessively about how much worse things might have been. This is called *downward* CFT.

CFT tends to occur when an outcome is negative, unexpected and upsetting, particularly when the result constitutes a near miss. Wolfson (2002) discusses the example of the 1998 World Cup quarterfinal, when David Beckham was famously dismissed for kicking out at an Argentinian player after an aggressive tackle. The England team was by no means certain to win had Beckham remained on the pitch; however, England's loss was almost universally attributed to his actions, and the UK press and public engaged in an 'orgy' of CFT, focusing on the likely outcome of the championship had the incident not taken place. Interestingly, had England been clearly losing at the time, probably little attention would have been given to Beckham's action – this illustrates the importance of the near miss in activating CFT.

Both upward and downward CFT can lead to positive and negative consequences. Upward CFT can be a depressing experience if it just leads us to relive unhappy and humiliating experiences. However, it can also be helpful in pointing us in the direction of improvement. Thus, a batsman who takes a thrashing from a bowler using a high bounce might feel humiliated and dwell on this, thinking about what might have happened if he had survived the over (an example of upward CFT) or what might have happened if the ball had hit him and damaged his brain (an example of downward CFT). However, if it

Figure 8.7 After this incident in 1998, the country engaged in counterfactual thinking.
Copyright © Russell Boyce/Reuters/Corbis

leads him to work on his defence, it may improve his performance in the long run.

Downward CFT has a defensive function, and may make us feel better after something has gone wrong; for example, a footballer who breaks an ankle after a tackle might comfort himself with the thought that if the tackle had been higher there might have had serious knee damage ending his career altogether. However, there is a risk that downward CFT can lead to complacency. Thus, the martial artist who scrapes through a brown belt grading and then dwells on this achievement, ignoring the nearness of failure and the harder task of gaining a black belt, is likely to lose the necessary motivation to continue training hard (this is known as the 'brown belt blues'). Martial arts instructors often introduce new challenges and work students particularly hard after a grading in order to avoid this.

Pathological motivation and sport

It is unusual to be involved in sport psychology if we don't feel positively about sport. One of the consequences of this is that we often find it difficult to consider sporting behaviour in a bad light. Most of the time, we think that being highly motivated to participate and achieve in sport is a good thing. However, sometimes when it is possible to be *too* motivated. We might think of motivation as pathological when it leads to overtraining and burn-out, or when athletes compromise their health in pursuit of sporting excellence, as in effecting rapid weight loss.

Burn-out

The phenomenon of burn-out was first described by Freudenberger (1974). It is not unique to sport but can occur in any situation in which people respond to pressure by overworking. Its symptoms are depersonalisation (becoming emotionally cut off from other people), impaired performance and satisfaction, and emotional exhaustion (feeling weary and resigned). There has been relatively little research into burn-out in athletes (the most researched group are teachers). Gould et al (1996) have studied burn-out in young tennis players. They concluded that young athletes are under considerable pressure to succeed, and that those particularly vulnerable to burn-out are those who take on too many commitments in order to please others. Parental expectations emerged as a particularly significant factor in burn-out. Burn-out is thus not simply a result of the fatigue of overtraining and competing, but is also the emotional consequence of stress.

Burn-out is associated with the personality characteristic of perfectionism. A degree of perfectionism is of course essential in maintaining the motivation to perform at elite level. However, there appear to be different types of perfectionism, and not all are positive. Frost et al (1993) distinguish between positive achievement strivings and maladaptive evaluation concerns. *Positive achievement strivings* are associated with high personal standards and organisation. They broadly represent the positive aspects of perfectionism. *Maladaptive evaluation concerns*, on the other hand, are associated with excessive concern over mistakes, self-doubt and concern with parental criticism. It appears to be maladaptive evaluation concerns that are associated with burn-out.

Eating disorders

Sporting performance is associated with *aesthetic* satisfaction; that is, it is appreciated as a form of beauty. Some sports, such as diving and gymnastics, are partially scored on aesthetics. Cheerleading, which can be considered a sport in itself (LeUnes & Nation, 2002), is a predominantly aesthetic activity. The problem with this emphasis on appearance is that it creates pressure for athletes to conform to narrow definitions of attractiveness, often requiring weight loss. In this case, the motivation for sporting excellence can directly lead to unhealthy behaviours. Gymnastics creates particular problems, as it requires a particular body type, and at the elite level maintenance of this body type is short-term and associated with long-term health problems such as osteoporosis (brittle bones). Participants in combat sports such as boxing and wrestling, in which there are many weight classes, may also be at risk, as athletes can be required to lose weight extremely rapidly to shift to a different competition weight. Weight loss is usually achieved by restricting food intake (as in anorexia) or by using vomiting and laxatives to prevent food uptake (as in bulimia).[1]

Surveys have been conducted to assess body dissatisfaction and symptoms of eating disorders in athletic populations. Dobie (2000) surveyed American high-school athletes and found that 5.4% overall and 6.6% of girls reported sufficient symptoms to be diagnosed as having an eating disorder. Body dissatisfaction, the athlete's sense of being overweight, is much more common. In a survey of 155 American cheerleaders, Reel & Gill (1996) reported that 84% of respondents felt under pressure to maintain a low weight, and 40% agreed that they would be better cheerleaders if they lost weight. Given that body

---

[1] These are oversimple definitions of bulimia and anorexia. For a more specialist account, see Jarvis et al (2002), *Angles on atypical psychology*, published by Nelson Thornes.

dissatisfaction is associated with the development of eating problems, these statistics are very worrying. Surveys of coaches (e.g. Turk et al, 1999) suggest that as a group they are not well informed about the early signs of eating problems or in encouraging healthy eating habits. This represents a serious failure among professionals and a role for sport psychology.

Summary and conclusions

Human motivation is complex, and it has been addressed by a series of theories. An important distinction is that between intrinsic and extrinsic motivation. Contemporary research shows that intrinsic motivation is the more important factor for most participants in sport, and that in most cases adding extrinsic motivation reduces rather than enhances overall levels of motivation. In a classic theory, Maslow has produced a broad spectrum of human motives in an attempt to describe the entire range of human motivation. The main usefulness of Maslow's approach is in illustrating the breadth of motives for taking part in sport.

Modern theories of motivation are narrow in focus and concentrate on the cognitive aspects of motivation. The most influential theory is currently Nicholls' theory of achievement orientations. This distinguishes between athletes who focus on the mastery of skills and those who focus more on their performance relative to others. The former is widely agreed to be the more successful style, and psychologists have an important role to play in fostering mastery orientations. Two other approaches have emerged as important in working with athletes to improve motivation. Attribution theories are concerned with the ways in which athletes decide why they performed as they did. By reattribution training, we can help athletes develop healthier attributions; that is, to attribute failure to effort rather than ability. Self-efficacy is the individual's belief in his or her abilities. Success, feedback, verbal persuasion and reattribution training can all boost self-efficacy. Of course, all the traditional theories of motivation assume that high levels of motivation are a good thing. A radical alternative approach considers the harm that can result from very high levels of motivation, including burn-out and eating problems.

Self-assessment questions

1. What is meant by intrinsic motivation? From research findings, assess its importance.

2. To what extent does the additive principle hold up?
3. Evaluate the usefulness of Maslow's hierarchy of needs.
4. Describe one study showing the importance of achievement orientations.
5. Compare the theories of self-efficacy and attribution as explanations of sporting motivation.
6. What is meant by counterfactual thinking? Why is it important to athletes?
7. Under what circumstances is motivation to achieve excellence in sport not a good thing?

Further reading

- Chase M (1998) Sources of self-efficacy in physical education and sport. *Journal of Teaching in Physical Education* 18, 76–89.
- Cox R (2001) *Sport psychology: concepts and applications.* Boston, MA, McGraw-Hill.
- Harwood C & Biddle S (2002) The application of achievement goal theory in youth sport. In Cockerill I (ed) *Solutions in sport psychology.* London, Thomson Learning.
- Weinberg R & Gould D (1995) *Foundations of sport and exercise psychology.* Leeds, Human Kinetics.
- Wolfson S (2002) Reflections on past events: the role of social cognition in sport. In Cockerill I (ed) *Solutions in sport psychology.* London, Thomson Learning.

Skill acquisition and expertise 9

Learning objectives

By the end of this chapter, you should able to:

- distinguish between skills and abilities, and understand a range of ways in which skills and abilities can be classified
- critically consider the concept of superability and be aware of its relationship to the nature–nurture debate in sport psychology
- describe and evaluate Fitts & Posner's (1967) stage model of skill acquisition
- discuss information-processing approaches to skill acquisition with particular reference to the work of Welford, Anderson and Adams
- understand the differences between expert and novice performers, with particular regard to knowledge, anticipation and metacognition
- discuss the effect of practice on sporting expertise with particular regard to Ericsson's theory

Those who have participated in any sport at any level will be well aware that they have a certain level of proficiency in that sport. They will also be aware that, as they learn a sport, at whatever level, they develop existing and new skills. Each sport requires a different range of skills. Thinking more generally, we all have a set of basic physical abilities, including speed and strength, which underlie our skills. The aim of this chapter is to explore the nature of skills and abilities, and to look at how we might enhance our own sporting skills and those of other athletes. First, it might be helpful to look more closely at precisely what psychologists mean when they use the terms 'ability' and 'skill'.

Definitions

A widely accepted definition of a skill comes from Knapp (1963): 'the learned ability to bring about pre-determined results with maximum certainty, often with the minimum outlay of time, energy or both' (p 4). As we develop a sporting skill, we are aiming to combine speed, power, accuracy and economy of movement, whilst also minimising the possibility of a catastrophic error. The 'trick' in fulfilling one's potential level of skill is to achieve these ideals simultaneously. Take, for example, the technique of a tennis serve. If novices or even moderately skilled players serve with all the speed and power they can muster, the chances are high that they will waste a lot of energy and land the ball outside the target area.

An *ability*, by contrast, describes the physical attributes that affect our potential for a given sport. Abilities are important because they put limits on the degree of skill we can acquire in a given sport. If you wish to become an elite athlete, it is also a good idea to match up your abilities with an appropriate sport. If, for example, your upper body strength and aerobic fitness are excellent but you have poor manual dexterity and spatial awareness, you may be better suited to rugby than snooker. Table 9.1 shows some motor abilities and the skills that depend on those abilities.

Table 9.1 Examples of motor abilities and dependent skills

Motor ability	Skills dependent on ability
Dynamic strength	Power-lift, full-body tackle, bear-hug
Reaction time	Karate block, sprint start, tennis return
Manual dexterity	Bowling, basketball manipulation

Classifying abilities

Fleishman (1964) has provided a way of looking at abilities, distinguishing between two types of motor ability: gross motor abilities and psychomotor abilities. *Gross* motor abilities are physical attributes such as speed, strength, stamina and flexibility. *Psychomotor* abilities involve perception as well as physical attributes. An example of a psychomotor ability is reaction time, which requires that we perceive a stimulus, initiate the appropriate response and carry out the motor response. All sports require a blend of gross motor abilities and psychomotor abilities, but some sports have a particular requirement for particular abilities. Dynamic strength is particularly important for a weightlifter; psychomotor abilities less so (Figure 9.1).

Figure 9.1
Weightlifting requires
the ability of dynamic
strength.
Copyright © Reuters/
Corbis

The idea that a set of innate abilities underlies sporting skills has many useful applications, such as choosing the sports in which we might find it easiest to compete seriously. It is also certainly true to say that having certain abilities makes it easier to acquire certain skills. However, we should not take the idea of innate and unchangeable abilities too much to heart. Regular weight training does not merely increase our lifting skills (although it does so), but it also increases our dynamic strength, which in turn allows us to develop further our skills of tackling. In this case, the motor ability is certainly not fixed and unchangeable, but can in fact be enhanced by hard training.

Classifying skills

A number of systems for classifying motor skills have been developed in psychology. We can briefly examine some of the most influential distinctions.

Gross and fine skills

Figure 9.2 Examples of sporting skills ranging from gross to fine.

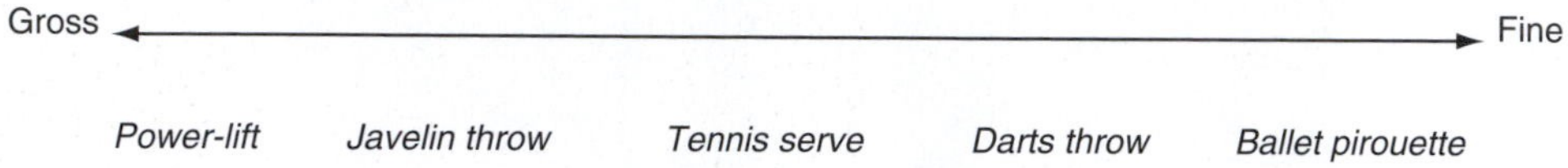

The fineness of a motor skill is defined as how much precision is required in the movement. Gross skills are those which require large muscular movement. For example, the major skill involved in the high jump is an upward thrust by the leg muscles. Fine skills require tiny muscular movements, such as are required for an elite standard gymnastic performance. Figure 9.2 shows the continuum of gross to fine motor skills.

Gross ◄───► Fine

Power-lift   Javelin throw   Tennis serve   Darts throw   Ballet pirouette

Open and closed skills

We define how closed a motor skill is by how predictable and unchanging the environment is in which it is performed. Sports such as shooting, dance and gymnastics involve highly predictable environments. By contrast, ball and contact sports tend to be far less predictable; hence, they involve open skills. Picture yourself in the boxing ring facing an opponent. One of the major obstacles you will have to overcome is that you don't know what is coming next. Will, for example, your opponent circle or attack; punch high or low, straight or roundhouse? Dealing with this involves responding to your opponent's plan of attack whilst formulating and implementing your own at the same time. The skills needed to achieve these goals are open.

Training for open skills may involve using open and closed scenarios. Closed training scenarios are particularly useful when very complex motor skills need to be learnt – they would simply be too difficult to learn in an open situation. The martial arts provide a good example of closed training techniques that can be helpful in preparation for open situations. Typically, training involves unvarying sequences of moves, called *kata* or *forms* according to the style. Kata involve entirely closed skills, because the karateka knows precisely what is coming next (Figure 9.3). However, practitioners of the martial arts involving kata believe that this approach to skill acquisition helps them greatly in open situations.

Discrete, continuous and serial skills

This distinction is based on the extent to which there are clear beginning and end points to a movement. Whatever your sport or sports, you probably have to use some discrete skills and some continuous skills. *Discrete* skills involve brief actions that have a clear beginning and end. Examples of discrete skills include a goalkeeper's dive, a fielder's throw and a rugby player's drop kick. *Continuous* skills are defined as those that do not have discrete beginnings and ends. They may thus be stopped at any point without the movement's being left incomplete. Examples of continuous skills include running and cycling. Of course, much of the time we need to perform a series of different movements in sequence. These skills do not fall neatly into the categories of either discrete or continuous skills. We classify such skills as a third category, called serial skills. Serial skills in sport include gymnastic routines and combination punches.

Figure 9.3 This martial artist is practising a closed skill, but with sufficient practice should be able to use it in an open situation. Copyright © A. Inden/ zefa/Corbis

External and internally paced skills

A further system for classifying skills is founded upon the extent to which the timing of the movement is under the control of the athlete. Movements which are largely under the athlete's control are known as *internally paced* movements. The more an athlete's timing is determined by external events, the more *externally paced* the skill is said to be. A good example of a skill that is highly internally paced is the cricketer's bowl. The bowler is not constrained by anything else happening on the pitch and has the freedom to choose the pace of the ball. The batsman, by contrast, has to respond to the pace dictated by the bowler. Batting is thus a more externally paced skill.

Two linked issues: the existence of superability and the nature–nurture debate in sport

An interesting question for researchers has been the extent to which different physical abilities tend to go together in the same people (the general motor ability hypothesis), and the extent to which different athletes have quite different strengths (the specificity hypothesis). Many current researchers tend to believe that there is a *superability* factor, which has some effect on, but does not directly determine, specific motor abilities. This means essentially that there is a broad tendency for athletes who score highly in one ability also to score highly in others. The existence of superability is linked to the nature–nurture debate, which concerns the extent to which sporting skill is in the genes and the extent to which it develops as a result of experience. Those who believe in superability tend to see it as innate, whereas those who place more emphasis on specific skills tend to see them as acquired by experience. These debates have important political dimensions as well as practical applications. The idea of athletes as generally superior by virtue of their genetic make-up makes many of us uncomfortable because of its historical association with extreme right-wing politics – this idea of genetic superiority was favoured by Nazi Germany and the eugenics movement.

The existence of superability

Research into expertise in general has tended to find that it is highly *domain specific*. Put simply, this means that being good at one thing does not usually mean that one will be equally skilful in other tasks, even those that are superficially similar. This is tricky to reconcile with the belief, widely held amongst athletes and the professionals that work with them, in *superability*, a general factor or set of factors that underlie athleticism and lead it to generalise from one sport to another.

Unfortunately, there is a lack of empirical research into superability, so we must rely on case examples and critical thinking in order to look at the debate. Much of the reason for the popularity of the idea of superability comes from anecdotal accounts, for example, of school football teams who, come the summer term, turn out also to be the cricket team! On the one hand, in spite of the obviously differing demands of football and cricket, individuals who are fit, quick and well coordinated are advantaged in both sports. On the other hand, consider the range of social and motivational factors that might also affect the situation. Those who made it into the football team are probably more likely to have the confidence to try out for the cricket team than other youngsters. They may also have more positive relationships with PE staff, and may even be personally invited to try out for the cricket team. In addition, their general interest in sport will probably have been enhanced by their experience in the football team, and so they will be more likely to be highly motivated to participate also at team level in cricket. Finally, after a season in a cohesive football team, it is likely that many young athletes' social lives are tied up with the school team.

There are thus several good reasons that have nothing to do with ability that might account for the overlap in school team membership. At the elite level, this sort of crossover between different sports is much less common. There are isolated examples of elite athletes that achieved expertise in quite different sports. For example, it was widely believed that cricketer Ian Botham could have had a successful career in professional football, and tennis player Mats Wilander went on to become a competent professional golfer. However, there are many other examples of athletes who failed to make this kind of move. Moran (2004) cites the examples of Nigel Mansell (Formula One), Terry Dicks (football) and Ivan Lendl (tennis), all of whom tried and failed to become successful golfers.

The nature–nurture debate: are successful athletes born or made?

Running through many areas of psychology is the nature–nurture debate. This concerns the extent to which our individual characteristics, including abilities, are the product of our genetic make-up (nature) and to what extent they result instead from our experience (nurture). In the same way that many in the sporting community believe in superability on the basis of anecdote, so there is a widespread belief in the overriding importance of innate talent. This assumption is built in to the very language with which we discuss ability – phrases such as 'gifted', 'God-given talent' and 'a natural' all reflect a bias toward the nature side of the argument. However, as psychologists, we should not take such factoids for granted. Actually, there is a healthy debate in sport psychology over the relative importance of nature and nurture in the development of sporting excellence, and in the past decade the balance has shifted away from the nature position toward an emphasis on effective training. On the one hand, there is no doubt that our dynamic strength and psychomotor abilities are influenced by our genes – we are not all born equally strong, fast

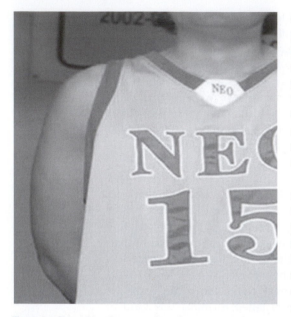

Figure 9.4 This child basketball prodigy did not develop the necessary physical characteristics for adult competition.

or well coordinated. Moreover, particular, genetically determined physical characteristics are beneficial for particular sports – for example, height for basketball. On the other hand, there is no doubt that investing time in training can also enhance both strength and psychomotor abilities, so there is clearly a role for nurture as well as nature.

Perhaps more importantly, sporting expertise is associated as much with expert knowledge of a sport as physical characteristics. It is easy to fall into the trap of watching Beckham free-kick or Agassi return a serve and thinking, 'I could never do that.' However, although we might assume that these feats are the result of innate talent, we may, in doing so, underestimate the role of training time and training effectiveness, not to mention other factors such as motivation. As Moran (2004) points out, some of the feats regularly achieved by elite athletes would be impossible if they relied on physical abilities. For example, top tennis players can return serves that literally travel too fast for the human eye to follow. This is achieved by a learnt strategy – judging the ball's trajectory by means of the opponent's body position and limb movements. To what extent the potential to learn to use this type of strategy is genetically influenced is unclear, but research certainly suggests that a great deal of practice is needed. We can return to the role of practice in a discussion of expertise later in this chapter (p 174).

There is an important third argument against the 'nature' side of the debate. Contrary to popular belief, there is actually little evidence to suggest that elite athletes generally possess better physical abilities than less successful competitors. In one recent study, for example, Ward & Williams (2003) compared the visual abilities of elite and non-elite child footballers and found no difference between the two groups. Similar findings have emerged on reaction times (Moran, 2004).

Stages of skill acquisition

Those who have ever learnt a new sport will be aware that their new skills develop gradually, and that they have to concentrate less and less on what they are doing with time. From this starting point, Fitts & Posner (1967) have produced a three-stage model of skill acquisition.

The cognitive stage

In the early stages of trying to acquire a new skill, we tend to focus on understanding the nature of the task. We use higher mental processes to analyse what we intend to achieve and how to go about this. The aim of the cognitive stage is to develop a *motor programme*, that is, a mental representation of the skill and how to perform it. We use various mental 'tools' to help us with this. We might *discuss* the skill with other learners or more experienced performers. We will make use of our *visual* abilities in several ways at this stage. We watch our limbs closely as we attempt movements. We will probably watch more expert performers. We may also mentally rehearse movements and visualise ourselves performing them correctly. The coach plays an important role in directing visual techniques, as by giving demonstrations and telling us exactly what to look for when observing. Once the cognitive stage is complete, we have a motor programme and we can perform the necessary actions to practise the skill.

The associative stage

This is the intermediate stage of acquiring a skill. Once we have developed an effective motor programme, our next task is to practise the skill. With practice, we tend to need to think less and less about the skill in order to perform it successfully. During the associative stage we rely less on the visual sense and become more dependent on *proprioception*, which is the sense by which we feel what is happening to our bodies. In everyday life, we use proprioception to be aware of our position and movement. When learning a motor skill, proprioception becomes critical as we learn to *feel* whether our movements are correct without looking. During the associative stage, practice allows us to reduce the frequency of errors and improve our speed, accuracy and consistency.

The autonomous stage

This is achieved when we have mastered the skill. By now, performing the skill requires little conscious effort. In fact, thinking about the skill and consciously attempting to improve on it generally *worsens* our performance. Once we can perform the skill without thinking, we are free to concentrate on other things, such as our strategy (individual or team). Fischman & Oxendine (1993) cite the example of Michael Jordan, the elite basketball player, who could dribble the ball at full speed and change direction without any conscious effort, leaving him free to focus on the positions of other players and determine the best strategy to reach the basket.

The general principle that practice allows us to perform actions automatically, and that automatic processing requires little conscious effort is supported by contemporary cognitive psychology (e.g. Eysenck & Keane, 2000). Furthermore, the model is extremely useful to coaches and teachers. Clearly, by understanding what stage a performer has reached, we can provide the optimum balance of demonstration, and direct instruction and practice. This becomes particularly important when we suggest that an experienced performer return to the cognitive stage in order to relearn a basic technique (a common occurrence when an athlete changes coach).

However, whilst the principles underlying the model are sound, and whilst it undoubtedly has useful applications, there is some question as to how *complete* an explanation it provides of skill acquisition. As Fischman & Oxendine (1993) point out, no amount of practice will take athletes to the autonomous stage if they are not sufficiently motivated. The model also fails to address individual differences in learning style. Some athletes are more dependent on their visual sense; others, on proprioception. Some of us are extremely analytic whilst others like to 'just do it'. Despite these limitations, however, Fitts & Posner's model remains an influential and useful account of skill acquisition.

Reflective exercise

This should help develop your skills of creative thinking. Imagine you are coaching in your chosen sport. Devise a training plan for your students, incorporating the principles of the Fitts & Posner model.

The information-processing approach to skills

The information-processing approach in psychology refers to the study of cognitive processes by analogy with the computer. Since computers were developed in the 1950s, psychologists have found it useful to look at human mental processes as if they were the operations of a computer. The first psychologist to apply the information-processing approach to skill acquisition was Welford (1968). Like a computer operation, a human skill is seen as having three stages: the input of information (perception), throughput (decision making) and output (response). A simplified version of Welford's model is shown in Figure 9.6.

The information-processing approach, as exemplified by Welford's model, is useful to sport psychologists because it allows them to break down skills and skill acquisition to their component parts. Incoming information comes in several forms. Visual information is particularly important in open situations, in which we need to be able to respond to what is going on around us. In general, the more closed the skill, the less important visual information is. As a bowler in cricket, you would need some visual information to bowl in the right direction, but the last thing you would wish is to be distracted by the crowd. Indeed, athletes who perform very closed routines, such as weightlifters, frequently report that they have little or no awareness of what is going on around them whilst performing.

Another important source of incoming information comes from the sense of proprioception. This is important regardless of whether we are practising an open or a closed skill. Proprioception allows us to sense our own position and movements. It becomes particularly important when we have mastered a skill. As a skilled performer, we can respond automatically to proprioception without making conscious decisions.

We use the six senses, sight, hearing, taste, smell, touch and

Figure 9.6 Welford's information-processing model.

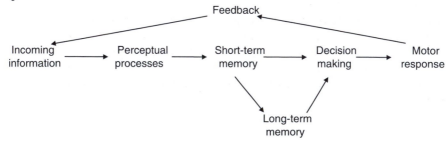

proprioception, to receive sensory information. Information enters the information-processing system via all of these senses. To avoid being overloaded by this information, we have the ability to attend selectively to important information and filter out irrelevant material. We generally attend to material that we are expecting, that which is particularly relevant to the situation and that which is particularly striking.

Welford conceived short-term memory not just as a store of information but also as the point in the information-processing system at which thinking and decision making occurs, using information from perceptual processes and long-term memory. Decision making occurs once the necessary information has been processed in short-term memory, and signals are sent to the muscles in order to effect the appropriate motor response. In this sense, Welford was ahead of his time, anticipating the modern understanding of short-term memory, as proposed in Alan Baddeley's working memory model (Baddeley, 1986).

The essential principle outlined by Welford, namely, that we can break down skills to their components by comparing them to the workings of a computer, remains sound today. In general, the sequence of events outlined by Welford is confirmed by contemporary research. However, more recent research into information processing has revealed some issues not addressed by Welford's approach. The issue of *automatic processing*, for example, is not satisfactorily explained. If a stimulus can be responded to without conscious attention, the model fails to explain at what point in the system it is filtered out from consciousness and what precisely happens to this information. Similarly, the Welford model does not address the factors that put limits on how much information we can process at once and respond to with simultaneous actions.

Memory

The nature of human memory is of interest to sport psychologists, because it is integral to understanding how motor skills are stored and retrieved. Memory is also important because it determines how we learn from experience, bringing information from past experiences to bear on the current situation. A useful information-processing model addressing the general nature of memory comes from Anderson (1983).

Anderson's multistore model of memory

Several theories of memory have been based on the idea that there are a number of different memory systems that interact. This is known as the *multistore approach* to memory. Anderson (1983) proposed that there are three, functionally separate aspects of memory. In short-term memory, incoming information is processed, and conscious thinking and decision making take place. Short-term memory interacts with two separate long-term stores. The procedural store comprises our knowledge of motor skills. The declarative store comprises our memory for facts. A simple version of Anderson's model is shown in Figure 9.7.

The declarative store constantly receives information about what is currently occurring. This information is stored for later use. When we need to make a strategic decision, we draw on the information in the declarative store. This might, for example, have information on our strengths and weaknesses and those of the opponent. It might also contain information about alternative strategies we have tried in the past or seen others try. The purpose of the procedural store is quite different. When we learn a new skill, we form a mental representation of that skill, what Fitts & Posner called a motor programme. This motor programme is kept in the procedural store. When the skill is required, we access the motor programme and retrieve the information necessary to perform the skill.

Anderson's theory represents quite well cognitive psychologists' beliefs about the 'functional architecture' of memory. There is considerable evidence for the existence of three separate parts to the memory system. Evidence comes in the main from cases of brain-

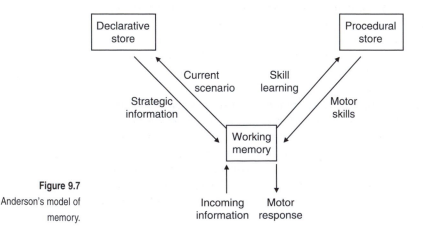

Figure 9.7
Anderson's model of memory.

damaged patients who have lost or partially lost one of the three systems but have the other two still intact (e.g. Groome, 1999; Eysenck & Keane, 2000). The theory explains well how we function in sporting situations. For example, because of the separate mental pathways needed to make strategic decisions, by using the declarative store, and operate motor skills, by using the procedural store, it is obvious that we should be able to perform these two mental tasks simultaneously, *provided* that the motor skill has become automatic and thus does not require much of the capacity of working memory. In novices, who require working memory to process motor skills consciously, strategic planning cannot be carried out simultaneously.

Levels of processing

Craik & Lockhart (1972) suggested a radically different way of looking at memory. Rather than looking at the role of different memory stores, they focused instead on the different ways information can be processed, and how this can affect how well information is remembered. Information that is *deeply* processed, that is, thought deeply about, is likely to be well remembered. Craik & Lockhart suggested three levels at which information is processed.

1. structural processing, that is, processing information about what things look like
2. phonetic processing, that is, processing information about what something sounds like
3. semantic processing, that is, processing information about what something means.

Semantic processing (in which material is analysed for meaning) is the *deepest* form of information processing; that is, material processed in this way undergoes the most processing. Material that is semantically processed is likely to be the best remembered. Structural processing is the *shallowest* form of information processing and tends to result in the least material being remembered.

The levels of processing approach is a useful supplement to the multistore approach to memory, forcing us to bear in mind that there is more to memory than transferring information from one store to another. There is some support for the idea that processing information semantically does involve more cognitive work than other forms of processing. Nyberg (2002) reviewed brain-scanning studies of information processing and memory. It was concluded that activity in the frontal and temporal lobes of the brain is greater when information is semantically processed. This suggests that these regions are doing 'more work' when information is processed for meaning.

Theories of motor learning

Whereas Anderson's theory provides us with a good overview of the processes of memory, there are also theories addressing the more specific issue of the storage and retrieval of motor skills. Two theories have emerged as particularly significant: closed loop theory and schema theory.

Closed loop theory

Adams (1971) proposed the closed loop theory that two separate types of information are stored, and these interact to bring about the motor response. The *memory trace* contains the information needed to initiate the movement or movements. The *perceptual trace* contains the information as to what the movement should *feel like* if it is performed correctly. Once the movement begins, information from the muscles is fed back to the perceptual trace. If it does not match the memory of what the movement *should* feel like, this information is passed on to a central control centre, which amends the movement accordingly. This feedback loop is shown in Figure 9.8.

You can see from Figure 9.8 why the theory is called the closed loop. Muscle movement is regulated by a closed feedback loop, involving the two types of stored information.

The closed loop approach would explain well the familiar experience in which you commence a technique, such as a tennis serve or a golf drive, and immediately become aware that it is not going to be successful. It certainly seems likely that both types of information proposed by Adams are indeed stored. However, as Schmidt (1975) pointed out, some motor responses are simply too quick to involve a

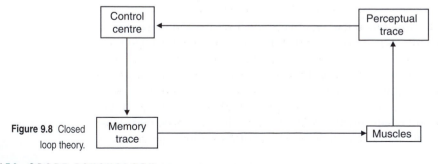

Figure 9.8 Closed loop theory.

feedback loop to perfect the movement. Closed loops are thus not *universal* in motor skills.

Schema theory

Schmidt (1975) proposed schema theory, an alternative approach to that of Adams. A schema is a packet of information containing all the information we have in relation to one subject. Most cognitive psychologists support the notion that knowledge is stored in schemas. Schmidt went further and proposed that motor skills are stored in schemas as well. Schmidt proposed that when we perform an action we store four types of information. The initial conditions include any information about the environment in which the action was performed, the position and state of the body, and the circumstances in which that action was performed. Certain aspects of the movement, such as its speed, force and direction, are also stored. Schmidt's third type of recorded information concerns the results of the action. Clearly, if we are to plan, we need to know what actions will have what effects. Finally, we store the sensory consequences of the action, that is, how it felt.

Each action practised will generate two schemas, a recall schema, which contains the information needed to reproduce the movement, and a recognition schema, which compares the movements generated with those expected from past experience of performing the action. Recognition schemas are similar to Adams' perceptual traces. There are two principal differences between schema theory and closed loop theory. Firstly, schema theory does not suggest a feedback loop; thus, the recognition schema does not automatically provide feedback to the recall schema. Secondly, unlike Adams' memory traces, a schema as proposed by Schmidt corresponds to a single movement, not merely a movement in a single situation in a single sport. Thus, the skill of sprinting has a single schema that can be activated in a variety of sporting situations, from track athletics to cricket and rugby.

Like closed loop theory, schema theory can explain how we can sense when a move is going awry. The great virtue of schema theory, as opposed to closed loop theory, is its *cognitive economy*. A general principle of cognitive psychology is that if we could have developed two ways of performing a cognitive process, the chances are that we have evolved the simpler, more efficient system. Because schemas are generalised and can be activated in a variety of situations, they use considerably less processing capacity than perceptual traces, one of which would need to be constructed for every action in every sport. Most contemporary psychologists therefore broadly support schema theory.

Expert performance

Since we have examined some of the basic processes of skill acquisition, it is now worth looking a stage further and considering what makes an athlete not just competent but *expert*. Having demolished the assumption that what defines elite performers are their innate abilities, we must understand what really determines sporting expertise. Modern research has suggested a number of ways in which expert performers seem to differ cognitively from novices.

The role of knowledge

Perhaps the most fundamental difference concerns the knowledge athletes have concerning their sport. Think back to Anderson's model of memory, in which two types of knowledge are stored, declarative and procedural. Experts have more knowledge in both the procedural domain – that is, they have a better knowledge of how to do things – and in the declarative domain – that is, they know more facts about sport, including rules and strategies. This was demonstrated in a study by Abernathy et al (1994), in which snooker players of different standards were compared on their procedural knowledge (how to perform a shot) and their declarative knowledge (how to plan ahead to set up future shots). Expert players emerged as superior in both these senses.

It appears that the *amount* of knowledge is not the only factor distinguishing experts from novices. Experts also appear to be more skilled at using the knowledge they have. Think back to the levels of processing approach to understanding memory (p 169). Woll (2002) suggests that experts process information relevant to their sport more deeply than do novices. Research has also demonstrated that experts assimilate relevant information more efficiently than novices. For example, Bedon & Howard (1998) showed karateka of various grades a range of karate techniques, and then questioned them about what they had seen. Although the novices recalled as many techniques as the higher grades, the more expert practitioners had better recall for the frequency with which each technique had been performed and in what context.

The role of anticipation

Another way in which experts differ from novices appears to be in their ability to anticipate events before they happen. This is important because at top levels athletes have to respond to movements the speed of which exceed the fast human reaction times. It takes 0.2 seconds for a sensory message to reach the brain and a motor impulse to be sent to the muscles. This is too long for a goalkeeper to have time to follow the trajectory of a penalty ball and move to intercept it. However, some penalties are saved because goalkeepers become expert at judging from cues in the movements of the player taking the penalty and thus move the right way at the instant the boot connects with the ball.

A fascinating recent study set out to test the extent to which anticipation develops over time. Tenenbaum et al (2000) followed a group of Israeli tennis players of different levels of experience, testing their anticipation abilities by temporal occlusion tasks, in which video footage was shown with the ball's flight path disguised. The participants' task was to anticipate the ball's direction just with the information from the body position and movements of the opponent. Although more expert performers were better at this task, there were substantial individual differences amongst the novices. This could suggest that anticipation is influenced by genetic factors; alternatively, it could mean that anticipation is affected by other activities undertaken before commencing formal training in tennis.

The role of metacognition

Metacognition is an area currently generating tremendous interest in modern psychology. The term refers to our insight into our own mental processes. Larkin (2002) defines metacognition as 'a form of cognition, a second or higher-level process. It involves both a knowledge of our cognitive processes (how am I thinking about this?) and a conscious control and monitoring of that processing (would it be better if I thought about this differently?)' (p 65). Flavell (1985) suggests that we make use of three categories of metacognitive knowledge; personal knowledge, task knowledge and strategy knowledge.

- *Personal knowledge* concerns the knowledge and beliefs athletes have about their individual cognitive characteristics. For example, we know what techniques and strategies we are most comfortable with. To use a footballing example, we know whether we prefer to run the ball ourselves or play long passes.
- *Task knowledge* concerns what we know about the sporting task we are engaged in. For example, we are aware when we play football that the task of tackling an attacking player differs in its requirements from that of putting an effective corner into the penalty area.
- *Strategy knowledge* refers to the awareness of the strategies we have available to us to progress on a sporting task and the ability to select the most appropriate strategy. For example, if we are on the

attack in a football match, we should have a range of strategies for getting the ball and players into a scoring position.

Research has shown clearly that expert athletes make more use of metacognitive knowledge. For example, in one study, McPherson (2000) compared novice and expert tennis players on the frequency with which they planned strategies between points. This was a measure of their metacognitive use of strategy knowledge. The experts emerged as far superior, using strategy knowledge three times as frequently as the novices.

Enhancing skill and expertise: the role of practice

It is generally agreed that practice forms an essential part of skill acquisition. As Fitts & Posner (1967) found in their model of skill acquisition, once the basic technique can be performed (the cognitive stage), the bulk of training will consist of practice (the associative stage). Athletes, coaches or teachers have various decisions to make regarding practice, such as whether it should be massed or distributed, whole or part, and physical or mental.

Massed and distributed practice

In *massed practice*, the skill to be mastered is repeated over an extended period. For example, a set of rugby backs might spend a 2-hour session just running the line. The alternative to massed practice is *distributed practice*, in which practice of the skill to be mastered is interspersed with other training. Massed practice has the advantage that the athlete probably forgets less between practices, but also has the disadvantage of leading to boredom. Too much massed practice with young or inexperienced athletes and we run the risk of demotivating them and potentially losing them to the sport. In some cases, massed practice also risks injury; thus, techniques that put particular strain on a joint (such as karate kicks) are best distributed rather than massed.

Whole and part practice

A second issue concerns whether to practise skills in their complete form (whole-skill practice), or whether to break them down to their component parts (part-skill practice). With *continuous skills*, this is not really an issue – there is little point in practising a single step in running or a single peddle in cycling. However, *serial skills* can sometimes benefit from separate practice of each part. Take, for example, a boxer's combination punches. The combination will not work unless each punch is correct in technique, aim and pace. It is thus well worth perfecting each punch separately. However, if there is too much emphasis on part skill practice, there is a risk that the flow of the whole skill may be lost.

Physical and mental practice

It goes without saying that physical skills are enhanced by physical practice. However, an interesting issue concerns the usefulness of *mental* practice, in which athletes visualise themselves performing the skill. In a recent study, Smith et al (1998) asked participants to imagine performing a finger exercise 20 times a day for 4 weeks. Finger strength improved by an average of 16%. However, mental practice alone is not equivalent to physical practice. In is the Smith et al study, participants who *actually performed* the finger exercise increased their strength by 33%. It is generally believed that a combination of physical and mental practice is most useful to athletes, but that physical practice is the more important and should make up the bulk of training.

Box 9.1 Ericsson's theory of deliberate practice

In recent years, the emphasis of sport psychologists studying practice has shifted from analysing different types of practice to looking at what makes practice effective in the development of skills. A particularly influential view of this comes from Ericsson et al's (1993) deliberate practice theory. Ericsson was not concerned specifically with sporting expertise but with expertise in general, and his early work studied childhood musical prodigies. The starting point of Ericsson's work was the principle that innate talent does not lead to expertise without practice. However, not all practice is effective in enhancing skill. Ericsson suggests four criteria for deliberate practice:

- Practice targets particular skills that are associated with good performance.
- Practice involves sustained concentration and hence extended periods of hard training.
- Practice involves activities that are not enjoyable in themselves, such as massed practice.
- Practice involves feedback from a specialist in order to identify the gap between current and desired performance.

Ericsson also suggests that expertise develops in the following stages:

- Stage 1: athletes are introduced to a sport and they play for recreation.
- Stage 2: they undergo formal training. Deliberate practice begins at this stage.
- Stage 3: they move from introductory training to high-level specialist training. The amount of deliberate practice increases at this stage.

A number of criticisms have been levelled at Ericsson's research methods. Apart from the obvious problem of an emphasis on non-sporting contexts, Ericsson has relied on retrospective accounts of early training rather than direct observation of young people at the start of their career. Research has supported some aspects of Ericsson's theory, but not others. For example, there is little doubt that time spent in effective practice is strongly correlated with athletic success (Starkes, 2001). Much more questionable is Ericsson's belief – based on observing the lack of enjoyment in young musicians practising scales – that effective practice is unenjoyable. Young & Salmela (2002) tested this idea by asking middle-distance runners to rate various training practices for effort, concentration and enjoyment. Although, in line with Ericsson's theory, the runners regarded the activities involving most effort and concentration as the most useful, they also said these were highly enjoyable – in direct contradiction to Ericsson.

Reflective exercise

This should help develop your critical thinking abilities. Consider Ericsson's deliberate practice theory, in particular the following points:

1. What sort of evidence are his ideas based on? Are these a sound basis?
2. To what extent does empirical evidence support him?
3. Does the theory have practical applications?
4. Is there anything important not addressed by the approach?

Guidance

As Ericsson suggests, effective practice takes place not in isolation, but in the presence of a coach or teacher who can offer guidance. Guidance refers to any information we give learners in order to help them develop their skills. Guidance can be visual, in the form of demonstrations, diagrams, film, etc.; verbal, in the form of instructions; or manual, in the form of physical support or adjustment of posture. These may of course be used in conjunction. An example of this would be guidance to an archer on the correct posture from which to shoot. The coach may begin by demonstrating the stance, then give verbal instructions to improve the learner's position, and finally make tiny adjustments by hand. Demonstration is a good general form of guidance, and often a way of beginning a lesson. However, verbal prompts are often needed to improve position and movements. Sometimes, verbal instructions are simply too clumsy, and for fine adjustments manual guidance may be needed.

Feedback

Feedback is any information we receive after an action. Feedback is important in skill acquisition, as it is the knowledge of how an action we perform compares to our *intended* action that allows us to perfect skills. Feedback can be intrinsic or extrinsic. Intrinsic feedback comes directly through our sense. You can, for example, hear when you hit a tennis ball with the frame of the racket. The jarring sensation in your arm will similarly tell you when your golf drive has ploughed straight into the ground! Extrinsic feedback comes from others, and is a particularly important part of coaching. Extrinsic feedback comes in two forms, knowledge of performance and knowledge of results. *Performance feedback* comes in the form of information about the skill with which we performed an action. *Results feedback* comes in the form of points, goals, times, etc. The effective coach focuses on performance feedback. In the early stages of skill acquisition, before athletes have learned to use proprioception to tell them whether an action was performed correctly, performance feedback is particularly critical.

Summary and conclusions

When we learn a new sport, we acquire proficiency by making use of our general abilities and acquiring specific skills. Skills are central to sporting proficiency, and they can be classified according to the predictability of the environment, the presence of clear beginning and points to the movement, and the factors that determine the pace at which the action is carried out. Some researchers have proposed distinct stages to the acquisition of skills, beginning with gaining an understanding of the task and progressing with practice. There are significant debates surrounding ability and skill, in particular the existence of superability and the related nature–nurture debate over the relative importance of innate talent and training.

The information-processing approach to psychology allows us to break down skills and analyse them in the same way as we analyse the functions of a computer. In particular, an understanding of memory, has proved useful to understanding skill acquisition. We believe that long-term memory involves two separate stores, one of which, called procedural memory, deals with motor skills. There have been attempts to explain in more detail the nature of procedural memory, including two particularly influential theories, closed loop theory and schema theory. Psychologists have applied their understanding of skill acquisition to the process of coaching, improving our knowledge of practice, guidance and feedback. In particular, it has been important to identify the components of effective practice. Our understanding of this area has been influenced greatly by Ericsson's theory of deliberate practice; however, it is important to recognise the limitations of Ericsson's approach.

Self-assessment questions

1. Define the term 'ability'. To what extent do you believe in the concept of superability?
2. Explain the nature–nurture debate as regards the development of sporting excellence.
3. Explain with examples how our understanding of memory has enhanced our understanding of skill acquisition.
4. Critically compare the closed loop and schema theories.
5. What factors explain the differences between expert and novice performers?
6. Discuss Ericsson's theory of deliberate practice.

Further reading

- Fischman M & Oxendine J (1993) Motor skill learning for effective coaching and guidance. In Williams J (ed) *Applied sport psychology*. Mountain View, CA, Mayfield.
- Magill R (1993) *Motor learning: concepts and applications*. Madison, WI Brown and Benchmark.
- Moran A (2004) *Sport and exercise psychology: a critical introduction*. London, Routledge.
- Starkes J & Ericsson KA (eds) (2003) *Expert performances in sport: advances in research on sport expertise*. Champagne, IL, Human Kinetics.

Research methods
in sport psychology 10

Learning objectives

By the end of this chapter, you should able to:

- understand the distinction between quantitative and qualitative research
- describe the experimental method and discuss its use in sport psychology research
- describe the correlational method and discuss its use in sport psychology
- describe survey methods, including questionnaires, interviews and focus groups, and discuss their use in sport psychology
- outline the case study method and discuss its use in sport psychology
- discuss the use of archived data in sport psychology research
- critically discuss the usefulness of systematic review and meta-analysis as ways of drawing conclusions from multiple studies.

This chapter is devoted to understanding the sort of research conducted in sport psychology. There are two purposes of this. First, it should give you a slightly deeper understanding of the research you will come across in this and other books whilst studying sport psychology. For example, you might wish to understand better why a study was done the way it was, or what the strengths and limitations are of the different research methods. Second, it should help you begin to plan your own research. There is no attempt to include everything you might ever want to know about carrying out research; that would be a book in itself, and there are several good books of that sort. However, it should give you a sound background in some basic principles.

Quantitative and qualitative research

Hayes (2000) defines quantitative methods as those 'which involve the manipulation of numerical data' (p 239). In other words, the researchers are dealing with information in the form of numbers. Qualitative approaches, on the other hand, attempt to draw out the *meanings* of data; that is, they interpret that when people say something that they are revealing something important. Some research methods such as experiments generate mostly quantitative data, whilst others such as interviewing are looking mainly for qualitative information. Of course, sometimes we can extract some interesting numbers from interviews (e.g. the percentage of people answering a particular way), and sometimes some of the most interesting findings from experiments are not so much the numbers we obtain but observations of comments participants make about the procedure.

Some psychologists have very strong feelings about the usefulness of qualitative and quantitative research. Some qualitative researchers believe that quantitative methods are clumsy and miss uncovering the most important details available from research. On the other hand, some quantitative researchers see qualitative methods as informal and lacking in scientific rigour. A simple and pragmatic way of thinking about the qualitative–quantitative debate is that we need both approaches because they tell us different things. When we want to know whether two variables, say, extraversion and success as a track athlete, are related, or whether there is a difference in the numbers of goals scored in home and away games, we are clearly dealing with variables that can be measured numerically. In these cases, there is no doubt that quantitative data should be gathered. However, if we are using a focus group method to find out about people's motives for taking up sport, we will soon find that if all we analyse is the frequency with which people identify a particular reason, we will begin to ignore some of the most important things our participants are telling us. In this case, we would do well to concentrate on collecting qualitative data. The vast bulk of sport psychology research collects quantitative data, and so most space in this chapter is devoted to quantitative methods.

The experimental method

The aim of an experiment is to establish a cause-and-effect relationship between two or more variables, that is, whether one (called the independent variable) causes an effect on the other (known as the dependent variable). For example, we might investigate experimentally whether high levels of team cohesion affect the team's scores. This is achieved by comparing two or more conditions, whilst keeping other factors constant. In the above example, we might compare the performance of teams known to be high and low in team cohesiveness, or see how performance changes after a change in cohesiveness. There are some variations in the ways we could test this experimentally.

Pre-experiments, true experiments and quasi-experiments

Pre-experiments (also known as pre-post-test comparisons) involve measuring the dependent variable before and after the manipulation of the independent variable in a single group of participants. For example, we might assess team cohesiveness, then follow a programme known to increase team cohesiveness, and finally reassess the team's performance. This allows us to infer (that is, make a logical judgement) that any improvements in team performance are a result of the increase in team cohesiveness. The limitation of the pre-post-test design is that we can *infer* only that any change is the result of the course. In a real-life sporting setting, many other variables also have effects on athletic performance over time, and it may be that any change in performance is due to other factors.

An alternative to the pre-post-test comparison is the *true experiment*. A true experiment involves the random allocation of participants to conditions, including a control condition. The purpose of this randomisation is approximately to match all the relevant variables between the experimental and control groups, making the experimental and control groups truly equivalent. When this has been achieved, it is possible to attribute differences to the variations in the independent variable.[1] In the team cohesiveness example, to test the hypothesis that high levels of team cohesiveness lead to good team performance, we could randomly allocate athletes to teams, manipulate their cohesiveness to create teams high and low in cohesiveness, and then compare their performance. In fact, this has been done. Grieve et al (2000) randomly assigned 222 male, university student, basketball players to three-person basketball teams, and manipulated the interactions of each team in order to create either high or low levels of team cohesiveness. Each team was then assessed for cohesiveness, given a series of games and then assessed again for

---

[1] In practice, we can only be certain that experimental and control groups are equivalent if group size is large.

cohesiveness. No relationship emerged between early cohesiveness and later performance.

The third experimental design is the *quasi-experiment*. We conduct quasi-experiments whenever we compare two groups that already exist as distinct groups, as opposed to having been randomly allocated. We could, for example, compare the performance of existing sports teams who are high and low in team cohesiveness. This is the quickest and easiest way of investigating the effect of cohesiveness on performance, and it has the advantage of looking at real teams in the real-life situation of their sporting league as opposed to in the artificial settings in which randomly allocated teams perform.

There are many cases where we have to adopt a quasi-experimental design because we cannot create two truly equivalent groups. Say we wanted to compare the crowd behaviour of fans of two football clubs. We cannot randomly allocate fans to two clubs because by the time they are football fans their loyalty to one team is already established. All we can do is to compare existing football fans. Similarly, if we want to compare men and women in the ability to perform a sporting technique, we cannot randomly allocate them to conditions because they are already male or female.

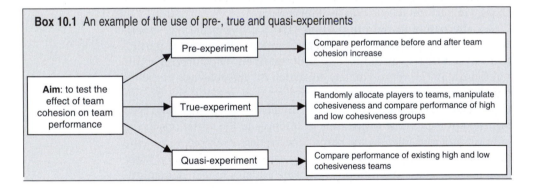

Box 10.1 An example of the use of pre-, true and quasi-experiments

Reflective exercise

Practise your creative and critical thinking on the experimental method.

1. With reference to the issue of self-efficacy and performance, suggest how you could use pre-experimental, true-experimental and quasi-experimental methods to study the effect of self-efficacy on performance.
2. Critically evaluate each method of investigating the effect of self-efficacy on performance.

Laboratory and field experiments

Another important distinction is that between laboratory experiments, that is, those carried out in artificial and controlled conditions, and field experiments, which are carried out in the natural environment of the participants. There are advantages to both these procedures. Take the issue of social loafing. Heuze & Brunel (2003) tested whether the reputation of an opponent affects the likelihood of social loafing. They conducted an experiment in which students threw darts under four conditions. In one condition, they had no opposition. In the other three conditions, fictitious opponents were created who were inferior, equal or superior in standard. This sort of study could be carried out fairly easily in a laboratory or the field. The advantage of doing it in the laboratory is that we can control the conditions, whereas in the field all sorts of factors can affect performance. The natural environment of the darts player is the pub. Here, anything from the quality of the beer to the attractiveness of the bar staff can affect concentration and hence performance. In the laboratory, we can make sure that there are no distractions, and so we can be more certain that all that actually varies between the four conditions is the independent variable in which we are interested. On the other hand, what we gain in experimental control in the laboratory we can lose in realism. When athletes are performing in their natural environment, they are more likely to behave naturally. There is thus a trade-off, and it is important to carry out experiments in both the laboratory and the field.

Discussion of the experimental method

Experiments are the most direct way of testing cause and effect, and they form a very important part of sport psychology. Despite their usefulness, however, there are a range of problems that limit the validity of experimental findings, and it is important to be aware of these. One particular problem in experimental research is the *Hawthorne effect*. This occurs when participants in an experimental condition realise they are the subjects of study and accordingly perform better than those in the control condition. The Hawthorne effect may lead researchers to attribute more importance to the experimental condition than is justified. This can be made worse by a statistical phenomenon called *regression to the mean*. This means that low pre-test scores have a general tendency to become higher in post-test assessment, further exaggerating the significance of pre-post-test differences.

The correlational method

The aim of correlational research is to establish relationships between two or more measured variables. Wherever a psychological variable felt to have a bearing on performance is measurable, such as personality traits, motivational style or team cohesion, it becomes possible to assess its relationship to other variables, most obviously measures of performance outcome such as team scores, league positions or individual statistics. We might also look for relationships between these apparently independent variables, to see, for example, whether a personality trait is associated with a motivational style. Correlations are usually presented as a coefficient, that is, a figure between 0 and 1. The nearer it is to 1, the stronger is the relationship between the variables. This may also be presented in graph form. Some examples are shown in Figure 10.1.

In Figure 10.1 (a), there is a positive correlation between two variables. A sporting example of a positive correlation would be that between team cohesiveness and performance. In (b), there is a negative correlation. A sporting example of a negative correlation would be that between number of goals scored and the size of the opposing team's crowd. In (c), there is a curvilinear relationship between two variables. An example of a curvilinear relationship is that between arousal and performance (at least under certain circumstances; see p 121). In (d), there is no correlation between the two variables. Two unrelated variables in sport psychology are performance and hair length.

As well as the obvious use of correlation to look for relationships between individual and team characteristics and outcome measures, it

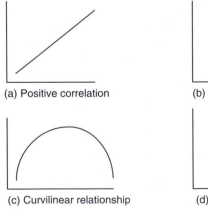

(a) Positive correlation

(b) Negative correlation

Figure 10.1 Some correlation patterns.

(c) Curvilinear relationship

(d) No correlation

can also be used to look at the relationships between independent variables and *process* variables. For example, we know that the personality trait of conscientiousness is positively related to athletic performance. However, this raises the question of why this might be. One likely explanation is that highly conscientious people spend more time training. We can investigate this by correlational techniques, and it is important to do so because if we find that it is really training time, not personality, that affects performance, we can overcome the problem of athletes low in conscientiousness by supervising their training more closely. There are a range of correlational techniques that we could apply to this situation.

Partial correlation

Partial correlation can be used to assess the relationship between two variables whilst controlling for a third. For example, we might be interested in the relationships between conscientiousness, training time and individual performance. If we suspect that the relationship between conscientiousness and performance is the result of the influence of a third factor of time spent training, we could carry out a *partial correlation* in which the relationship between conscientiousness and performance is calculated while *controlling for training time*. If there is still a relationship once training time is controlled for, we may infer that there is a direct relationship between the two variables. If there is not, we would conclude that conscientiousness is important only because it affects training time.

Multiple regression

Multiple regression (or *multiple correlation*) is another variation on the basic correlational procedure. In multiple regression, a set of variables are all intercorrelated. This is useful when we want to know about a range of factors that might be related to a dependent variable. For example, we might be interested in a range of factors underlying the performance of boxers, including their aggression, conscientiousness, achievement orientation, team cohesiveness and the quality of their relationship with their coach. By multiple regression, we can in one calculation compare the strength of the relationship between each of these variables and the boxers' performance. In addition, multiple regression also allows us to see the relationships between each of these variables – for example, whether achievement orientation is associated with personality traits.

To return to our example of the relationship between conscientiousness, training time and performance, we could use multiple regression to calculate the correlation between each of the three variables. Thus, we would know the strength of the relationship between conscientiousness and training time, between conscientiousness and performance, and between training time and performance. Looking at the strength of these three relationships together will give us a sophisticated understanding of the relationship between these three variables.

Cross-lagged correlation

Sometimes we have the opportunity to measure two or more variables across time and look at the relationships between each at the beginning, middle and end of a period. For example, we might wish to measure the relationship between team cohesion and performance. Measuring the relationship on one occasion (assuming we find a significant correlation) will not give us much of a clue as to whether the cohesion actually *caused* the performance, because, of course, it may be that the converse is true – team cohesiveness increases as a result of good results. We can get around this problem by cross-lagging our correlation. Slater & Sewell (1994) did just this when they assessed team cohesiveness in 60 university-level hockey players from six teams, early, midway and at the end of the season. The relationship between early cohesiveness and later success and between early success and later cohesiveness could thus be calculated. It was found that, whilst early success was related to later cohesion, the stronger relationship was between early cohesiveness and later success. This suggests that there is a two-way causal relationship – team cohesiveness does affect performance, but performance also affects cohesiveness, though to a lesser extent.

Cross-lagged correlation can also give us some insights into our example of the relationship between conscientiousness, training time and performance. If we were to measure the three variables at the start, middle and end of a season, we could see whether conscientiousness at the start of the season influenced training time and performance later in the season. If these were strongly related, this would suggest that the conscientiousness *caused* the training time and performance. If, however, performance early in the season correlated more strongly with later conscientiousness, this would suggest that the early success caused the later conscientiousness – this is certainly possible.

Discussion of the correlational method

Where we are dealing with measurable variables and are interested in whether one thing is related to another, correlational techniques are invaluable. They are particularly important when we are dealing with multiple variables. Say, for example, we want to know about the relationship between performance and several factors that might affect it, such as achievement motivation, conscientiousness and the relationship with the coach. We could establish a quasi-experiment with nine conditions (e.g. condition 1: mastery orientation, extravert, conscientious). However, this would be a very complex business to organise, and results would still be in the form of comparisons between extremes – this would not necessarily tell us much about the *relationship* between performance and the three other variables. In this sort of case, multiple regression would be a better way of analysing the data.

The major limitation of the correlational methods is that we need to be a little cautious about using them to infer cause-and-effect relationships. Just because training time is positively correlated with performance does not necessarily mean that it directly causes it. Success may be highly motivating, and this may lead an athlete to spend more time on training. Alternatively, a third factor might underlie both variables. For example, athletes with a good relationship with their coaches may wish to train harder to please them *and* are likely to learn technique from them more efficiently. Nevertheless, we can use correlational techniques such as cross-lagging and partial correlation to give us a better idea of causal relationships. The problems of using correlational methods to make judgements about cause and effect are sometimes exaggerated, but they are still worth bearing in mind.

Survey methods

Sometimes in sport psychology what we are interested in is not so much 'what is' as what people think, feel or believe. In this case, the most direct way of finding out what we want to know is to ask them. This is done by survey. We can survey people on paper or electronically by questionnaires. Alternatively, we can speak to them individually in an interview or in focus groups. Questionnaires, interviews and focus groups tend to generate different sorts of data and are useful in different situations.

Questionnaires

There are several ways of asking questions in a questionnaire. You might, for example, simply ask open questions and leave a space for answers. This is useful when you don't really know what people are going to say, but it can make analysis of the results harder because answers will not come in the form of neat categories. Alternatively, you might prefer closed questions, which require a choice between a number of options. Examples of open and closed questions are shown in Box 10.2.

Box 10.2 Examples of open and closed questions

1. **Open**: What do you think the most important purpose of a coach is?

....

....

....

2. **Closed**: The most important purpose of a coach is (tick one box)

To encourage and support you   [   ]
To develop your technique   [   ]
To make you train hard   [   ]

Sometimes, particularly when we are measuring emotional responses or attitudes, we want to know the strength of participants' responses. For example, if we are using a questionnaire to measure attitudes to boxing, we want to know not just whether they are pro or anti but how strong their views are. We can do this by means of Likert scales and semantic differentials. These are described in Chapter 4 (p 59).

There are strengths to questionnaires. They can be distributed to large numbers of people with little effort or expense. They can easily be designed to generate quantitative data, meaning that they can be used in correlational and experimental designs. On the other hand, response rates to questionnaires are typically quite poor (except for 'captive audiences', less than half of people who receive a questionnaire typically complete and return it). There is also little chance to collect interesting ideas that people would like to tell you but for which there is not an obvious place on the questionnaire.

Interviews

Interviews are verbal interactions that can be conducted face to face or by telephone. Interestingly, some studies (e.g. Donovan et al (1997)) have found that people are less truthful in telephone interviews. Interviews can be used to collect quantitative or qualitative data, but they are best suited to the latter – there is little advantage to using an interview rather than the much quicker questionnaire method to collect quantitative data. For this reason, interviews are more likely than questionnaires to have open rather than closed questions.

We can think about four major types of interview. In *structured* interviews, the format of questioning has been worked out in advance, and all respondents are asked the same questions in the same order using the same wording. *Unstructured* interviews are more open; respondents are asked the same questions, but they are allowed to diverge considerably from these when they respond. In *non-directive* or *clinical* interviews, there are no fixed questions, and the interviewer just identifies the broad area, and then respondents explore the issues according to their own thinking. *Focused* interviews are used to assess responses to a particular experience. As far as possible, they are non-directive; however, the interviewer identifies a hypothesis in advance and aims to test this by looking at respondents' answers.

Focus groups

Focus groups are group interviews in which the interactions between group members stimulate the generation of ideas and opinions and add to the information gathered (Wilson, 1997). The use of focus groups has advantages over traditional interviews. Participants speak in a group of peers and are thus more inclined to speak freely. They are also prompted by others to think of a view that, alone and put on the spot, they might have thought about too late to be recorded. On the other hand, it is possible that respondents are more influenced by the social desirability of particular answers.

Reflective exercise

Practise your creative and critical thinking by designing a study to investigate people's attitudes to the inclusion of non-traditional sports in the Olympics. Try designing an interview study, a questionnaire study and a focus group study. Consider the following issues:

---

1. What sort of data will each method produce? What can each contribute to our understanding of the issue?
2. What number of participants is necessary and easily achievable for each type of study?
3. How might the social desirability of potential answers affect responses in each type of study?
4. How convincing do you think people will find the results of each type of study?

Discussion of survey methods

Often, what we are interested in are people's opinions, motives, feelings, attitudes, etc. When these are the focus of our research, it is advisable to use a survey method to determine them. It is possible to design experiments to demonstrate that people behave in a particular way and so presumably have a particular attitude. However, this is usually inadvisable, as there can often be a significant difference between people's attitudes and behaviour. They might, for example, like sport but not bother to participate (see p 65 for a discussion of theories of the attitude–behaviour relationship). However, the reverse is also true – surveying people's attitudes and beliefs will not tell you how they will behave in a particular situation. For that, you require a different approach, perhaps an experiment.

Case studies

A case study involves the detailed analysis of a single case; this may involve a single athlete or a team in a particular set of circumstances. We may, for example, be concerned with how a particular athlete responded to an anxiety-management technique, or how a football team responded to the sacking of its manager. The sort of data we gather in a case study can vary widely, but it typically involves pre-experimental designs in which the athlete or team is compared before and after an event. It is also likely to involve some sort of surveying.

Some cases trace change in an individual athlete or team after a targeted intervention strategy. These studies can be thought of as pre-experimental, because the effect of an independent variable is being observed. For example, we might track motivational change in an athlete whose coach is using goal setting for the first time. Such case studies are sometimes called *n=1* experiments, *n* being the number of participants.

Case studies provide rich information with which we can understand a situation; in some cases, they provide the only available data with which to understand the effect of independent variables. This is particularly so when a situation is highly unusual or cannot be replicated for ethical reasons. For example, a football team traumatised by the unexpected death of the manager will have a complex emotional response requiring in-depth analysis. Such a situation is sufficiently unusual for it to be impractical to gather a large sample size, and it is obviously impossible to replicate experimentally – we can't go around murdering managers just to see what happens!

The limitations of case studies are clear, however. They are one-offs, and it is impossible to know whether the results can be generalised to other individuals or institutions. Take the above hypothetical case of the athlete newly introduced to goal setting. It is very likely that whilst tracking one case might reveal improved motivation and performance, another apparently similar case might not show any change at all.

Archival studies

Sometimes in sport psychology research, we are interested in analysing sporting statistics – for example, the percentage of wins under different circumstances such as when playing at home and away. Sometimes we are interested in slightly more subtle statistics such as number of fouls. In such cases, we could sit through a season's worth of games and systematically note the fouls, goals, final scorelines, etc. However, in many cases, this would be a waste of time because those statistics are already gathered and archived. When we want to access this sort of data, it is easier simply to go to a source of archived data and analyse it.

Archived data facilitate correlational and quasi-experimental research. For example, we might be interested in the relationship between the number of fouls a team commit and the number of goals they score – a positive correlation would suggest that aggressive play is beneficial to a team. Comparison of scores in home and away matches is a quasi-experimental design, because we are looking at the effect of an independent variable (where the game is played) on a dependent variable (the score), comparing two conditions that already exist as opposed to being experimentally set up.

Reliable archived data may be extremely useful, as a large body of information can be accessed instantaneously without the time and effort involved in collecting it. However, the key word here is 'reliable'. It is important that you can trust the source of your archived data. Generally, national professional bodies such as the Football

Association are highly competent at collecting and recording match statistics. However, local associations or more amateur outfits, such as your university or college magazine, may not be so skilled at data management, and you should be more wary about relying on their archived data.

Review methods

Often when you go to the sport psychology literature, you find, as well as papers describing individual studies, review papers that aim to overview a field of research, perhaps attempting to reach conclusions about what the bulk of studies say about an issue. Some research reviews are relatively informal – rather like the way issues are tackled in this book, with a selection of relevant studies and their findings being described. Typically, these papers finish with a tentative conclusion about what the bulk of studies point toward and identify directions for future research. However, two formal review methods are worth looking at in more detail.

Systematic review

A systematic review is, as the name suggests, rather more systematic than an informal review. Whereas informal reviews may aim to provide a general overview of the state of play in a field, systematic reviews tend to have one or more highly specific aims – for example, to identify the most commonly used or most effective psychological strategies with which to intervene in a sporting situation. They are most useful when there has been a large volume of research in an area, but results are variable and overall conclusions are different to reach.

The first stage in conducting a systematic review is to define precisely the area that is being researched and to gather as many studies as possible that seem relevant to that issue. Typically, this is done by manual searches (going through the journals in a university library), electronically by keyword searches of databases such as PsycINFO, and by consulting experts. In some fields, this stage can generate several hundred studies; however, sport psychology is a relatively small discipline, and usually a more manageable number will be turned up. The next task is to cut down the number of studies being examined. There are two parts to this. First, studies that appear from their titles to be relevant but in fact have a different focus are discarded. Then more rigorous criteria are applied to eliminate studies that are relevant to the research question but not methodologically up to the highest standards. This is the most tricky part of a systematic review; by deciding that a particular approach to researching a problem is not appropriate, you may find that you are taking a leading researcher or team of researchers out of the reckoning altogether. Finally, a small number of studies are left that focus precisely on the issue being examined and have been carried out to the highest standards. Looking at their findings, it is possible to come to a conclusion about what the research in this field shows.

Meta-analysis

If systematic review is a qualitative method of arriving at overall conclusions from large numbers of studies, meta-analysis is its quantitative equivalent. A large proportion of sport psychology research involves small samples studied in a particular situation, which may or may not generalise more widely. Meta-analysis involves combining the results of a number of smaller studies, weighting each for sample size, and arriving at an overall figure. For example, we might have 20 small-scale studies concerned with the effectiveness of team building in boosting team performance. Combining their results can have several benefits. First, we end up with a large sample size encompassing a good range of situations. Second, the statistical method of meta-analysis expresses findings as an *effect size*. This allows us to see just how powerful are the benefits of team building. Effect size is expressed in standard deviations, and plotted on a normal distribution curve (Figure 10.2).

For example, in Figure 10.2, meta-analysis shows a shift of one standard deviation. A psychological intervention with an effect size of one standard deviation would move an athlete or team, on average, from the 2nd percentile (that is, the bottom 2% of the population) to

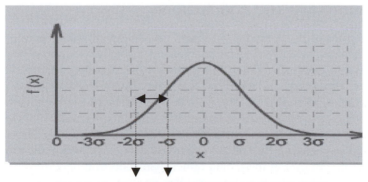

Movement of 1 standard deviation through the population

Figure 10.2 An effect size of one standard deviation.

the 34th percentile, putting them in the top two-thirds of the population. Thus, this would be highly effective.

Discussion of review methods

Systematic review and meta-analysis have been a tremendous step forward in understanding the factors affecting sporting outcome and the success of various psychological interventions. Small-scale studies, rather that being limited in usefulness by their size and the specific situation in which they were conducted, become part of a greater whole. However, there are important limitations to both techniques. First, the validity of the results depends on the quality of the data analysed. As computer programmers say, 'garbage in, garbage out'. Combining the results of methodologically poor studies may simply compound the problems of each. Although the researcher can try to select the 'best' studies, in practice there is never universal agreement on which studies are in fact the best. Moreover, there is a serious risk of bias in the selection of studies, meaning that reviewers or meta-analysts can influence their findings (unconsciously or deliberately) by favouring one research tradition over another. The knack of using systematic reviews and meta-analyses effectively is to be able to look at the selection criteria of the studies included and decide for yourself whether they are fair.

Reflective exercise

This should help to develop your critical thinking skills. Choose a review or meta-analysis study and track down the original paper. Look at the selection criteria for studies. What types of research are excluded? Why might this be a problem?

Summary and conclusions

The majority of studies in sport psychology involve quantitative methods, particularly experimental and correlational approaches that seek to establish relationships between measurable variables. There are also occasions when we are primarily interested in people's motives, attitudes, etc. These are best researched by survey methods, including questionnaires, interviews and focus groups. Sport psychology is unusual in that sport statistics are archived by professional bodies, meaning that reliable archived data exist, and many studies involve analysing these data rather than collecting new information. Where there are numerous studies around an issue, we can use systematic review and meta-analysis to try to arrive at some conclusions using this accumulated data.

Self-assessment questions

1. Why does most research in sport psychology collect quantitative data?
2. Distinguish between true experiments and pre- and quasi-experiments.
3. Discuss the view that correlational methods cannot be used to inform us about cause-and-effect relationships.
4. Discuss the relative strengths and weaknesses of interview and questionnaire methods.
5. Archived data are treated with suspicion in most branches of psychology. Discuss with examples why this is less of an issue in sport psychology.
6. Critically compare systematic review and meta-analysis as methods of drawing conclusions from multiple studies.

Further reading

- Hayes N (2001) *Doing psychological research*. Milton Keynes, Open University Press.
- Oppenheim AN (1992) *Questionnaire design, interviewing and attitude measurement*. London, Pinter.
- Russell J & Roberts C (2001) *Angles on psychological research*. Cheltenham, Nelson Thornes.
- Rust J & Golombok S (1999) *Modern psychometrics: the science of psychological assessment*. London, Routledge.

Writing essays in sport psychology 11

If you are studying sport psychology at college or university, the chances are that you will be assessed at some point by essays. This may take place in the form of a routine term-term assignment or in your examinations. The aim of this chapter is to introduce you to the skills of writing a scientific essay of the type that will impress a psychologist marker. First, let us waste no time in identifying what you may be doing wrong. The following are some common but serious errors that you need at all costs to avoid.

Seven deadly sins of essay writing

1. *Plagiarism*: Plagiarism is the theft of material, the copyright of which is owned by another author. Your tutor or librarian will be able to provide more details on what technically constitutes plagiarism, but a simple rule is that you should never copy something word for word as it appears in a published book or article unless you are quoting it.

2. *Buying the essay on the Internet*: This is the worst form of plagiarism, as it means you haven't even bothered to weave the plagiarised material into your own work. Be aware that tutors may well have seen the same downloaded essays before, so the probability of being caught is extremely high and the consequences will be severe.

3. *Personalisation*: You will probably have strong opinions on some of the issues you write about (you can probably recognise some of mine in reading this book). That is a good thing – it shows you have engaged fully with the subject matter. However, if you want to present a particular viewpoint, you have to make a scientific case, using scientific argument and scientific language. 'Evidence from laboratory experiments points to' sounds much better than 'I think' or, worse, 'I feel'. Unless the assignment specifically asks you to refer to your experience, it is normally a bad idea in a scientific essay to say 'I' at all.

4. *Disjointing the text*: The art of essay writing is to say everything that needs to be said in continuous prose. This means that you should avoid at all costs devices such as subheadings, bullet points or numbered lists that break up the text. This means that essay writing is quite distinct from writing a report. You may well be learning to write essays and reports at the same time, so remember that they have different conventions.

5. *One-sentence paragraphs*: Each paragraph should broadly address one idea. If an idea is worth mentioning, you should have more than one thing to say about it. Therefore, you should never have a paragraph consisting of just one sentence. Lots of one-sentence paragraphs give an essay a bitty feel and make it hard to follow your train of thought.

6. *The Blue-Peter syndrome*, as in 'here's one I prepared earlier. Unfortunately, that's not what the question asked for!' This is most common in examination situations when students have learnt one area really well and are thrown by a question that is in the same ballpark but not focused precisely on the material they are expecting. It can also be a problem in essay assignments, however. It is extremely important to answer the question, researching new information if necessary, and not just offer vaguely relevant knowledge because you have it at your fingertips.

7. *Factoid*: A factoid is a pseudo-fact, something that may be a widely held belief but for which there is little evidence, or perhaps it is the subject of some debate. There are many factoids in psychology and sport science. A classic example is 'sport is character building'. This

is not necessarily untrue, but it is actually a complex issue and the subject of considerable research (see p 46). To suggest that this is a *fact* is a gross oversimplification and will suggest to your tutor that your understanding of the issue is unsophisticated.

This is all rather negative. To put it more positively, what do you have to do to impress in an essay? Consider the following four variables:

- content: *what* you write
- structure: *where* you place each idea
- style: *how* you put your ideas across
- conventions: spelling, grammar, referencing, etc.

Content

There are some basics to observe when selecting your content for an essay. Firstly, it should be of the right length. This may sound obvious, but once you start writing it can be tricky to say just enough to answer the question in a particular number of words. Usually, the word length you are given has a tolerance of 10%, so a 2000-word essay should be between 1800 and 2200 words. If it is shorter than 1800 words, it is unlikely that you are providing the level of detail expected. If it is longer than 2200, you are effectively claiming an unfair advantage over your peers by giving more detail than they are able to. You are also giving your tutor additional work, which will not be appreciated! Secondly, the content should be relevant to the question. A poorly focused essay, where it is not clear how what you are writing ties in to the title, gives the impression either that you didn't fully understand the question or that you didn't take the trouble to locate the material that would have answered it correctly. If you believe that what you are writing is relevant but are concerned that the marker won't agree, be explicit. Say 'this is important in understanding . . . because . . .'.

Demonstrating your thinking skills

What tutors are largely interested in is how deeply you are thinking about the material. An essay will give you the chance to demonstrate a number of distinct thinking skills. There are several *taxonomies* of thinking skills available. Perhaps the most influential comes from Bloom et al (1956). This is shown in Figure 11.1.

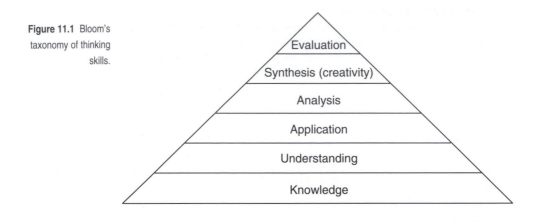

Figure 11.1 Bloom's taxonomy of thinking skills.

Evaluation

Synthesis (creativity)

Analysis

Application

Understanding

Knowledge

Bloom et al saw these skills as a hierarchy, with knowledge as the most basic skill and evaluation as the highest. Consider how you can demonstrate each of these.

- *Knowledge*: You demonstrate your knowledge of a subject by identifying, defining and describing psychological ideas, theories and studies. The more detailed your description, the more knowledge is suggested to the marker. You can impress with your knowledge if you go beyond the obvious sources of information and describe additional details not in the main texts. Another tip is to focus as far as possible on up-to-date theory and research.

- *Understanding*: You demonstrate understanding when you rephrase, clarify, explain and draw conclusions from the material you are writing about. The phrase, 'the teacher learns from the student', is not just for tacky martial arts films! Tutors genuinely learn to see theories, studies and sport itself differently, having seen the range of ways they are interpreted by students. Therefore, do think about what you are writing about, and describe things as you see them, not just how they are explained in books.

- *Application*: You apply your understanding of theory and research in sport psychology when you use it to explain a real-life situation. This might be a particular incident (such as a notable sporting success or failure) or a regular phenomenon (such as the home advantage effect). You can also demonstrate your ability to apply your knowledge and understanding when you make recommendations.

- *Analysis*: You demonstrate your skills of analysis when you break down a situation in order to clarify it. You might, for example, suggest the reasons that might lie behind a phenomenon or identify problems and propose solutions.

- *Synthesis*: This is roughly equivalent to the concept of creativity. You synthesise when you put ideas together in an imaginative way, perhaps designing a new programme or improving an existing theory or research method.
- *Evaluation*: You demonstrate your ability to evaluate, that is, your *critical thinking*, when you make judgements about an idea, theory, study or practice. How to evaluate theories and studies is addressed elsewhere (p 9). Briefly, you can evaluate a theory on the basis of its evidence base and testability, its practical application and its contribution to understanding an area. You can evaluate a study according to its sample size and characteristics, the setting in which it was carried out, how well results generalise to other sports and situations, and the validity of the measures used to record results.

Examples

Compare the following two paragraphs, taken from essays on the relationship between arousal, anxiety and performance. They are concerned with catastrophe theory (see p 123). Both paragraphs are clearly written and the content is by and large accurate.

(a) Fazey & Hardy (1988) proposed a theory to explain the relationship between cognitive and somatic anxiety and athletic performance. They point out that when an athlete is experiencing high cognitive anxiety (i.e. they are worried), even a small increase in arousal beyond the optimum level can bring about a massive fall-off in performance. Under conditions of low cognitive anxiety, i.e. when the athlete is not worried, the inverted-U hypothesis holds true; i.e. there is an optimum level of arousal, above or below which performance gradually declines. However, when cognitive anxiety is high, there comes a point just above the optimum level of arousal where performance drops off sharply. This is a performance catastrophe. Hardy (1994) demonstrated that the theory is correct in a study of crown-green bowlers, in which performance was seen to drop off sharply under conditions of high anxiety.

(b) Fazey & Hardy (1988) put forward their cusp catastrophe theory in an attempt to explain the role of cognitive anxiety in athletic performance, in particular the phenomenon of performance catastrophes. They suggested that under conditions of low cognitive anxiety the classic inverted-U hypothesis tends to hold true; i.e. there is an optimum level of arousal above or below which performance gradually declines. However, when cognitive anxiety is high, even a small increment of additional physiological arousal can result in a performance catastrophe.

Although catastrophe theory has proved useful in helping athletes mentally prepare for competition – Lew Hardy used it as team psychologist for the British Olympic Team in the 1996 games – the approach has its critics. Although Hardy (1994) has produced some empirical support for the idea that performance drops off suddenly under conditions of high cognitive anxiety, the theory is fairly resistant to empirical testing (Gill, 1992), and thus there is only a small body of supporting research. Moreover, Hardy's 1994 study relies on the validity of the CSAI–2 as a measure of anxiety (this is a matter of some debate), and the conceptual distinction between cognitive and somatic anxiety (this has recently been challenged by some psychologists). Hardy's results would be more convincing if they could be replicated using a variety of sports.

The second paragraph is somewhat longer (215 words compared to 145), but is still quite concise (whether a paragraph like this is *too* concise depends on the essay title and word limit). The real difference is that it is much more effective in demonstrating that the student has thought deeply about the topic. Both convey a degree of knowledge about the details of catastrophe theory. However, paragraph (a) is quite similar in phrasing to the relevant section of this book; thus, it misses an opportunity to demonstrate understanding by rephrasing. It also implies to the marker that the student has consulted only this book, suggesting laziness. There is some limited evaluation in the form of a study supporting the theory; however, the study itself is treated uncritically. There is no real analysis and no application or synthesis. Paragraph (b) is much richer. The greater degree of rephrasing demonstrates a sound understanding of the theory. In the first sentence, the skill of analysis is demonstrated, as the purpose of the theory is explored rather than being taken for granted. There is some practical application, although this is rather brief. What is more impressive is the depth of evaluation. The same empirical study is used as in paragraph (a) to support the theory; however, the study itself is subject to rigorous evaluation. Finally, the skill of synthesis is demonstrated as the student explores briefly beyond the existing evidence to suggest what *would* constitute convincing evidence.

Researching your content

Although books like this should provide you with a reasonable understanding of the basics of psychological theory and research, a tutor marking an essay expects to see evidence that you have read beyond the basics. As a bare minimum, you should look at a range of textbooks like this one when researching an essay. If you are studying at university level, you should also make use of more specialist books, journal articles and electronic resources. The databases PsycINFO and MEDLINE provide abstracts of studies in sport psychology. The university library should stock a range of specialist journals in sport science and sport psychology. The database Infotrac is also helpful in locating newspaper articles concerning specific incidents in matches to which you can apply a theoretical understanding.

Structure

An essay is not merely a collection of ideas, however well thought out these might be. You also have to structure them into a coherent sequence so that the reader can easily follow your train of thought and appreciate why you have made the points you have and what has led you to your conclusions. The first thing to consider is your introduction.

The introduction

There have always been rumours that tutors read only the introductions and conclusions of essays. This is absolutely false! However, it is true that first impressions count; therefore, if you want your essay to impress, begin with an impressive introduction. Your introduction should set out what you are going to write about, clearly and conventionally. You are setting the scene here, so background details (e.g. differing aims or background to alternative theories) about what you are going to be writing about are helpful. Details of theories and studies themselves are not – save that for the 'flesh' of the essay. Consider the three following introductions. All are from essays on theories of personality and sport, requiring comparison between two personality theories.

(a) In this essay, I am going to talk about the theories of Sigmund Freud and Hans Eysenck. They are very different approaches. Eysenck emphasised genetics while Freud thought childhood experience was more important. Eysenck's approach is more important in sport psychology.

(b) Theories of personality fall into broad categories. An interesting contrast is that between the trait approach, as typified by Hans Eysenck, and the psychodynamic approach of Sigmund Freud. To Freud, who developed his ideas from a blend of neurology and philosophy at the end of the nineteenth century before psychology was really established as a discipline, the personality consists of interacting elements and develops through an interaction between instincts and childhood experiences. To Eysenck, one of Freud's sternest critics, personality consists of genetically determined, measurable traits. Despite the radical differences between these theories, both have important applications in sport psychology.

(c) Eysenck (1951) developed a trait theory of personality. In the first version of his theory, he identified two traits, extraversion and neuroticism. Extraversion means lively, impulsive and sociable behaviour. Its opposite is introversion, more reserved and cautious behaviour. Neuroticism is emotional instability. Neurotic people are anxious and unstable. The opposite of neuroticism is stability. In his later work Eysenck added a third trait, psychoticism. This means tough-mindedness.

These three introductions give quite differing first impressions of what the essay is going to be like, and the tutor will form different impressions of the students writing them. Introduction (a) makes me think of the advertising slogan, 'it does exactly what it says on the tin'. It succeeds in making it clear what the essay is about and it gives some background to each approach before getting stuck into the flesh of the essay. However, it is very much a 'no frills' approach. It is very brief, and its short, simple sentences give the impression of a writer that thinks in simple terms. The classic phrasing, 'in this essay, I am going to', is not the worst sin in the world, but it lacks style and sophistication. Compare this to the approach taken in introduction (b). Here, in a much more effortless fashion, the writer makes it clear what two theories are going to be compared, and also introduces some interesting background material, such as the relationship between the two theorists, which serves to intrigue the reader and make the contrast between the theories more interesting. The last sentence, unlike that of introduction (a), suggests that a balanced account of the two theories is going to follow. Introduction (c), whilst a perfectly reasonable start to describing Eysenck's trait theory, would have been much better placed as the second paragraph of the essay. It completely fails to perform the functions of an introduction; it does not indicate the aim or approach taken in the essay as a whole, and it does not make clear what two theories will be discussed. Nor is there any clue to suggest that the essay is concerned with sport psychology. In case there is any doubt, introduction (b) is the way to go!

The conclusion

The point of the conclusion is to tie together the various strands you have been discussing and suggest what you can conclude from them. Remember that just because you are asked to draw conclusions does not mean that you are being forced to make hard and fast judgements. In the personality theories essay above, for example, it is not required that you come down in favour of one theory at the expense of the other. Quite tentative conclusions can often be more appropriate. Thus, 'Eysenck's theory has generated more empirical evidence in sport psychology; however, Freud's approach has a unique contribution to make in understanding the irrational aspects of sporting behaviour' is more considered than 'Eysenck's theory is better than Freud's. Moreover, don't panic about reaching the 'right' conclusion. You are reaching *your* conclusion based on *your* assessment of the evidence. Your tutors should prefer a well-thought-out argument with which they don't agree to a token effort at feeding them what they expect to hear. Consider the following conclusions, taken from essays on team cohesion:

(a) In spite of some inconsistencies in findings, there is sufficient empirical evidence to warrant the taking of team cohesion very seriously. Studies of the relationship between cohesion and performance consistently show that high levels of cohesion are associated with good performance. In addition, research has pointed clearly toward the strategies with which coaches can improve the cohesion of their team. Building cohesion is thus an important part of a coach's job, and psychological research can help with this.

(b) Although much research has been devoted to the much-vaunted construct of team cohesion, results have been equivocal, and, although there is an association between team cohesion and performance, the direction of causality is unclear. In addition, there are many recorded instances where teams with poor cohesion outperform those with good levels of cohesiveness; therefore, cohesion is clearly not the main factor in a team's performance.

Both of these are very reasonable conclusions that a student might reach having read the research concerning the importance of team cohesion. The first is clearly more positive and focuses on the consensus in findings and the practical applications of this area of research. The second is highly critical. Although critical thinking is important in psychology and can impress in an essay, don't play games and try to second-guess the marker. If an area of research enthuses you, go with that. Conclusions (a) and (b) would probably attract similar credit.

Planning an essay

Your essay will need a reasonable introduction and conclusion, but although these will help make a good impression, they won't let you off the hook as regards structuring the bulk of the essay that falls between the two. In order to place your ideas in a meaningful order, you will need an essay plan. There are various ways of planning an essay, and what works for you will depend on your learning style. For most people, the following approach is helpful because it makes use of your visual, as well as verbal, information processing.

1. Start by putting down all the broad categories of information you have to hand that appear relevant to the question. A spider diagram might be the best way of presenting this. For example, you might have to compare two theories of personality and discuss their relevance to sport.

Figure 11.2 A spider diagram.

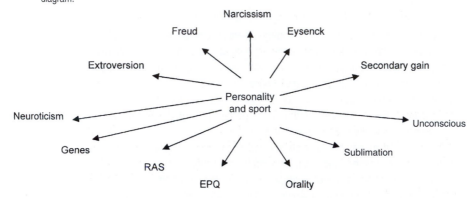

2. You can now begin to structure your ideas. There is always more than one way to structure an essay, but if you are comparing two essays, it is a good idea to deal with one and then the other, finishing by comparing and contrasting them. For example, an outline plan might look like this:

Introduction
↓
Eysenck's theory
↓
Freud's theory
↓
Comparison
↓
Conclusion

If the essay is not about theories, you need to find an equally logical way of dividing the material. For example, in an essay on team cohesion, you can take the argument for the importance of cohesiveness and then the argument against. The outline plan might look something like this:

Introduction
↓
Evidence for the importance of cohesiveness
↓
Limitations of the evidence
↓
Evidence for the lack of importance of cohesiveness
↓
Analysis of the argument
↓
Conclusion

3. You now have the outline plan. You just need to think about how to structure your ideas about each of the theories. One way of doing this is the TEE system (Eysenck, 2004). This stands for *theory*, *evidence* and *evaluation*. In your comparison of two theories of personality, for example, you might take Eysenck's theory first and apply the TEE method:

- **theory**: the traits, their neurological basis, their genetic origins and their measurement
- **evidence**: studies of Eysenck's traits in relation to sporting participation and success
- **evaluation**: comments on the theory based on its evidence, practical application, completeness, etc.

Style

This is perhaps the hardest aspect of essay writing to put across in a book. When you write an essay, you should attempt to sound authoritative, knowledgeable, scientific, unbiased and objective – in short, like a (good) psychologist. One way of learning to sound like a psychologist is to read plenty of psychology textbooks and articles. In fact, you will probably find that the more you read, the better your style will become. Consider the following two paragraphs, taken from essays on social and personality development, evaluating Freudian theory:

(a) Freud's influence in sport psychology has been fairly limited, and there are good reasons to challenge his ideas. His theory overemphasised the importance of human sexuality, and many of his ideas are difficult to test, meaning that there is little supporting evidence. He also emphasised the negative aspects of human personality, playing down our positive aspects. This is critical because it means that, rather than seeing sport as a positive thing, psychologists using Freud's ideas have pathologised sporting behaviour.

(b) Freud was a pervert and a cocaine addict. There is no evidence for any of his theories, and I think they are all wrong. Sport psychologists don't take any notice of them anyway. He said athletes were narcissistic; as an athlete, I find that very offensive. Eysenck's theory was much better.

Although both these writers are critical of Freud's ideas, and in fact have made quite similar points, their style is very different. The first suggests in a measured way that Freud's influence is limited and proposes some very sound reasons for this. There is a useful element of analysis in the linking together the separate but related ideas of testability and the availability of supporting evidence for Freudian theory. The point about Freud's negative view of human nature is explained fully, so that it is absolutely clear to the reader why this is relevant to sport psychologists. This is not to say that paragraph (a) is above criticism. The argument is quite one-sided, and, as some of the points are attributable to published work, I would have liked to see some referencing. However, the writing style is good – clear and analytic. The second paragraph is stylistically very poor. It begins with a personal attack on Freud, expressed in crude terms and unsupported by further argument. The second sentence introduces a gross oversimplification of the debate about the evidence base for Freud's ideas. It then goes on to introduce a highly personal opinion, again unsupported by evidence or coherent argument. More personal reaction without supporting argument follows, and the paragraph ends with a meaningless comparison to Eysenck. It is not that such comparisons are not useful, or that the writer was necessarily wrong to come down in favour of Eysenck's theory. The problem is that there is no analysis of *what* makes Eysenck's theory more useful in sport psychology. Without this argument, such a simplistic statement tells the reader nothing useful.

Conventions

Essay writing is a tradition, and with all traditions goes a set of conventions that you might find irritating. However, it is important to follow essay conventions as far as you can. There may of course be reasons why you find this particularly difficult – English may be a relatively new language to you, or you might have a specific learning difficulty such as dyslexia. If so, you should be allowed some leeway, and your college or university should be able to provide you with some specialist help.

SPAG

Spelling, paragraphing and grammar (SPAG) are important in any written work. You can check your spelling with a spellchecker programme, but remember that the programme won't recognise some of the technical terms we use in psychology. *Never* use the autocorrect facility on a word processor – this will replace many technical terms and authors' names with totally inappropriate substitutes. Similarly, don't use grammar checker programmes – they don't work, and if you let them, they will carefully rearrange your essay into complete nonsense.

Good paragraphing will make your essay considerably easier to read. There is some acceptable variation in the length and content of a paragraph, but if any of the following are true, you probably aren't doing it right:

- Your paragraph is only one or two sentences long.
- Your paragraph is over half a side long.
- What you are writing about at the end of your paragraph has nothing to do with what you started writing about at the beginning of the paragraph.

One more thing. *Never* try to hedge your bets by starting a sentence on a new line, so that it is 'sort of a new paragraph'. Consider the following section of an essay on aggression in sport, concerned with research into the relationship between aggression and sporting success. The wording of the three versions is exactly the same. All that differs is the number of paragraphs into which it is divided.

(a) It is widely believed amongst athletes and the public that aggression is a necessary aspect of sporting behaviour and that aggression wins games. A well-known American coach famously said, 'Nice guys finish last.' In fact, as Jarvis (2006) points out, this view might result from failure to distinguish between aggression – behaviour designed to harm another person – and assertiveness. A classic historical example of aggression in sport that did lead to improved performance is the bodyline controversy in cricket. In 1932, the England team developed the technique following a series of humiliating defeats at the hands of the Australians. They used the technique to great effect to win the Ashes 4–1. However, the technique, which involved bowling the ball to the leg stump in such a way as to bounce into the body of the batsman, was dangerous and left two Australian players with serious injuries. The affair became an international incident and led to a national falling out that lasted until the Second World War. Most contemporary research has been focused on the notoriously aggressive ice hockey. A study by Wankel (1973) of aggression in ice hockey found that the penalty times of winning and losing teams were no different, suggesting that the frequency of fouls did not affect game outcomes. On the other hand, McCarthy & Kelly (1978) found a positive correlation between the time taken for penalties and number of goals scored. Results are thus unclear.

(b) It is widely believed amongst athletes and the public that aggression is a necessary aspect of sporting behaviour and that aggression wins games. A well-known American coach famously said, 'Nice guys finish last.' In fact, as Jarvis (2006) points out, this view might result from failure to distinguish between aggression – behaviour designed to harm another person – and assertiveness.

A classic historical example of aggression in sport that did lead to improved performance is the bodyline controversy in cricket. In 1932, the England team developed the technique following a series of humiliating defeats at the hands of the Australians. They used the technique to great effect to win the Ashes 4–1. However, the technique, which involved bowling the ball to the leg stump in such a way as to bounce into the body of the batsman, was dangerous and left two Australian players with serious injuries. The affair became an international incident and led to a national falling out that lasted until the Second World War.

Most contemporary research has been focused on the notoriously aggressive ice hockey. A study by Wankel (1973) of aggression in ice hockey found that the penalty times of winning and losing teams were no different, suggesting that the frequency of fouls did not affect game outcomes. On the other hand, McCarthy & Kelly (1978) found a positive correlation between the time taken for penalties and number of goals scored. Results are thus unclear.

(c) It is widely believed amongst athletes and the public that aggression is a necessary aspect of sporting behaviour and that aggression wins games. A well-known American coach famously said, 'Nice guys finish last.'

In fact, as Jarvis (2005) points out, this view might result from failure to distinguish between aggression – behaviour designed to harm another person – and assertiveness.

A classic historical example of aggression in sport that did lead to improved performance is the bodyline controversy in cricket. In 1932, the England team developed the technique following a series of humiliating defeats at the hands of the Australians.

They used the technique to great effect to win the Ashes 4–1. However, the technique, which involved bowling the ball to the leg stump in such a way as to bounce into the body of the batsman, was dangerous and left two Australian players with serious injuries.

The affair became an international incident and led to a national falling out that lasted until the Second World War.

Most contemporary research has been focused on the notoriously aggressive ice hockey. A study by Wankel (1973) of aggression in ice hockey found that the penalty times of winning and losing teams were no different, suggesting that the frequency of fouls did not affect game outcomes.

On the other hand, McCarthy & Kelly (1978) found a positive correlation between the time taken for penalties and number of goals scored. Results are thus unclear.

The first of these combines three separate areas, the hypothesis that aggression is associated with success, the bodyline controversy and research into aggression in ice hockey, into a single paragraph. The second version successfully separates out these three issues, but without creating any tiny paragraphs that fail to put a whole idea across. The third version separates the text into a series of mini-paragraphs, giving the essay a bitty feel and making it hard to follow. Although the content is identical, I would mark version (b) the most generously and version (c) the most harshly.

Referencing

If you are studying at university level, you should receive information from your tutor about exactly what referencing system you are expected to follow. Generally, however, the following conventions are followed.

In the text of the essay

In the text, reference theories, studies, ideas and concepts. You might, for example, say, 'In a study by Wankel (1973) . . .' or 'Eysenck (1952) proposed that . . .'. If you are stating an idea briefly, it is also permissible to say something like 'Freud's theory has been criticised as pathologising all sporting behaviour' (Jarvis, 2005).

When you are quoting, you need to put in the page from which the quotation was taken, because the reader might well want to look at the original to see the context of the writer's statement. Your quotation should look something like this: 'Sport psychology is still seen by some as a Cinderella subject' (Clough et al, 2002: p 42). If you are quoting something that has been quoted already in a book or article and you have not read the original in full, you should indicate this by saying, 'cited in . . .'. It should look something like this: 'Not only is the efficacy of goal-setting assumed; it is also claimed that the technique is a fundamental psychological skill that all athletes must develop' (Hall & Kerr, 2001: p 183; cited in Moran, 2004: p 61).

At the end of the essay

You will need a references section at the end of your essay. This will normally contain the original source for every theory, study, comment, etc., that you referenced in the text. A marker will almost certainly check that you have a source listed for everything you referenced in the essay. Each entry in your list will need a name, date, title and journal title or publisher. In addition, journal articles need page numbers and books the place of publication. Entries should look something like this:

- Moran A (2004) *Sport and exercise psychology: a critical introduction.* London, Routledge.
- Henderlong J & Lepper MR (2002) The effect of praise on children's intrinsic motivation: a review and synthesis. *Psychological Bulletin* 128, 774–795.

Book and journal titles should be in italics. The order in which they are presented should be alphabetical, by the surname of the first author. Thus, if the two references above were to appear in your essay, Henderlong & Lepper should come first.

You may also be asked for a bibliography as well as a references section. Check this with your tutor if it is not clear from the course literature. The format of a bibliography is exactly the same, but what goes in it is rather different. The references section should contain details of everything you *referred* to in your essay. The bibliography is a list of what you actually read or dipped into, as opposed to what you read *about*. If, for example, you read about the Henderlong and Lepper study in Aidan Moran's book, but you didn't read the article in *Psychological Bulletin,* then Henderlong & Lepper should appear in the references and Moran in the bibliography. If you *did* read the original article and you mention it in the text, it should appear in the references *and* the bibliography. Moran's book will appear in the bibliography. It should also appear in the references section if you mention it in the text, but not otherwise.

Summary and conclusions

If you are studying sport psychology, you will almost certainly be assessed by essay. There are a number of things you should know about essay writing. Avoid the 'seven deadly sins' of scientific essay writing and consider what the marker will find impressive. In planning the content of your essay, think in particular about demonstrating your thinking skills. The higher thinking skills of analysis, application, synthesis and evaluation will be particularly important. However, don't just think about *what* you are going to write but also look at the structure and style of your essay. Finally, don't throw away marks by not sticking to essay conventions. Think in particular about paragraphing and referencing.

References

Abernathy BM, Neal RJ & Koning P (1994) Visual-perceptual and cognitive differences between expert, intermediate and novice snooker players. *Applied Cognitive Psychology* 8, 185–212.

Adams JA (1971) A closed loop theory of motor learning. *Journal of Motor Behaviour* 3, 111–150.

Ajzen I (1985) From intentions to actions: a theory of planned behaviour. In Kuhl J & Beckman J (eds) *Action-control: from cognition to behaviour*. Heidelberg, Springer.

Ajzen I & Fishbein M (1980) *Understanding attitudes and predicting social behaviour*. Englewood Cliffs, NJ, Prentice-Hall.

Amorose AJ & Horn TS (2001) Intrinsic motivation: relationships with collegiate athletes' gender, scholarship status and perceptions of coaches' behaviour. *Journal of Sport and Exercise Psychology* 22, 63–84.

Anderson CA, Deuser WE & DeNeve KM (1995) Hot temperatures, hostile affect, hostile cognition and arousal: tests of a general model of affective aggression. *Personality and Social Psychology Bulletin* 21, 434–438.

Anderson JR (1983) *The architecture of cognition*. Cambridge, MA, Harvard University Press.

Anderson KL (2001) Snowboarding: the construction of gender in an emerging sport. In Yiannakis A & Mellnick MJ (eds) *Contemporary Issues in Sociology of Sport*. Champaign, IL, Human Kinetics.

Anshel MH (1994) *Sport psychology from theory to practice*. Scottsdale, AZ, Gorsuch Scarisbrick.

Anshel MH (1992) The case against the certification of sport psychologists: in search of the phantom expert. *Sport Psychologist* 6, 265–286.

Apter MJ (1993) Phenomenological frames and the paradoxes of experience. In Kerr JH, Murgatroyd S & Apter MJ (eds) *Advances in reversal theory*. Amsterdam, Zwets & Zeitlinger.

Apter MJ (1997) Reversal theory, what is it? *Psychologist*, May 217–220.

Arms RL, Russell GW & Sandilands ME (1979) Effects of viewing aggressive sports on the hostility of spectators. *Social Psychology Quarterly* 42, 275–279.

Arndt J, Schimel J & Goldenberg JL (2003) Death can be good for your health: fitness intentions as a proximal and distant defence against mortality salience. *Journal of Applied Social Psychology* 33, 1726–1746.

Aronson E, Wilson TD & Akert RM (1994) *Social Psychology*. New York, HarperCollins.

Ashford B, Biddle S & Goudas M (1993) Participation in community sport centres: motives and predictors of enjoyment. *Journal of Sport Sciences* 11, 249–256.

Atkinson JW (1964) *An introduction to motivation*. New York, Van Nostrand.

Azuma H & Kashiwagi K (1987) Descriptors for an intelligent person:

A Japanese study. *Japanese Psychological Research* (29)1, 17–26.

Baddeley AD (1986) *Working memory.* Oxford, Oxford University Press.

Baghurst T, Thierry G & Holder T (2004) Evidence for a relationship between attentional styles and effective cognitive strategies during performance. *Athletic Insight 6* np (online).

Bakker FC, Whiting FTA & Van Der Brug H (1990) *Sport psychology: concepts and applications.* Chichester, Wiley.

Bandura A (1973) Aggression: a social learning analysis Oxford, Prentice-Hall.

Bandura A (1977) *Social learning theory.* Englewood Cliffs, NJ, Prentice-Hall.

Bandura A (1982) Self-efficacy mechanism in human agency. *American Psychologist* 37, 122–147.

Bandura (1990) Perceived self-efficacy in the exercise of personal agency. *Journal of Applied Sport Psychology* 2, 128–163.

Baron R (1977) *Human aggression.* New York, Plenum.

Baron R & Byrne D (2002) *Social psychology, the study of human interaction.* Boston, MA, Allyn & Bacon.

Baron RA & Richardson DR (1992) *Human aggression.* New York, Plenum.

Baumeister RF (1984) Choking under pressure: self-consciousness and the paradoxical effects of incentives on skilled performance. *Journal of Personality and Social Psychology* 46, 610–620.

Baumeister RF & Steinhilber A (1994) Paradoxical effects of supportive audiences on performance under pressure: the home field disadvantage in sports championships. *Journal of Personality and Social Psychology* 47, 85–93.

Beal B (1996) Alternative masculinity and its effects on gender relations in the subculture of skateboarding. *Journal of Sport Behaviour* 19, 204–220.

Bedon BG & Howard DE (1998) Memory for the frequency of occurrence of karate techniques: a comparison of experts and novices. *Bulletin of the Psychonomic Society* 30, 117–119.

Beedie CJ, Terry PC & Lane AM (2000) The profile of mood states and athletic performance: two meta-analyses. *Journal of Applied Sport Psychology* 1, 249–268.

Bell GJ & Howe BL (1988) Mood state profiles and motivations of triathletes. *Journal of Sport Behaviour* 11, 66–77.

Bem DJ (1967) Self-perception: an alternative interpretation of cognitive dissonance phenomena. *Psychological Review* 74, 183–200.

Berkowitz L (1989) *Aggression: its causes, consequences and control.* Philadelphia, Temple University Press.

Biddle S & Hill AB (1992) Relationships between attributions and emotions in a laboratory-based sporting contest. *Journal of Sport Sciences* 10, 65–75.

Billings AC, Halone KK & Denham BE (2002) 'Man, that was a pretty shot.' An analysis of gendered broadcast commentary surrounding the 2000 Men's and Women's NCAA Final Four Basketball Championships. *Mass Communication and Society* 5, 295–315.

Bowers KS (1973) Situationalism in psychology: an analysis and a critique. *Psychological Review* 80, 307–336.

Breivik G (1996) Personality, sensation seeking and risk taking among Everest climbers. *International Journal of Sports Psychology* 27, 308–320.

Burak LJ & Burckes-Miller M (2000) Weight control beliefs and behaviours of middle school athletes. *International Journal of Adolescence and Youth* 8, 287–297.

Caron SL, Halteman WA & Stacy C (1997) Athletes and rape: is there a connection? *Perceptual and Motor Skills* 85, 1379–1393.

Carron AV (1993) The sport team as an effective group. In Williams J (ed)

Applied sport psychology. Mountain View, CA, Mayfield.

Carron AV, Widmeyer WN & Brawley LR (1985) The development of an instrument to assess cohesion in sport teams: the group environment questionnaire. *Journal of Sport Psychology* 7, 244–266.

Carron AV, Spink KS & Prapavessis H (1997) Team building and cohesiveness in the sport and exercise setting: use of indirect interventions. *Journal of Applied Sport Psychology* 9, 61–72.

Cattell RB (1965) *The scientific analysis of personality*. Baltimore, MD, Penguin.

Chelladurai P (1993) Styles of decision-making in coaching. In Williams JM (ed) *Applied sport psychology*. Mountain View, CA, Mayfield.

Chirivella EC & Martinez LM (1994) The sensation of risk and motivational tendencies in sports: an empirical study. *Personality and Individual Differences* 16, 777–786.

Clough P, Earle K & Sewell D (2002) Mental toughness: the concept and its measurement. In Cockerill I (ed) *Solutions in sport psychology*. London, Thomson Learning.

Collins D (1998) 'In the event': how does anxiety affect performance? *Proceedings of the British Psychological Society* 6, 104.

Conroy DE, Silva JM, Newcomer RR, Walker BW & Johnson MS (2001) Personal and participatory socialisers of the perceived legitimacy of aggressive behaviour in sport. *Aggressive Behaviour* 27, 405–418.

Costa PT & McCrae RR (1985) *The NEO personality inventory manual*. Odessa, FL, Psychology Assessment Resources.

Cottrell NB (1968) Performance in the presence of other human beings: mere presence, audience and affiliation effects. In Simmel EC, Hoppe RA & Milton GA (eds) *Social facilitation and imitative behaviour*. Boston, MA, Allyn & Bacon.

Cox R (1998) *Sport psychology: theory and application*. New York, McGraw-Hill.

Cox R (2001) *Sport psychology*. New York, McGraw-Hill.

Craft LL, Magyar TM, Becker BJ & Feltz DL (2003) The relationship between the competitive state anxiety inventory-2 and sport performance: a meta-analysis. *Journal of Sport and Exercise Psychology* 25, 44–65.

Craig KM (2000) Defeated athletes, abusive mates? Examining perceptions of professional athletes who batter. *Journal of Interpersonal Violence* 15, 1224–1232.

Craik FIM & Lockhart RS (1972) Levels of processing: a framework for memory research. *Journal of Verbal Learning and Verbal Behaviour* 11, 671–684.

Culos-Reed SN, Gyurcsik NC & Brawley (2001) Using theories of motivated behaviour to understand physical activity. In Singer RN, Hausenblas HA & Janelle CM (eds) *Handbook of sport psychology*. New York, Wiley.

Cunningham GB (2000) Trait anxiety among students in a college golf course. *Perceptual and Motor Skills* 91, 693–695.

Curry TJ, Arriagada PA & Cornwell B (2002) Images of sport in popular nonsport magazines: power and performance versus pleasure and participation. *Sociological Perspectives* 45, 397–413.

Daley A & O'Gara A (1998) Age, gender and motivation for participation in extra-curricular physical activities in secondary school adolescents. *European Physical Education Review* 4, 47–53.

Daniels K & Thornton E (1990) An analysis of the relationship between hostility and training in the martial arts. *Journal of Sport Sciences* 8, 95–101.

Davis H (1991) Criterion validity of the athletic motivation inventory: issues in professional sport. *Journal of Applied Sport Psychology* 3, 176–182.

Diehm R & Armatas C (2004) Surfing: an avenue for socially acceptable risk-taking, satisfying needs for sensation seeking and experience seeking. *Personality and Individual Differences* 36, 663–677.

Dollard JL, Doob W, Miller NE, Mowrer OH & Sears RR (1939) *Frustration and aggression*. New Haven, CT, Yale University Press.

Dru V (2003) Relationships between an ego orientation scale and a hypercompetitive scale: their correlates with dogmatism and authoritarianism factors. *Personality and Individual Differences* 35, 1509–1524.

Duck JM (1990) Children's ideals: the role of real life versus media figures. *Australian Journal of Psychology* 42, 19–29.

Dunn JGH & Causgrove Dunn J (1999) Goal orientations, perceptions of aggression, and sportspersonship in elite male youth ice hockey players. *Sport Psychologist* 13, 183–200.

D'Urso V, Petrosso A & Robazza C (2002) Emotions, perceived qualities and performance of rugby players. *Sport Psychologist* 16, 173–199.

Elman WF & McKelvie SJ (2003) Narcissism in football players: stereotype or reality? *Athletic Insight* 5, np (online).

End CM, Kretschmar J, Campbell J, Mueller DG & Dietz-Uhler B (2003) Sports fans attitudes toward war analogies as descriptors for sport. *Journal of Sport Behaviour* 26, 356–367.

Englehardt GM (1995) Fighting behaviour and winning national hockey league games: a paradox. *Perceptual and Motor Skills* 80, 416–418.

Engler B (1999) *Personality theory and research*. Boston, MA, Houghton-Mifflin.

Ericsson KA, Krampe RT & Tesch-Romer C (1993) The role of deliberate practice in the acquisition of expert performance. *Psychological Review* 100, 363–406.

Eriksson SG (2002) *On football*. London, Carlton.

Ewing ME, Gano-Overway LA, Branta CF & Seefeldt VD (2002) The role of sports in youth development. In Gatz M & Messner MA (eds) *Paradoxes of youth and sport*. Albany, NY, State University of New York Press.

Eysenck HJ (1952) *The scientific study of personality*. London, Routledge & Kegan Paul.

Eysenck HJ (1966) *Fact and fiction in psychology*. Baltimore, MD, Penguin.

Eysenck HJ (1975) *The inequality of man*. San Diego, CA, Edits Publishers.

Eysenck HJ, Nias DKB & Cox DN (1982) Sport and personality. *Advances in Behavioural Research and Therapy* 4, 1–56.

Eysenck MW (2004) Trait anxiety, repressors and cognitive biases. In Yiend J (ed) *Cognition, emotion and psychopathology: Theoretical, empirical and clinical directions* (pp 49–67). New York, NJ, Cambridge University Press.

Eysenck MW & Calvo MG (1992) Anxiety and performance: the processing efficiency theory. *Cognition and Emotion* 6, 409–434.

Eysenck M & Keane M (2000) *Cognitive psychology: a student handbook*. Hove, LEA.

Fazey J & Hardy L (1988) The inverted U hypothesis: a catastrophe for sport psychology? *British Association of Sport Sciences Monograph 1*. Leeds, National Coaching Foundation.

FEPSAC (1996) Position statement of the FEPSAC. I. Definition of sport psychology. *Sport Psychologist* 10, 221–223.

Ferraro T (1999a) A psychoanalytic perspective on anxiety in athletes. *Athletic Insight* 1, np (online).

Ferraro T (1999b) Aggression among athletes: an Asian versus American comparison. *Athletic Insight* 1, np (online).

Ferraro T & Rush S (2000) Why athletes resist sport psychology. *Athletic Insight* 2, np (online).

Festinger LA (1957) *A theory of cognitive dissonance*. New York, HarperCollins.

Festinger LA, Schachter S & Back K (1950) *Social pressures in informal groups: a study of human factors in housing*. New York, Harper.

Fiedler F (1967) *A theory of leadership effectiveness*. New York, McGraw-Hill.

Finkenberg ME & Moode FM (1996) College students' perceptions of the purposes of sports. *Perceptual and Motor Skills* 82, 19–22.

Fischman M & Oxendine J (1993) Motor skill learning for effective coaching and guidance. In Williams J (ed) *Applied sport psychology*. Mountain View, CA, Mayfield.

Fitts PM & Posner MI (1967) *Human performance*. Belmont, CA, Brooks/Cole.

Flavell JH (1985) *Cognitive Development*. Englewood Cliffs, NJ, Prentice Hall.

Fleishman EA (1964) *The structure and measurement of physical fitness*. Englewood Cliffs, NJ, Prentice-Hall.

Fortier MS, Vallerand RJ, Brière NM & Provencher PJ (1995) Competitive and recreational sport structures and gender: a test of their relationship with sport motivation. *International Journal of Sport Psychology* 26, 24–39.

Francis LJ, Kelly P & Jones SJ (1998) The personality profile of female students who play hockey. *Irish Journal of Psychology* 19, 394–399.

Freixanet MGI (1999) Personality profile of subjects engaged in high physical risk sports. *Human Performance in Extreme Environments* 4, 11–17.

Freud S (1905) *Three essays on sexuality*. London, Hogarth.

Freud S (1914) *The psychopathology of everyday life*. London, Hogarth.

Freud S (1919) *Lines of advance in psychoanalytic therapy*. London, Hogarth.

Freudenberger HJ (1974) Staff burnout. *Journal of Social Issues* 30, 159–165.

Frost RO, Heimberg RG, Holt CS, Mattia JI & Neubauer AL (1993) A comparison of two measures of perfectionism. *Personality and Individual Differences* 14, 119–126.

Garland DJ & Barry JR (1990) Personality and leader behaviours in collegiate football: a multidimensional approach to performance. *Journal of Research in Personality* 24, 355–370.

Geisler GWW & Leith LM (1997) The effects of self-esteem, self-efficacy and audience presence on soccer penalty shot performance. *Journal of Sport Behaviour* 20, 322–337.

Gernigon C & Le Bars H (2000) Achievement goals in aikido and judo: a comparative study among beginner and experienced practitioners. *Journal of Applied Sport Psychology* 12, 168–179.

Gervis M (1991) Children in sport. In Bull S (ed) *Sport psychology, a self-help guide*. Marlborough, Crowood.

Giges B (1998) Psychodynamic concepts in sport psychology: comment on Strean & Strean (1998). *Sport Psychologist* 12, 223–227.

Gill DL (1986) *Psychologicval dynamics of sport*. Champaign, IL, Human Kinetics.

Gill DL (1992) A sport and exercise perspective on stress. *Quest* 46, 20–27.

Gill DL (2000) *Psychologicval dynamics of sport*. 2nd edn. Champaign, IL, Human Kinetics.

Golby J, Sheard M & Lavallee D (2003) A cognitive-behavioural analysis of mental toughness in national rugby league football teams. *Perceptual and Motor Skills* 96, 455–462.

Gould D & Krane V (1992) The arousal-performance relationship: current status and future directions. In Horn TS (ed) *Advances in sport psychology*. Champaign, IL, Human Kinetics.

Gould D, Udry E, Tuffey S & Loehr J (1996) Burnout in competitive junior tennis players. I. A quantitative analysis. *Sport Psychologist* 10, 332–340.

Gould D, Guinan D, Greenleaf K, Medbery R & Peterson K (1999) Factors affecting

Olympic performance: perceptions of athletes and coaches in more and less successful teams. *Sport Psychologist* 13, 371–394.

Graydon J & Murphy T (1995) The effects of personality on social faciliation whilst performing a sports related task. *Personality and Individual Differences* 19, 265–267.

Grieve FG, Whelan JP & Meyers AW (2000) An experimental examination of the cohesion-performance relationship in an interactive sport. *Journal of Applied Sport Psychology* 12, 219–235.

Grogan S, Evans R, Wright S & Hunter G (2004) Femininity and muscularity: accounts of seven women body builders. *Journal of Gender Studies* 13, 49–61.

Groome D (1999) *An introduction to cognitive psychology: processes and disorders*. Hove, Psychology Press.

Gross R (2005) *Psychology, the science of mind and behaviour*. London, Hodder & Stoughton.

Grouios G (1992) Mental practice: a review. *Journal of Sport Behaviour* 15, 42–59.

Guillet E, Sarrazin P & Fontayne P (2000) 'If it contradicts my gender role I'll stop': introducing survival analysis to study the effects of gender typing on the time of withdrawal from sport practice: a 3-year study. *European Review of Applied Psychology* 50, 417–421.

Hagger M (1997) Children's physical activity levels and attitudes towards physical activity. *European Physical Education Review* 3, 144–164.

Hagger MS, Chatzisarantis NLD & Biddle SJH (2002) A meta-analytic review of the theories of reasoned action and planned behaviour in physical activity: predictive validity and the contributions of additional variables. *Journal of Sport and Exercise Psychology* 24, 3–32.

Hall HK & Kerr AW (1998) Predicting achievement anxiety: a social-cognitive perspective. *Journal of Sport and Exercise Psychology* 20, 98–111.

Hall HK, Kerr AW & Matthews J (1998) Precompetitive anxiety in sport: the contribution of achievement goals and perfectionism. *Journal of Sport and Exercise Psychology* 20, 194–217.

Hanin Y (1986) State-trait anxiety research on sports in the USSR. In Spielberger C & Dias-Guerrero R (eds) *Cross-cultural anxiety*. Washington, DC, Hemisphere.

Hanton S, Jones G & Mullen R (2000) Intensity and direction of competitive state anxiety as interpreted by rugby players and rifle shooters. *Perceptual and Motor Skills* 90, 513–521.

Hardy L (1996) Testing the predictions of the cusp catastrophe model of anxiety and performance. *Sport Psychologist* 1, 140–156.

Hardy L, Parfitt G & Pates J (1994) Performance catastrophes in sport: a test of the hysteresis hypothesis. *Journal of Sport Sciences* 12, 327–334.

Harris DV & Williams JM (1993) Relaxation and energising techniques for regulation of arousal. In Willimans JM (ed) *Applied sport psychology*. Mountain View, CA, Mayfield.

Hassmen P, Koivula N & Hansson T (1998) Precompetitive mood states and performance of elite male golfers: do trait characteristics make a difference? *Perceptual and Motor Skills* 86, 1443–1457.

Hastie PA & Sharpe T (1999) Effects of a sport education curriculum on the positive social behaviour of at-risk rural adolescent boys. *Journal of Education for Students Placed at Risk* 4, 417–430.

Hayes N (2000) *Doing Psychological Research*. Milton Keynes, Open University Press.

Heuze JP & Brunel PC (2003) Social loafing in a sporting context. *International Journal of Sport Psychology* 1, 246–263.

Holt NL & Sparkes AC (2001) An ethnographic study of cohesiveness in a college soccer team over a season. *Sport Psychologist* 15, 237–259.

Hull CL (1943) *Principles of behaviour*. New York, Appleton-Century-Crofts.

Husman BF & Silva JM (1984) Aggression in sport: definitional and theoretical considerations. In Silver JM & Weinberg RS (eds) *Psychological foundations of sport*. Champaigne, IL, Human Kinetics.

Inlay GJ, Carda RG, Stanborough ME, Dreiling AM & O'Connor PJ (1995) Anxiety and performance: a test of zones of optimal functioning theory. *International Journal of Sport Psychology* 26, 295–306.

Jack SJ & Ronan KR (1998) Sensation seeking amongst high and low risk sports participants. *Personality and Individual Differences* 25, 1063–1083.

Jacobsen E (1929) *Progressive relaxation*. Chicago, University of Chicago Press.

Jambor EA (1999) Parents as children's socialising agents in youth soccer. *Journal of Sport Behaviour* 22, 350–359.

Janis IL (1982) *Victims of groupthink*. Boston, MA, Houghton Mifflin.

Jarvis M (2000) *Theoretical approaches in psychology*. London, Routledge.

Jarvis M (2004) *Psychodynamic psychology: classical theory and contemporary research*. London, Thomson Learning.

Jarvis M, Putwain D & Dwyer D (2002) *Angles on atypical psychology*. Cheltenham, Nelson Thornes.

Johnson SR, Ostrow AC, Perna FM & Etzel EF (1997) The effects of group versus individual goal setting on bowling performance. *Sport Psychologist* 11, 190–200.

Jones G (1991) Recent developments and current issues in competitive state anxiety research. *Psychologist* 4, 152–155.

Jones G, Hanton S & Connaughton D (2002) What is this thing called mental toughness? An investigation of elite sport performers. *Journal of Applied Sport Psychology* 14, 205–218.

Jones G, Swain A & Hardy L (1993) Intensity and direction dimensions of competitive state anxiety and its relationship to performance. *Journal of Sport Sciences* 11, 525–532.

Jowett S & Cockerill I (2001) The coach athlete relationship: an Olympic perspective. In Papaionnu A, Theodorakis Y & Goudas M (eds) *Proceedings of the 10th World Congress* 3, 235–237.

Jowett S & Cockerill I (2002) Incompatibility in the coach–athlete relationship. In Cockerill I (ed) *Solutions in sport psychology*. London, Thomson Learning.

Jowett S & Meek GA (2000) Coach–athlete relationships in married couples: an exploratory content analysis. *Sport Psychologist* 14, 157–175.

Jowett S & Meek GA (2000) Outgrowing the family athlete–coach relationship: a case study. Paper presented at the First International Conference of Sport Psychology, Halmstad, Sweden.

Kenyon GS (1968) Six scales for assessing attitudes towards physical activity. *Research Quarterly* 39, 566–574.

Kerr JH (1997) *Motivation and emotion in sport*. London, Taylor & Francis.

Kirkcaldy BD, Shephard RJ & Siefen RG (2002) The relationship between physical activity and self-image and problem behaviour among adolescents. *Social Psychiatry and Psychiatric Epidemiology* 37, 544–550.

Kirkpatrick SA & Locke EA (1991) Leadership: do traits matter? *Academy of Management Executive* 5, 48–60.

Knapp B (1963) *Skills in sport*. London, Routledge & Kegan Paul.

Kobasa SC (1979) Stressful life events, personality and health: an inquiry into hardiness. *Journal of Personality and Social Psychology* 37, 1–11.

Krane TD, Marex MA, Zaccaro SJ & Blair Z (1996) Self efficacy, personal goals and wrestlers' self regulation. *Journal of Sport & Exercise Psychology* 18, 36–48.

Krane V (1998) Sport: experiences in diversity or diverse experiences. *Proceedings of the British Psychological Society* 6, 109.

Kremer J & Scully D (1994) *Psychology in sport*. London, Taylor & Francis.

Lakes KD & Hoyt WT (2004) Promoting self-regulation through school-based martial arts training. *Journal of Applied Developmental Psychology* 25, 283–302.

Lantz CD & Schroeder PJ (1999) Endorsement of masculine and feminine gender roles: differences between participation in and identification with the athletic role. *Journal of Sport Behaviour* 22, 545–557.

Larkin M (2002) Using scaffolding instruction to optimize learning. *ERIC Digest*.

Ledwidge B (1980) Run for your mind: aerobic exercise as a means of alleviating anxiety and depression. *Canadian Journal of Behavioural Science* 12, 126–140.

Leith L (1991) Aggression. In Bull S (ed) *Sport psychology, a self-help guide*. Marlborough, Crowood.

Lemieux P, McKelvie SJ & Stout D (2002) Self reported hostile aggression in contact athletes, no contact athletes and non-athletes. *Athletic Insight* 4, np (online).

LeUnes AD & Nation JR (2002) *Sport Psychology* (3rd edition). Belmont, CA, Wadsworth Publishing.

Lewin K, Lippitt R & White PR (1939) Patterns of aggressive behaviour in experimentally created social climates. *Journal of Social Psychology* 10, 271–299.

Likert RA (1932) A technique for the measurement of attitudes. *Archives of Psychology* 140, 1–55.

Locke EA & Latham GP (1985) The application of goal-setting to sports. *Journal of Sports Psychology* 7, 205–222.

Lore RK & Schultz LA (1993) Control of human aggression. *American Psychologist* 48, 16–25.

Lorenz K (1966) *On aggression*. New York, Harcourt, Brace and World.

Marchant DB, Morris T & Anderson MB (1998) Perceived importance of outcome as a contributing factor in competitive state anxiety. *Journal of Sport Behaviour* 21, 71–91.

Marcus BH & Simkin LR (1993) The stages of exercise behaviour. *Journal of Sports Medicine and Physical Fitness* 33, 83–88.

Maslow A (1954) *Motivation and Personality*. New York, Harper & Row.

Martens R (1977) *Sport competition anxiety*. Champaign, IL, Human Kinetics.

Martens R, Burton D, Vealey R, Bump LA & Smith D (1990) Development and validation of the Competitive State Anxiety Inventory-2. In Martens R (ed) *Competitive anxiety in sport*. Champaign, IL, Human Kinetics.

McCarthy JF & Kelly BR (1978) Aggressive behaviour and its effects on performance over time in ice hockey athletes: an archival study. *International Journal of Sport Psychology* 9, 90–96.

McClelland DC, Atkinson JW, Clark RW & Lowell EL (1953) *The achievement motive*. New York, Appleton-Century-Crofts.

McGhee P (2001) *Thinking psychologically*. Basingstoke, Palgrave.

McLean L (1998) *The Guv'nor*. London, Blake.

McKelvie S, Lemieux P & Stout D (2003) Extraversion and neuroticism in contact athletes, no contact athletes and non-athletes: a research note. *Athletic Insight* 5, np (update).

McNair DM, Lorr M & Droppelman LF (1972) *Profile of mood states manual*. San Diego, CA, Educational and Industrial Testing Service.

McPherson SL (2000) Expert-novice differences in planning strategies during intercollegiate singles tennis competition. *Journal of Sport and Exercise Psychology* 22, 39–62.

Michaels JW, Blommel JM, Brocato RM, Linkous RA & Rowe JS (1982) Social facilitation and inhibition in a natural setting. *Replications in Social Psychology* 2, 21–24.

Middleton SC, Marsh HW, Martin AJ, Richards GE, Savis J, Perry C & Brown R (2004) The Psychological Performance Inventory: is the mental toughness test tough enough? *International Journal of Sport Psychology* 35, 91–108.

Miller JL & Levy GD (1996) Gender role conflict, gender-typed characteristics, self-concept and sports socialisation in female athletes and non-athletes. *Sex Roles* 35, 111–112.

Miller Brewing Company (1983) *The Miller Lite report on American attitudes towards sports*. Milwaukee, WI, author.

Mischel W (1968) *Personality and adjustment*. New York, Wiley.

Mischel W (1990) *Introduction to personality*. New York, Holt, Rinehart and Winston.

Moorhead G & Griffin RW (1998) *Organizational behaviour*. Boston, MA, Houghton Mifflin.

Moran AP (2004) *Sport and exercise psychology: a critical introduction*. London, Routledge.

Morgan LK, Griggin J & Heywood VH (1996) Ethnicity, gender and experience effects on attributional dimensions, *Sport Psychologist* 10, 4–16.

Morgan WP (1979) Prediction of performance in athletics. In Klavora P & Daniels JV (eds) *Coach, athlete and sport psychologist*. Champaign, IL, Human Kinetics.

Muir KB & Seitz T (2004) Machismo, misogyny and homophobia in a male athletic subculture: a participant-observational study of deviant rituals in collegiate rugby. *Deviant Behaviour* 4, 303–327.

Mummery WK & Wankel LM (1999) Training adherence in adolescent competitive swimmers: an application of the theory of planned behavior. *Journal of Sport and Exercise Psychology* 21, 313–328.

Murgatroyd S, Rushton C, Apter M & Ray C (1978) The development of the telic dominance scale. *Journal of Personality Assessment* 12, 519–528.

Nevill AM & Cann GJ (1998) Does home advantage peak with crowd sizes? *Proceedings of the British Psychological Society* 6, 112.

Nicholls JG (1984) Concepts of ability and achievement motivation. In Ames R & Ames C (eds) *Research in motivation in education: student motivation*. New York, Academic Press.

Nideffer R (1976) Test of attentional and interpersonal style. *Journal of Personality and Social Psychology* 34, 394–404.

Ntoumanis N & Jones G (1998) Interpretation of competitive trait anxiety symptoms as a function of locus of control beliefs. *International Journal of Sport Psychology* 29, 99–114.

Nyberg L (2002) Levels of processing: a view from functional brain imaging. *Memory* 10, 345–348.

Oppenheim AN (1992) *Questionnaire design, interviewing and attitude measurement*. London, Pinter.

Orbach I, Singer R & Price S (1999) An attribution training programme and achievement in sport. *Sport Psychologist* 13, 69–82.

Osgood CE, Suci G & Tannenbaum P (1957) *The measurement of meaning*. Urbana, IL, University of Illinois Press.

Pennington DC, Gillen K & Hill P (1999) *Essential social psychology*. Oxford, Oxford University Press.

Pensgaard AM (1999) The dynamics of motivation and perceptions of control when competing in the Olympic Games. *Perceptual and Motor Skills* 89, 116–125.

Pervin L (1993) *Personality theory and research*. New York, Wiley.

Peterson TR & Aldana SG (1999) Improving exercise behaviour: an application of the stages of change model in a workplace setting. *American Journal of Health Promotion* 13, 229–232.

Petruzello SJ, Flanders FJ & Salazar W (1991) Biofeedback and sports/exercise performance: applications and limitations. *Behaviour Therapy* 22, 379–392.

Phillips DP (1986) Natural experiments on the effects of mass media violence on fatal aggression: strengths and weaknesses of a new approach. In Berkowitz L (ed) *Advances in experimental social psychology*. Orlando, FL, Academic Press.

Piedmont RL, Hill DC & Blanco S (1999) Predicting athletic performance using the five-factor model of personality. *Personality and Individual Differences* 27, 769–777.

Prapavessis, H (2000) The POMS and sports performance: a review. *Journal of Applied Sport Psychology* 12, 34–48.

Prochaska JO & DiClemente CC (1983) Stages and processes of self-change in smoking: towards an integrative model of change. *Journal of Consulting and Clinical Psychology* 51, 390–395.

Randle S & Weinberg R (1997) Multidimensional anxiety and performance: an exploratory examination of the zone of optimal functioning hypothesis. *Sport Psychologist* 11, 160–174.

Rascle O, Coulomb G & Pfister R (1998) Aggression and goal orientations in handball: influence of institutional sport context. *Perceptual and Motor Skills* 86, 1347–1360.

Rathvon N & Holmstrom RW (1996) An MMPI-2 portrait of narcissism. *Journal of Personality Assessment* 66, 1–19.

Reifman AS, Larrick IP & Fein S (1991) Temper and temperature on the diamond: the heat-aggression relationship in major league baseball. *Personality and Social Psychology Bulletin* 17, 580–585.

Richards B (1994) The glory of the game. In Richards B (ed) *Disciplines of delight*. London, Free Association Books.

Rotter JB (1966) Generalised expectancies for internal versus external control of reinforcement. *Psychological Monographs: General and Applied* 80.

Russell GW (1993) *The social psychology of sport*. New York, Springer-Verlag.

Russell WD & Cox RH (2000) A laboratory investigation of positive and negative affect within individual zones of optimal functioning theory. *Journal of Sport Behaviour* 23, 164–180.

Ryan RM & Deci EL (2000) Self-determination theory and the facilitation of intrinsic motivation, social development and well-being. *American Psychologist* 55, 68–78.

Saul H (1993) Dying swans? *Scientific American* December, 25–27.

Schmidt RA (1975) A schema theory of discrete motor skill learning. *Psychological Review* 82, 225–260.

Schunk DH (1991) Self-efficacy and academic motivation. *Educational Psychologist* 26, 207–232.

Schurr KT, Ashley MA & Joy KL (1977) A multivariate analysis of male athlete characteristics: sport type and success. *Multivariate Experimental Clinical Research* 3, 53–68.

Searle A (1996) Group psychology, valuable lessons from our 'new-fangled' subject. *Psychology Review* 2, 34.

Sevcikova L, Ruzanza S & Sablova M (2000) Neuroticism, physical activity and nutritional habits in schoolchildren. *Homeostasis in Health and Disease* 40, 143–144.

Shields EW (1999) Intimidation and violence by males in high school athletics. *Adolescence* 34, 503–521.

Sidney KH & Shephard RJ (1983) Attitudes towards exercise and sports: sex and age differences, and changes with endurance training. *Journal of Sport Sciences* 1, 195–210.

Slater MR & Sewell DF (1994) An examination of the cohesion-performance relationship in university hockey teams. *Journal of Sport Sciences* 12, 423–431. ·

Smith D & Stewart S (2003) Sexual aggression and sports participation. *Journal of Sport Behaviour* 26, 384–395.

Smith D, Holmes P, Collins D & Layland K (1998) The effect of mental practice on muscle strength and EMG activity. *Proceedings of the British Psychological Society* 6, 116.

Smith MB, Bruner JS & White RW (1964) *Opinions and personality*. New York, Wiley.

Spielberger CD (1966) *Anxiety and behaviour*. New York, Academic Press.

Starkes J (2001) The road to expertise: can we shorten the journey and lengthen the stay? In Papaionnaou A, Goudas M & Theodorakis Y (eds) *Proceedings of the International Society of Sport Psychology's 10th World Congress of Sport Psychology* 3, 198–205.

Stein GL, Raedeke TD & Glenn SD (1999) Children's perceptions of parent sport involvement: it's not how much but to what degree that's important. *Journal of Sport Behaviour* 22, 591–601.

Sternberg RJ (1999) A comparison of three models for teaching psychology. *Psychology Teaching Review* 8, 37–43.

Strean WB & Strean HS (1998) Applying psychodynamic concepts to sport psychology practice. *Sport Psychologist* 12, 208–222.

Sturman TS & Thibodeau R (2001) Performance-undermining effects of baseball free agent contracts. *Journal of Sport and Exercise Psychology* 23, 23–36.

Sutton J (1994) Aggression and violence. In McKnight J & Sutton J (ed) *Social psychology*. Sydney, Prentice-Hall.

Swain A (1996) Social loafing and identifiability: the mediating role of achievement goal orientation. *Research Quarterly for Exercise and Sport* 67, 337–351.

Swain A & Jones G (1993) Intensity and frequency dimensions of competitive state anxiety. *Journal of Sport Sciences* 11, 533–542.

Tenenbaum G, Stewart E & Singer RN (1997) Aggression and violence in sport: an ISSP position stand. *Sport Psychologist* 11, 1–7.

Thelwell RC & Maynard IW (2000) Professional cricketers' perceptions of the importance of antecedents influencing repeatable good performance. *Perceptual and Motor Skills* 90, 649–658.

Theodorakis Y (1992) Prediction of athletic participation: a test of planned behaviour theory. *Psychology and Motor Skills* 74, 371–379.

Thirer J (1994) Aggression. In Singer RN, Murphy M & Tennant LK (eds) *Handbook of research in sport psychology*. New York, Macmillan.

Thurstone LL & Chave EJ (1929) *The measurement of attitudes*. Chicago, University of Illinois Press.

Triplett N (1898) The dynamogenic factors in pacemaking and competition. *American Journal of Psychology* 9, 507–553.

Tucker LW & Parks JB (2001) Effects of gender and sport type on intercollegiate athletes' perceptions of the legitimacy of aggressive behaviours in sport. *Sociology of Sport Journal* 18, 403–413.

Tuckman BW & Jensen MA (1977) Stages of small-group development revisited. *Group and Organisational Studies* 2, 419–427.

Turman PD (2003) Coaches and cohesion: the impact of coaching techniques on team cohesion in the small group sport setting. *Journal of Sport Behaviour* 26, 86–103.

Tutko TA & Ogilvie BC (1966) *Athletic motivation inventory*. San Jose, CA,

Institute for the Study of Athletic Motivation.

Vealey RS (1989) Sport personology: a paradigmatic and methodological analysis. *Journal of Sport and Exercise Psychology* 11, 216–235.

Vealey RS & Walter SM (1993) Imagery training for performance enhancement and personal development. In Williams J (ed) *Applied sport psychology*. Mountain View, CA, Mayfield.

Waller NG, Koietin BA, Bouchard TJ, Lykken DT & Tellegan A (1990) Genetic and environmental influences on religious interests, attitudes and values: a study of twins reared together and apart. *Psychological Science* 1, 138–142.

Wankel LM (1973) An examination of illegal aggression in intercollegiate hockey. In Williams I & Wankel LM (eds) *Proceedings of the Fourth Canadian Psychomotor Learning and Sport Psychology Symposium*, 531–542.

Wankel LM, Mummery WK, Stephens T & Craig C (1994) Prediction of physical activity intention from social psychological variables: results from the Campbell's survey of well-being. *Journal of Sport and Exercise Psychology* 16, 56–69.

Wann D, Carlson JD & Schrader MP (1999) The impact of team identification on the hostile and instrumental verbal aggression of sport spectators. *Journal of Social Behaviour and Personality* 14, 279–286.

Wann D, Haynes G, McLean B & Pullen P (2003) Team identification and willingness to consider anonymous acts of hostile aggression. *Aggressive Behaviour* 29, 406–413.

Ward P & Williams AM (2003) Perceptual and cognitive skill development in soccer: the multidimensional nature of expert performance. *Journal of Sport and Exercise Psychology* 25, 93–111.

Waxmonsky J & Beresin EV (2001) Taking professional wrestling to the mat: a look at the appeal and potential effects of professional wrestling on children. *Academic Psychiatry* 25, 125–131.

Weinberg & Gould (1995) *Foundations of sport and exercise psychology*. Madison, WI, Human Kinetics.

Weinberg RS, Bruya LD, Jackson A & Garland H (1987) Goal difficulty and endurance performance: a challenge to the goal attainability assumption. *Journal of Sport Behaviour* 10, 82–93.

Weinberg RS & Weigand DA (1993) Goal-setting in sport and exercise: a reaction to Locke. *Journal of Sport and Exercise Psychology* 15, 88–96.

Weinberg RS, Yukelson D, Burton S & Weigand D (2000) Perceived goal setting practices of Olympic athletes: an exploratory investigation. *Sport Psychologist* 14, 279–295.

Weinberg RS, Butt J & Knight B (2001) High school coaches' perceptions of the process of goal setting. *Sport Psychologist* 15, 20–47.

Weiner B (1992) *Human motivation: metaphors, theories and research*. Thousand Oaks, CA, Sage.

Welford AT (1968) *Fundamentals of skill*. London, Methuen.

Wells CM, Collins D & Hale BD (1993) The self-efficacy–performance link in maximum strength performance. *Journal of Sport Sciences* 11, 167–175.

Widmeyer WN, Brawley LR & Carron AV (1985) *The measurement of cohesion in sport teams: the Group Environment Questionnaire*. London, Sports Dynamics.

Widmeyer WN & McGuire EJ (1997) Frequency of competition and aggression in professional ice hockey. *International Journal of Sport Psychology* 28, 57–66.

Wilson P & Eklund RC (1998) The relationship between competitive anxiety and self-presentational concerns. *Journal of Sport and Exercise Psychology* 20, 81–97.

Wolfson S (2002) Sports' participants reflections on past events: the role of social cognition. In Cockerill I (ed) *Solutions in sport psychology*. London, Thomson Learning.

Woll S (2002) *Everyday thinking: memory, reasoning and judgement in the real world*. Hillsdale, NJ, Lawrence Erlbaum.

Wright EF, Voyer D & Wright RD (1995) Supporting audiences and performance under pressure: the home-ice disadvantage in hockey championships. *Journal of Sport Behaviour* 18, 21–28.

Yerkes RM & Dodson JD (1908) The relationship of strength and stimulus to rapidity of habit formation. *Journal of Comparative Neurology and Psychology* 18, 459–482.

Young BW & Salmela JH (2002) Perceptions of training and deliberate practice of middle distance runners. *International Journal of Sport Psychology* 33, 167–181.

Young K (1993) Violence, risk and liability in male sports culture. *Sociology of Sport Journal* 10, 373–396.

Zajonc RB (1965) Social facilitation. *Science* 149, 269–274.

Zuckerman M (1978) *Sensation seeking: beyond the optimum level of arousal*. Hillsdale, NJ, LEA.

Index

skill
  classification, 158–9
  definition, 156
  information-processing
    approach, 166–7
  practice and, 174–7
  stages of acquisition,
    163–5
social desirability
  beliefs about, 70
  participation and, 67
  of sport, 71
social development,
    influence on, 40–2
social facilitation, 2, 97–102,
    110
social learning theory, 36–7,
    53, 80–2, 89
  aggression and, 86, 88
  application to sport, 37–40
  attitudes, 62–3
  attitudes to competition,
    64–5
  catharsis and, 89
  influences, 40–2
  patterns of sport-related
    behaviour, 37
  punishment and, 88
  trait anxiety, 119
social loafing, 102–3, 110
social needs, 139, 140
social perspective, 8, 9
social psychology, 6, 7
socialisation, 40
  cultural differences in,
    42
somatic anxiety, 114–15, 117,
    118, 133
Soviet psychology, 2–3
specificity hypothesis, 160
spectators
  aggression and, 75, 89
  aggression in sport and,
    87–8
  gender and attitudes to, 63
spider diagram, 206
Sport Behaviour Inventory,
    83

Sport Competition Anxiety
    Test (SCAT), 115,
    116–17
state anxiety, 119
stereotypes, 58
stimulus control, 68
strategy knowledge, 173–4
stress
  definition, 114
  factors inducing, 118–20
  management, 127–33
structural processing, 169
structured interviews, 189
sublimation, 51, 52
success, careers, sport and,
    46
superability, 160–1, 177
survey (research method), 6,
    187–90
synthesis as thinking skill,
    201
systematic review, 192–3

TARGET system, 143
task knowledge, 173
task orientation, 85, 142,
    143
team
  aggression and, 89
  building, 42, 97, 98
  cohesiveness, 110
  culture, 41
  definition, 93–4
  factors, group
    cohesiveness and, 96
  identification with,
    aggression and, 83–4
  membership, negative
    effects, 102–4
team prayers, group
    cohesiveness and, 96
technical assistance, group
    cohesiveness and, 96
TEE system, 207
telic dominance, 24–5
Telic Dominance Scale
    (TDS), 24, 25
telic states, 24